Brickwork 3

Brickwork 3

W. G. Nash, MCIOB

First published in 1970 by Hutchinson Education
Second edition 1983
Revised second edition 1988
Reprinted in 1990 by Stanley Thornes (Publishers) Ltd

Reprinted in 2002 by:
Nelson Thornes Ltd
Delta Place
27 Bath Road
CHELTENHAM
GL53 7TH
United Kingdom

04 05 06 / 17 16 15 14 13 12 11 10

A catalogue record for this book is available from the British Library

ISBN 0 7487 0310 1

Printed in Croatia by Zrinski

Contents

Preface

This book progresses from *Brickwork 1* and *2* and takes the reader up to the advanced craft certificate and beyond into craft foremanship studies. It is also intended for students following courses for construction technicians. Each chapter has been specially written to assist the ambitious craftsman and questions have been set to test the reader's knowledge of the subject and encourage further study.

The author would like to record his sincere thanks to the following organizations for generously providing up-to-date information and so kindly allowing their products to be described and illustrated:

Acrow (Engineers) Ltd, Paddington, London W2
Frankipile Ltd, Croydon, Surrey
Hilger and Watts Ltd, London W1
Lafarge Aluminous Cement Company Limited, London W1
Phoenix Surveying Equipment, Bristol BS17 5NH
True Flue Ltd, London W1

Finally, may readers find pleasure and satisfaction in all their future studies and work.

W. G. Nash
1983

Chapter 1

General preliminary work

After reading this chapter you should be able to:

1 Have an appreciation of the power and responsibilities of a local authority.
2 Know how to apply for outline planning permission; and planning permission for a structure.
3 Understand the procedure for obtaining byelaw approval.
4 Have an understanding of the scope of the Building Regulations.
5 Know the procedure for obtaining services on a building site.
6 Appreciate the necessity for erecting a hoarding around a site and the procedure for applying for permission to erect a hoarding over a public footway; and to know the rules applicable to such a hoarding.
7 Understand the rights of adjoining owners.
8 Have a good understanding of the scope of the Working Rule Agreement.

The local authority

The local authority is responsible for providing many services for the people who live within its area. These services include education, libraries, sewage disposal, refuse collection, baths, public lands and recreation grounds, health services, housing, town and country planning, street lighting, police, fire service, and water supply. Much of the money for these services is collected from rates, which are charges made by the local authority on the various premises within its area or under its control.

The local authority is also responsible for the siting and the quality of the new buildings which are built within its area. Therefore, certain procedures have to be adopted before any new work or alterations to existing buildings can begin. Although these procedures are basically the same in all authorities, they do vary in detail, and you should find out the actual method of making applications for permission to build or alter existing structures from the area authority in which you live.

Outline planning permission

.The local authority is divided into various departments. Each department is responsible for specific services and experts are employed to handle the work. For example, the planning department is concerned with the planning control of a structure and if a piece of land were to be developed they would require an outline application form to be completed and sent, giving the following details:

1 Name and address of the developer.
2 Location of the land to be developed.
3 Description of the proposed development.

4 Previous uses of the land.

5 Whether a new access would be required from the highway.

The planning department would probably also need the following drawings and plans with the application:

1 Plan or sketch to show the site to which the application refers.

2 1:100 or 1:200 drawing to give a clear picture of the new building or alteration.

Where both new and existing work are shown on the same drawing, the new work should be distinctly coloured.

Generally two copies of all plans should be sent, together with two application forms. Additional copies may be called for in certain cases.

The planning department will ensure that certain areas within its area will be scheduled for specific purposes so that residential areas are kept separate from industrial and other areas. Once the planning department has approved the proposed development, then a recommendation would be made to the local council to grant permission to build. This is often done through a planning sub-committee elected by the local authority.

Planning permission

Once the outline permission has been obtained, then the developer may go ahead with preparing all the details of the proposed new structure or alteration. When these are completed, a further application must be made to the local authority for planning permission. In addition to the information that would be submitted on the outline planning application form, the following extra information would also be needed:

1 The purpose for which the new structure will be used.

2 The number of habitable rooms.

3 The total floor area of the non-residential part, if any.

4 Means of water supply.

5 Number of water closets.

6 Estimated cost of proposed building works.

7 Name and address of builder.

If the building is to be for industrial or commercial use, the nature of the business, the total floor area, provision for unloading and loading vehicles, and the means of disposal of any trade effluent must also be considered.

Usually this application has to be in triplicate and four sets of plans (one of which must be on linen) must be submitted to the local authority. Plans should be drawn in ink and copies reproduced in a clear and intelligible way on suitable durable material.

The plans and drawings should include the following:

A site plan

This should be to an appropriate scale, that is, 1:2500, 1:10,000.

A layout plan

This should be not less than 1:1250 and should show:

1 The boundaries of the land, the existing and proposed layout of the structure(s).

2 The position of existing and proposed buildings, roads, streets and the widths and levels of any proposed roads.

3 The maximum heights of new buildings.

4 The proposed use of each building and the use of any land not built upon.

5 The maximum number of habitable rooms.

6 The total floor area for commercial or industrial developments.

7 The approximate contours of the land at 3 metre vertical intervals.

8 The approximate lines of the water supply pipes.

9 The lines of drains and sewers giving sizes and gradients.

10 The situation of the land in relation to the nearest road, giving the width of such road and any access that may be required.

11 Any trees or natural features to be preserved.

In certain cases the local planning authority may not need the layout, but this must first be checked with the authority before action is taken.

Block and building plans

The block plans should be to a scale of not less than 1:500 and the building plans to a scale of not less than 1:100 unless permission is given by the local authority for a smaller scale to be used. They should show:

1 The boundaries of the plot.
2 The position of the existing and proposed buildings.
3 The position and width of existing and proposed means of access.
4 The position and size of every yard and space belonging to the building.
5 The position of every water closet, urinal, and cesspool in connection with the building.
6 Existing and proposed foul water and surface water drains, manholes, catchpits, intercepting chambers, indicating size, depth, inclination and means of ventilation.
7 The position and level of the outfall of the drains, the connection of the drain with the sewer, and the position of the sewer.

When the local authority is satisfied that the proposed structure is in accordance with its planning requirements, it may grant planning permission for the structure.

Bye-law approval

Once the planning approval has been obtained, bye-law approval must be sought. Application is usually made with three copies of the necessary plans (one on linen) and by sending the following particulars:

1 The class or nature of the building.
2 The method of drainage; foul, surface and subsoil water.
3 Means of water supply.
4 Particulars of construction of the walls, materials, damp-proof courses, colour and external finish.
5 Estimated cost of proposed building work.
6 Name and address of builder.

The plans should also include the following:

1 A plan of every floor, and sections of every storey floor and roof, to a scale of not less than 1:100.
2 A block plan of the building to a scale of not less than 1:500.
3 A key plan showing the position of the site when it is not identifiable from the block plan.

These plans should show:

(a) The level of the site of the building, the lowest floor, damp-proof courses, and of any street adjoining the curtilage of the building, in relation to one another and above some known datum.
(b) The position, form and dimensions of the foundations, walls, floors, roofs, chimneys, and the several parts of the building.
(c) The form and dimensions of every water closet and urinal in connection with the building, and their position.
(d) The size and position of the building and of the appurtenances of the properties immediately adjoining the building.
(e) The position and width of every street adjoining the curtilage of the building.
(f) The size and position of every yard and open space belonging to the building.
(g) The position of the sewer and where the drain is intended to be connected.

Building Regulations requirements

This application together with the accompanying drawings and specification of the proposed new structure or alteration will be carefully checked by The Technical Services Department to ensure that the details comply with the minimum standards recommended by the Building Regulations. Such checking may also be carried out by an 'Approved Inspector' who may be an Architect, Chartered Builder, Control Officer, Engineer or Surveyor who is engaged in private practice.

Copies of these Regulations may be obtained from HM Stationery Office, 49 High Holborn, London WC1 or through booksellers.

British Standards and Codes of Practice play an important part in these Regulations and in some cases are mandatory, therefore all applications should comply with the requirements of any

British Standards or Codes of Practice which may affect the Structure. In some cases new materials may be required to be used for which there is no British Standard. In these instances, it would be advisable to have an Agrément Certificate for each of the materials concerned.

The following are brief outlines of the sections which are included in the Building Regulations.
General Requirements:
Development of building control
Control of building work
Application to Inner London
Relaxation of Building Regulations
Exempt buildings and works
Notices and plans
Approved Inspectors
Work undertaken by public bodies
Materials and workmanship.

Approved Document A Structure covers the requirements for foundations, ground movement, timber floors, ceilings and roofs, thickness of walls, imposed loads, construction materials and workmanship, openings and recesses, masonry chimneys. It also covers the calculation of loading for work above ground in steel, aluminium, reinforced and prestressed concrete, bricks, blocks and stone.

Approved Document B Fire includes the fire resistance of various types of structures. The prevention of internal and external fire spread. The construction of stairways, shafts, walls, ceilings and roofs, fire stopping, separating walls and means of escape.

Approved Document C Site Preparation and Resistance to Moisture Subsoil drainage, resistance to weather and ground moisture. Hardcore. Suspended ground floors. Protection of walls against moisture.

Approved Document D Toxic Substance Cavity insulation. Urea formaldehyde. Timber framed structures.

Approved Document E Sound Insulation Refuse chutes. Solid masonry walls. Cavity masonry walls. Timber frame walls. Sound insulation of floors. Floor base with soft covering. Concrete base with floating layer. Masonry walls with abutting separating floors.

Approved Document F Ventilation and Con-

densation Right to light. Walls and roofs. Closed courts. Open courts. Mechanical ventilation. Condensation in low pitched and steep pitched roofs.

Approved Document G Hygiene Food storage. Bathrooms. Hotwater storage. Sanitary conveniences.

Approved Document H Drainage and Waste Disposal Sanitation pipework and drainage, traps. Branch discharge pipes. Junctions. Watertightness. Materials. Foul drainage layout, settlement, depth of cover, bedding and backfilling, flexible pipes. Cesspools and tanks. Septic and settlement tanks. Rainwater drainage. Solid waste storage, capacity, design and siting.

Approved Document J Heat Producing Appliances Solid fuel and oil burning appliances, ventilation. Balanced flue appliances. Flues and chimneys. Factory made insulated chimneys. Protection against fire and heat. Constructional hearths. Fireplace recesses. Walls and chimneys. Placing of appliances. Gas burning appliances.

Approved Document K Stairways, Ramps and Guards Rise and going. Common stairs. Headroom, treads, tapered treads, width, length of flights, handrails, landings, guarding flights. Ramps, protection from falling, vehicle barriers.

Approved Document L Conservation of Fuel and Power Resistance to passage of heat in dwellings and buildings. Thermal conductivity. Heating system controls. Boiler control. Insulation of heating services. Warm air ducts. Hot water storage vessels.

Approved Document M Facilities for Disabled People Ramps and steps. Doors and internal access. Lifts. Staircases. Water closets. Fire escape.

The provision of services

Water

One of the first services that will be required on a site will be water, and an application must be made to the local authority if the water is publicly run, or to the water undertaking direct if privately run.

The usual information that is likely to be required will include the following:

1   A description of the road, the type of surface, and whether it is kerbed and channelled.

2 The purpose for which the new main is required.
3 The name of the owner of the land.
4 The number of houses to be built on the site and their net annual value.

As soon as the water undertaking have the particulars, they will prepare an estimate of cost to provide the main water supply into the site. When this estimate has been accepted, the local water authority will make the necessary connection to the main supply and run a pipe into the site with a meter installed just inside the boundary. It is the responsibility of the builder to provide full protection for such a meter, either by means of a small brick chamber or a stop tap pipe (see *Brickwork 2*, Chapter 13). The builder can then take off supplies from the meter to any part of the site.

Drain connection to a sewer

When a connection to a sewer is needed, an application must be made to the local authority. In some cases the local authority will open up the road, make the connection, reinstate the road, and make a charge to the builder. In other cases the builder will have to open up and make the connection under the supervision of the local authority, and then reinstate the road. In this case, the local authority will reinstate the surface of the road. A nominal charge is then made by the local authority to the builder for the connection to the sewer, and another charge for the reinstatement of the road surface. This will vary according to the type of surface. A further charge will be made for the footway reinstatement, if it has been necessary.

It is important to note at this stage that when opening up a road surface, the correct road signs must be placed at proper positions in relation to the roadworks.

Electricity, gas and telephone services
Applications are made to the various public authorities for the services which are required. The applications are similar to those made for the supply of water. Charges will be made according to the length of the main required and the amount of work to be done.

Access
The builder may also need a new access to the site and an application for one must be made to the local authority. The local authority will make a nominal charge for this service.

Hoardings

When the work has started, it is usual for the builder to erect a hoarding around the site to prevent the public from having a free access, and to safeguard the structure and building materials.

In some instances, particularly in urban areas, where the building is adjoining a footway, it may be necessary to erect the hoarding on the footway. This, however, cannot be done until permission has been obtained from the local authority. When applying for a hoarding licence, a drawing should be submitted showing the position of the proposed hoarding and its construction. The period for which it will be required must also be stated.

A licence usually takes about 7–14 days to obtain and may be subject to certain requirements which could include the following:

1 The method of construction to be used is approved by the local authority.
2 The position authorized is accurately situated on site when it is erected.
3 A deposit is paid. Some local authorities reinstate the footway at a nominal cost to the builder which may be deducted from the deposit. A nominal fee is charged for the hoarding licence. These are usually valid for one month and then must be renewed. (Some local authorities will grant licences for longer periods.) Licences are also required for any scaffolds which may be erected on a footway. The fee for these may be charged according to the number of standards which are erected.
4 Fan-boarding, lighting and fender baulks for the protection of the public must be provided.
5 A double boarded decking must be secured at the first scaffold lift above the footway, if the public are allowed to walk underneath.

The boards on each layer must run in different directions.

6   Lighting should be provided at night-time for both hoardings and scaffolds. Some local authorities require that hoardings are painted white.

7   The ends of hoardings should be splayed off at 45 degrees wherever possible.

8   No advertising is permitted on hoardings. If an advertising hoarding is required, planning permission is necessary, and the construction of the hoarding must satisfy the specified standard.

9   Any doors which are situated in a hoarding should either open inwards or be sliding doors.

10 If the footway is restricted so that it is not possible for pedestrians to use it with safety, permission must be obtained for a temporary footway to be erected within the roadway. In this case the temporary footway must be of a sound construction with a raised platform, handrails and fender and the access at each end by means of a ramp rather than by steps, and must be well lit at night.

Inspection of work

When planning permission is granted, a set of cards is issued to the builder as a convenient way of informing the local authority when certain stages of the work have been completed. This enables the representatives from the local authority to visit the site to verify that the work is of the specified standard and in accordance with the permits granted by the local authority. The same procedure also applies to the inspection of drains. When a drain has been completed and concreted in, the local authority drainage inspector should inspect the drain while it is still under test, and, if it is satisfactory, pass it as suitable for use.

Should any work be below the minimum standard required by the Building Regulations, or not in accordance with the original specification, then the local authorities can order that part of the work to be corrected or rebuilt.

Rights of adjoining owners

When a structure is being built next door to an existing building, the builder must not cause any undue inconvenience to the people living in that building. It is impossible to build without dust and noise but this should be kept to an absolute minimum, and the neighbouring property must not be damaged at all. If any damage is caused to the adjoining owner's property, the builder may be liable for the cost of the work to repair or replace the damaged items. If a site lavatory, for instance, had been put too close to an adjoining house and had not been kept clean, the owner could well claim that the building was offensive and could demand that the lavatory be removed or maintained in a sanitary condition.

When starting a new site, then, it is important to remember that neighbouring owners of properties are not unduly inconvenienced. Good relations, maintained from the beginning, can be a great asset on site.

The Working Rule Agreement

This is a set of rules which has been compiled and approved by the employers' federations and the operatives' unions, and it is the code under which all personnel on site should be employed.

The agreement embraces all aspects of employment and includes the following points:

1   The minimum wage rates for craftsmen, labourers, apprentices, young male labourers, watchmen and female operatives.

2   Differential margins between various categories of operatives and including such trades as bar-benders, fixers, and scaffolders.

3   Payment of annual and public holidays.

4   The payment of incentives to operatives on site.

5   Definition of *normal* working hours; allowance for meal intervals.

6   The application of the *guaranteed week*.

7   Termination of employment; the employers' and operatives' obligations.

8   Extra payments for work which causes discomfort, inconvenience and risk.

9   Payments for extra skill and responsibility.

10 Tool allowances which are payable to vari-

ous classes of tradesmen.

11 Travelling time and allowances which may be payable to operatives and the circumstances under which these may be paid to operatives; lodging allowances.

12 Supplementary rules for woodworking factories and shops.

13 Code of welfare conditions including:
The provision of shelter during bad weather
Accommodation for clothing
Accommodation and provision for meals
Provision of drinking water
Sanitary conveniences
Washing facilities
First aid requirements
General site conditions

14 Registration, employment and training of apprentices; attendance at further education classes.

15 Negotiating machinery; regional and local joint committees and their duties and responsibilities; machinery for settling disputes.

These points only give an outline of the contents of the Working Rule Agreement. For further information, copies of this may be obtained from either the employers' or operatives' secretary of a local or regional joint committee.

It is advisable for all site personnel, particularly those who are responsible for the organization of men and work, to be familiar with the contents of the agreement. Knowledge of the agreement often prevents disputes on site, which are costly, seriously affect output and impair good personnel relations.

Self-assessment questions

1 List the typical services which a local authority can provide and for which it is responsible.

2 What information is usually required by a local authority when making an application for outline planning permission?

3 How should the details of the work to be done be given when applying for outline permission?

4 When should planning permission be applied for and what information must be submitted?

5 What plans and drawings should accompany a planning application, and what details should be shown?

6 What is meant by 'bye-law approval' and what information should be provided when making an application to the local authority?

7 Why is it so important that those who are responsible for the erection of new buildings should have a good working knowledge of the Building Regulations?

8 Is it necessary for planning and bye-law permission to be obtained when alterations are required to an existing building?

9 State the information that may be required when making an application for water to be supplied to a site.

10 What other services may have to be applied for on a site?

11 Under what circumstances must a builder apply to the local authority for permission to erect a temporary hoarding?

12 What are the likely conditions that a local authority can lay down when granting permission for a hoarding to be erected?

13 What conditions may also be needed for permission to be granted for a scaffold to be erected over a footway and also for a temporary footway?

14 Has a local authority the right to inspect the work on a site?

15 If an owner of a building adjacent to a site complained about the noise and dust that was being made on the site, is it in order to ignore him and tell him to mind his own business? If not, what other procedure should be followed?

16 What is meant by 'the Working Rule Agreement'?

17 Why is it so important to have a good knowledge of the contents of the Working Rule Agreement?

Chapter 2

Planning and programming site works

After reading this chapter you should be able to:

1 Have a good understanding of the preparation of a site programme.
2 Know how elements of work for a programme are calculated.
3 Have an appreciation of labour constants, machine outputs and standard time.
4 Have a good appreciation of work measurement and method study.
5 Know how to prepare arrow diagrams, bar charts and progress charts.
6 Know how to arrive at targets for bonus schemes.

The best methods for carrying out the work which is to be done on a structure should be carefully thought out before the work begins. This is very important as hasty decisions may be very costly later on.

Once the overall programme has been decided and discussed with all the management personnel who will be concerned with its operation, it is most essential that the outlines be communicated to everybody concerned. Everyone must know exactly what the detailed programme covers. Some straightforward details need to be distributed, showing such information as:

1 The sequences of various operations or elements of work.
2 The periods of such operations.
3 Dates for ordering materials.
4 Dates when special materials should arrive on site.
5 Estimated plant requirements and dates for arriving on, and leaving, the site.
6 Dates for subcontractors to arrive on site.
7 Any other information that may be of use for increasing the efficiency on site.

Communication is one of the biggest problems on site. Therefore, good site management should make certain that all personnel must be kept well informed by efficient presentation.

Resources

In order to prepare a plan for the construction of the new building, it is essential to have some knowledge of the resources that will be available for use on the site. These include the number of men available, and for how long, in each trade. This is not an easy question to answer as quite a lot of labour in the building industry is casual labour, but many firms have a nucleus of staff regularly employed who can be relied upon for work within their firms. In other cases, companies utilize labour-only subcontracting gangs, and in many cases a close affinity is built up between the firms and such gangs, who can be relied on to carry out the work efficiently.

In some cases, the local labour exchange will provide excellent information regarding the availability of the various trades, and even the general trend of availability of various trades at different times of the year.

Types and amount of plant available

Some firms may have their own plant, while others may hire plant from specialist companies. In both cases, the jobs which the plant is required to do must be carefully thought out if money is not to be wasted.

As soon as the probable availability of resources has been estimated, the outputs of men and machines must be evaluated, so that the times for elements of work can be determined. These labour constants must be realistic and allowances must be made for rests, bad weather, tea breaks and other interferences with normal output.

Example 1

An element of work on site is 1000 m^2 of 1-brick internal walling. If the firm's estimated labour constant for this work is 1.50 man/h/m^2 then the number of man/h required for this work will be:

1000 m^2 × 1.50 man/h/m^2
= 1500 man/h

If 10 bricklayers are available in a gang, the time to be taken will be:

$$\frac{1500 \text{ man/h}}{10 \text{ men}}$$

= 150 h

If an 8 hour day is worked on site, this element will take 18¾ days to complete.

Example 2

An element of work on a structure is 1200 m^2 of cavity walling with facing bricks on the external leaf and common bricks on the inner leaf.

The estimated labour constant is 1.50 man/h for the face work and 1.0 man/h for the internal wall (including forming the cavity), making a total time of 2.50 man/h/m^2 of walling.

Total number of man/h required to build the walling will be:

1200 m^2 × 2.50 man/h/m^2
= 3000 man/h
= $\dfrac{3000 \text{ man/days}}{8}$

= 375 man/days

If the work is to be finished in 25 days, the number of men required will be:

$$\frac{375 \text{ man/days}}{25 \text{ days}}$$

= 15 men

Therefore, it can be seen that either time or resources can be calculated provided output constants are known.

Example 3
The following example is taken from a typical page from a bill of quantities showing a part of the brickwork section, how these items can be collected to determine the resources required, and the time allowed for carrying out the work.

Item	Semi-engineering bricks in cement mortar (1:3)				
A	One-brick wall	60	m^2		
B	One-and-a-half-brick wall	30	m^2		
C	Extra for fair-face and flush pointing as work proceeds	50	m^2		
D	Ditto in margins	30	lineal m		
	Common bricks in cement/lime mortar (1 : 1 : 6)				
E	One-brick wall	20	m^2		
F	Half-brick skin of hollow walls	300	m^2		
G	Extra for keyed bricks	40	m^2		
H	Labour and material for forming 50 mm (nominal) cavity between brick casings of hollow walls and including four galvanized steel ties per square metre placed in staggered positions	300	m^2		
I	Rough cutting	20	m^2		
J	Labour and material closing 50 mm (nominal) cavity at openings with half-brick in common bricks and strip of bituminous felt damp-proof course 112 m wide	150	lineal m		
K	Labour only rough cutting at eaves to one-brick wall	25	lineal m		
	Partition walls lightweight concrete blocks in cement mortar (1 : 4)				
L	100 mm partition	80	m^2		
M	Rough cutting 100 mm partition against soffit	35	lineal m		
N	Labour and materials bonding 100 mm partition to brickwork including forming pockets	25	lineal m		
	Damp-proof courses in slate laid breaking joint in cement mortar (1 : 3)				
O	Horizontally on brickwork	10	m^2		
P	Ditto 100 mm wide	45	lineal m		
	Sundries				
Q	Rake out joints of brickwork as key	60	m^2		
R	Bed wood-frames in cement mortar (1 : 3) and pointing to one side in mastic	80	lineal m		

Method of apportioning labour contents according to programme requirements

Bill item no.	Progress item no.	Brief description	Quantity	Labour constant	Man/hours	Gang	Gang hours	Gang days	Remarks
		Engineering bwk							
A		1-b.w.	60 m²	2.25	135				
B		1½-b.w.	30 m²	3.10	93				
C		Ex. for fair-faced work and pointing	50 m²	0.2	10				
D		Do. in margins	30 lin.m	0.15	4.5				
		Commons							
E		1-b.w.	20 m²	1.3	26				
F, G, & H		275 mm hol. wall	300 m²	1.6	480				
I		Ro. cutting	20 m²	0.65	13				
J		Closing cavity	150 m	0.3	45				
K		Ro. cut at eaves	25 m	0.25	6.25				
		Partitions							
L		100 mm partition	80 m²	0.7	56				
M		Ro. cut at soffit	35 m	0.15	5.75				
N		Form. indents	25 m	0.2	5				
		D.p.c.s							
O		Hor. d.p.c.	10 m²	0.3	3				
P		100 mm d.p.c.	14 m	0.04	0.56				
		Sundries							
Q		Rake out joints	60 m²	0.2	12				
R		Bad frames and point	80 m	0.25	20	assume a gang of 6 men	152.5	say 19 days	
					915.06				

If the same work had to be completed within 12 days, the number of men required would have been:

$$\frac{915.06}{12 \times 8} = 9.53 \text{ (say 10 men)}$$

An alternative method of apportioning the labour contents according to programme requirements

Bill item no.	Progress item no.	Brief description	Quantity	Labour constant	Man/ hours	Gang	Gang hours	Gang days	Remarks
		Engineering bricks							
A		1-b.w.	60 m²	2.25	135				
B		1½-b.w.	30 m²	3.10	93				
C		Ex. for f.f. work & p	50 m²	0.20	10				
D		Do. in margins	30 lin.m	0.15	4.5				
					242.5	6	40.4	5	
		Commons							
E		1-b.w.	20 m²	1.3	26				
F, G, & H		275 mm hol. w.	300 m²	1.6	480				
I		Ro. cutting	20 m²	0.65	13				
J		Closing cavity	150 m	0.3	45				
K		Ro. cut at eaves	25 m	0.25	6.15				
		D.p.c.s							
O		Hor. d.p.c.	10 m²	0.3	3				
P		112 mm d.p.c.	14 m²	0.04	0.56				
Q		Rake out joints	60 m²	0.2	12				
R		Bed frames and point	80 m²	0.25	20				
					605.71	6	say 101	say 13	
		Partitions							
L		100 mm partitions	80 m²	0.7	56				
M		Ro. cut at soffit	35 m	0.15	5.75				
N		Forming indents	25 m	0.2	5				
					66.75	4	16.7	2	

Plant and labour outputs

The following examples are typical of reasonable standard times for various operations, but these should be carefully checked and verified, and, if necessary, adjusted to suit any special conditions before applying them to actual work on site.

Machine excavation	*Cubic metres per hour*
Surface excavation not exceeding 300 mm deep 0.375 m³ bucket	11
Surface excavation not exceeding 300 mm deep 0.625 m² bucket	21
Surface excavation not exceeding 300 mm deep 0.375 m³ bucket	12
Surface excavation not exceeding 300 mm deep 0.625 m³ bucket	24
Excavate foundation trenches not exceeding 1.5 m deep 0.375 m³ bucket	6
Excavate foundation trenches not exceeding 1.5 m deep 0.625 m³ bucket	12
Excavate basements not exceeding 1.5 m deep 0.375 m³ bucket	9
Excavate basements not exceeding 1.5 m deep 0.625 m³ bucket	18
Excavate basements exceeding 1.5 m and not exceeding 3 m 0.375 m³ bucket	7.5
Excavate basements exceeding 1.5 m and not exceeding 3 m 0.625 m³ bucket	15

Hand excavation	*Hours per cubic metre*
Surface excavation not exceeding 1.5 m deep	2.0
Add for each additional 1.5 m of depth	0.75
Excavate trenches not exceeding 1.5 m deep	2.5
Add for each additional 1.5 m of depth	1.0
Excavate pits not exceeding 1.5 m deep	3.0
Add for each additional 1.5 m depth	1.25
Excavate spoil from heap and load into barrow	0.5
Wheel 20 m	0.25
Load excavated material into lorries	0.6
Spread and level in layers not exceeding 300 mm thick	0.3
Return fill and ram	0.85
Level and ram bottoms	0.06/m²

Planking and strutting	*Hours per square metre*
To excavations not exceeding 1.5 m deep:	
poling boards and struts	0.075
open boarding	0.2
close boarding	0.4
To excavations exceeding 1.5 m and not exceeding 3 m deep:	
open boarding	0.3
close boarding	0.8

Hardcore filling	*Hours per cubic metre*
Filling in making up levels	0.5
Consolidated in 150 mm layers	1.0

Concrete work	*Hours per cubic metre*
Mixing:	
By hand for small quantities	4–6
By machine allow 4–5 minutes per batch according to type of mixer	
Transporting:	
By hand in barrows and wheel not exceeding 18 m or raise not exceeding 3 m	1.5
By machine plant and labour to suit required output and placing conditions	

Placing and compaction	*Hours per cubic metre*
Foundations in trenches over 300 mm thick	0.5
Foundations in trenches not exceeding 300 mm thick	0.7
Isolated pier holes	1.0
Beds over 300 mm thick	0.75
Beds over 150 mm thick not exceeding 300 mm thick	1.0
Beds not exceeding 150 mm thick	1.25
Add to the above for working around reinforcement	1.0

Surface treatment	*Hours per square metre*
Grading to falls	0.3
Tamping	0.2
Trowelling	0.25

Brickwork

(The following outputs are based on the ratio of 2 bricklayers to 1 labourer)

		Man/hours per unit
General brickwork in plasticized or gauged mortar 60 bricks		1.0
General brickwork in cement mortar 60 bricks		1.1
General brickwork overhand in gauged mortar 60 bricks		1.1
Walling curved on plan exceeding 15 m not exceeding 22 m radius 60 bricks		1.5
Walling curved on plan exceeding 7.5 m not exceeding 15 m radius 60 bricks		1.66
Walling curved on plan exceeding 4.5 m not exceeding 7.5 m radius 60 bricks		1.75
Walling curved on plan exceeding 3 m radius		2.0
Underpinning 60 bricks		2.0
Rough arches 60 bricks		3.0
Form cavity including laying wall ties, and keeping cavity clean	per m²	0.25
Rough cutting	per m²	0.7
Close cavity	per lin. m	0.3
Cut chase for small pipe	per lin. m	0.6
Eaves filling	per lin. m	0.3
Engineering bricks	per 60 bricks	1.50

Face brickwork		Man/hours per unit
General facing bricks	per m²	1.25
Fair-faced walling	per m²	1.10
Rake out joints and point on completion	per m²	0.75
Fair straight cutting	per lin. m	0.3
Fair raking cutting	per lin. m	0.4
Fair curved cutting	per lin. m	0.5

Arches		Man/hours per unit
Soldier arches or brick lintels	per m²	3.6
Fair axed arches	per m²	5.5
Rubbed and gauged	per m²	12.25

Copings and sills		Man/hours per unit
Brick-on-edge coping including pointing	per lin. m	0.4
Two courses of tile creasing	per lin. m	0.6
Brick-on-edge	per lin. m	0.75

Partitions		Man/hours per unit
Clinker, concrete and hollow clay 50 mm thick per m²		0.5
Clinker, concrete and hollow clay 75 mm thick per m²		0.6
Clinker, concrete and hollow clay 100 mm thick per m²		0.7
Lightweight blocks 50 mm thick per m²		0.4
Lightweight blocks 75 mm thick per m²		0.5
Lightweight blocks 100 mm thick per m²		0.6
Bonding to brickwork per lin. m		0.2
Rough cutting at irregular angles and soffits per lin. m		0.15

Damp-proof courses	Man/hours per unit
Two courses of slates horizontal per m²	0.9
Two courses of slates vertical per m²	1.35
Bituminous felt per m²	0.3

Sundries	Man/hours per unit
Bed plates and sill per lin. m	0.1
Bed frame and point one side per lin. m	0.25
Bed frame and point two sides per lin. m	0.35
Rake out joints and point flashings per lin. m	0.3
Cut groove for asphalt skirting and point per lin. m	0.45
Fix metal windows including cut and pin lugs to brickwork not exceeding 0.4 m² each	0.5
Fix metal windows including cut and pin lugs to brickwork not exceeding 0.8 m² each	0.75
Fix metal windows including cut and pin lugs to brickwork not exceeding 1.6 m² each	1.0
Add for pointing one side per lin. m	0.08

	Man/hours per unit
Air bricks each	0.2
Flue linings per lin. m	0.6
Set chimney pot and flaunch each	1.0

Scaffolding	Man/hours per 100 m² erect and dismantle
Putlog scaffold up to 6 m high	25
Putlog scaffold 6–9 m high	30
Putlog scaffold 9–18 m high	35
Putlog scaffold over 18 m high	40
Independent scaffolds add 25 per cent to the above	

Drainage: *Stoneware drain pipes*		Man/hours		
		100 mm	*150 mm*	*225 mm*
Lay and joint 600 mm pipes per lin. m		0.45	0.6	0.75
Lay and joint 900 mm pipes per lin. m		0.35	0.45	0.6
Extra for bends	each	0.1	0.12	0.15
Extra for junctions	each	0.2	0.25	0.3
Gulleys	each	0.5	0.66	—
Interceptors	each	0.66	0.75	—

Concrete drain pipes	*225 mm*	*300 mm*	*375 mm*	*450 mm*
Lay and joint per lin. m	0.8	0.9	1.1	1.25
Extra for bends each	0.2	0.25	0.3	0.35

Manholes		*100 mm*	*150 mm*	*225 mm*
Channels	each	0.2	0.3	0.4
Three-quarter section channels	each	0.3	0.5	0.7
Covers and frames bedding and fixing	each	0.75		
Step irons	each	0.1		

Work study

The examples given show that calculations of time and resources for doing work need a fairly accurate knowledge of labour constants and machine outputs. Although fairly shrewd guesses can be made against each item, the whole programme will be disrupted if mistakes are made. Apart from this, the staff who are trying to carry out the programme on the site would tend to distrust such a plan and, in time, completely ignore it because it is unworkable. In fact, it is not unusual for a plan to be prepared and then *expect* the job to overrun the time allowed. Although contingencies must be allowed for unexpected items, it does not necessarily follow that all work *must* overrun its scheduled time.

The modern builder is beginning to understand, and apply, the techniques of work study in order to assist him in determining labour constants, both for planning and estimating purposes. Not all work-study techniques are suitable for building work but there are a number which are proving to be most useful, and many larger companies have work-study sections within their units.

Work study is merely a study of all the factors being investigated to determine the efficiency and economy of a particular operation, and, if possible, to improve the method of the operation and shorten the length of time it is going to take.

Method study

Method study is the systematic recording and critical examination of existing methods which are being used for carrying out a piece of work. It is also used as a means of developing and applying easier and more effective ways of doing the work, which will in turn reduce costs.

With method study the operation must first be carefully studied and analysed and the facts examined. When these facts are sorted out, unnecessary movements, or steps of the operation, must be adjusted. Gradually a new method can be devised, which should be more efficient and economical.

When the new method has been devised, it has to be installed, and, in order to ensure the most efficient operation, the staff must have a clear picture of what is required through precise individual instructions given to each person taking part. It may mean altering traditional methods of carrying out particular operations. This can be a major problem, as it is very difficult to change the habits of people, especially when they have been used to carrying out certain operations in set ways for many years. Therefore, this change has to be done with much skill and sometimes with patience. But most workmen will carry out reasonable requirements provided they are put clearly in the picture and are shown exactly what part they will have to play in the new scheme. The workman may well be quite sceptical about the whole affair, but it is up to the work-study supervisor to make out a good case for the new method.

Once the new method is under way, the work-study team and the supervisors must ensure that the new method is maintained and that the old method does not gradually creep back into use.

From the craftsman's or foreman's point of view, they should be prepared to accept new methods of carrying out work even though they may seem completely divorced from established practice. They must also be willing to co-operate with a work-study team when they advance new ideas for site operations.

Work measurement

This is to establish the time that is required for a qualified operative to carry out a specified job at a defined level of performance. Anybody who is capable of using their hands is generally able to do any job, provided there is enough time in which to do it. Consider the example of an amateur *do-it-yourself* enthusiast who is attempting to build a garage. Note the time that the amateur takes in laying the concrete floor and the bricks in the walls. It will soon be apparent that builders would quickly be out of business if their craftsmen took as long as amateurs. It is, therefore, quite reasonable to expect that certain minimum standard times for operations which are performed by qualified workers can be determined. The important thing about such times is that they *must* be realistic and take into account

all factors which might increase the time, and make due allowances for such items as reasonable rest periods, tediousness of an operation, awkward or difficult operations, and weather conditions.

This aspect of work study is probably the one which creates the most suspicion among operatives, and the work-study team must be scrupulously honest when they are carrying out a work-study operation. It will be readily seen that good labour relations can soon be ruined by suspicion. Therefore, it is essential that the members of a work-study team are completely fair and accurate in their findings. The objectives of good work measurement are:

1 More effective and economic planning of site operations.
2 Efficient production planning and control.
3 Reliable performance outputs which will allow for accurate estimating of prices.
4 Provision of reasonable targets for incentive schemes.
5 Economic use of a firm's resources.

These objectives can only be achieved if there is a right attitude of mind with everybody concerned. It is also essential that everyone has a genuine desire and determination to produce good results.

Operating costs will usually be the final test of the success of a method change and a detailed scrutiny of the existing costs of running a job can be a useful guide in selecting the work to be studied.

In addition to costs, the following indications of the need for method study should also be looked for:

1 Bottlenecks in production.
2 Excessive movement of materials or personnel.
3 Inefficient utilization of materials.
4 Wastage of labour.
5 Idle machinery and plant, or inefficient handling or usage.
6 Excessive handling of materials by manpower.
7 The need to provide an efficient incentive scheme.

It is not within the scope of this book to describe in detail the various techniques that may be adopted by a work-study engineer, but rather to indicate to the reader that work study is a method whereby greater efficiency can be achieved in the construction industry. Provided there is a good co-operation by everybody concerned, everyone will benefit from the improved efficiency.

Use of charts for programming and planning

As soon as the amount of resources which are to be allocated to a job have been determined, and the labour and machine constants calculated, times can then be allotted for each operation or element of work. The sequence in which these operations are to be carried out is then decided.

The next step is to plot these times and sequence of operations into some form that is readily understood by all of the supervisory personnel who are concerned with the control of the project.

Two types of charts which are most useful for this type of work are arrow diagrams and bar charts. Both of these are used on building sites either separately or, better still, in conjunction with each other.

Arrow diagrams

When arrow diagrams are used, the project is broken down into a series of stages or elements of work called *activities*. These are represented by arrows, the length of which have no significance. The head of an arrow indicates the finish of the operation or activity and the butt indicates the start of the same activity. Any junctions of activities are called *events* and are represented by circles or nodes. An event indicates the completion of one activity and the start of another one, with the exception of the first activity, which represents the start of the project, and the last activity, which indicates the completion only.

Assume that there are five operations (A, B, C, D, E) involved in a small project and these are to be carried out in a continuous sequence, as if a do-it-yourself enthusiast was working alone. (See Figure 1.)

Then each of the activities may be identified by

Table 1

Activity	Identity
A	1–2
B	2–3
C	3–4
D	4–5
E	5–6

the numbers of the beginning and end events as shown in Table 1.

On the other hand, if these five operations had been started and finished at the same time, it is not convenient to present them as an arrow diagram, as shown in Figure 2, because each has the same identity, viz. 1–2.

Therefore, in order to give each a separate identity, *dummy activities* must be introduced. These are shown by dotted lines ....(Figure 3). The series of operations may now be given as shown in Figure 3, and identified as shown in Table 2.

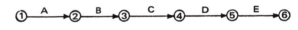

Figure 1

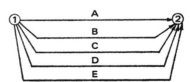

Figure 2

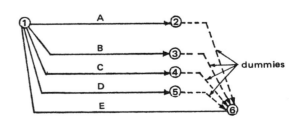

Figure 3

Table 2

Activity	Identity
A	1–2
B	1–3
C	1–4
D	1–5
E	1–6
dummy	2–6
dummy	3–6
dummy	4–6
dummy	5–6

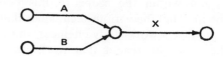

Figure 4

Figure 5

A dummy arrow has no duration and is used as a means of showing logical relationships which cannot otherwise be shown by activity arrows. They have no time and consume no resources, and are a means of transferring information from one event point to another. Arrows should always be identified by ascending order of numbers, so that the lower number is at the tail of the arrow, and the higher number at the head.

The questions which should be asked when setting out an arrow diagram for a project are:

What controls the start of each activity?
What controls its finish or end?
What job or jobs must be done before the next activity can be started?
What jobs must follow the activity?
What jobs can run concurrently?

The following are typical examples of the sequences which may be found in network analyses, and should be thoroughly understood before attempting arrow diagrams in full:

1   Activity X depends upon activities A and B (Figure 4).
2   Activities X and Y depend upon activities A and B (Figure 5).
3   Activity X depends upon activities A and B; and activity Y depends upon B only (Figure 6).
4   Activity Y depends upon activities A and B; and activity X depends upon A only (Figure 7).
5   Activity X depends upon A and B; and activity Y depends upon B and C (Figure 8).

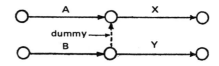

Figure 6

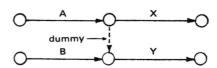

Figure 7

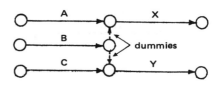

Figure 8

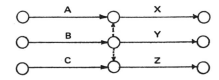

Figure 9

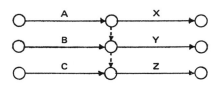

Figure 10

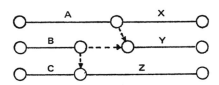

Figure 11

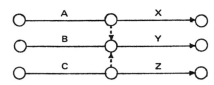

Figure 12

6 Activity X depends upon activities A and B; activity Z depends upon activities B and C; and activity Y depends upon B only (Figure 9).
7 Activity Z depends upon activities A, B and C; activity X upon A only; and activity Y upon A and B (Figure 10).
8 Activity Y depends upon activities A, B and C, activity X depends upon A only and activity Z depends upon activity C only (Figure 11).
9 Activity X depends upon activity A; activity Y depends upon activities A and B; and activity Z depends upon activities B and C (Figure 12).

Example: erecting a corner

Refer to Figure 13.

Activities
1 Raise scaffold
2 Deliver bricks from stack to scaffold
3 Place mortar boards
4 Mix mortar
5 Deliver mortar to scaffold
6 Build corner

In the preparation of the foregoing networks, we have so far been concerned with the placing of the activities in a logical order. It is now necessary to consider the time element and to apply this to the network in order to obtain the event times and the total project time. The duration of the activities should be written under each arrow. If the network is to be of value, these items must be carefully estimated, according to the work content contained within each activity.

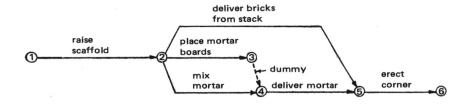

Figure 13

Earliest starting times

When the durations of the activities have been entered, the times of starting and finishing the events can be calculated. The earliest times for starting and finishing activities can be found by adding the duration of each activity to the finishing time of the previous activity. Begin at zero with the first activity and calculate each path separately. Where two or more paths meet at an event or node, the *longer* or *longest total time* must be taken as the earliest starting time of the next activity. An example of how to calculate earliest starting times is shown in Figure 14.

Latest starting times

This is a similar analysis carried out only in a *reverse* direction, which means beginning at the last event time and working backwards by deducting the activity time from the end event time. Where two or more paths meet at an event, the *shorter* or *shortest* time is adopted for the calculation of the latest starting time. The total times for each path have been indicated by the figures in circles, and it will be seen that the highest figures have been taken in each case.

Table 3

	Activity	Duration	Earliest	
			Start	*Finish*
A	1–2	15 days	0	15
B	1–3	10 days	0	10
C	1–4	12 days	0	12
D	1–6	29 days	0	29
	2–4	dummy	15	15
E	2–5	14 days	15	29
F	3–5	13 days	10	23
G	4–6	28 days	15	43
H	5–6	4 days	29	33
I	6–7	2 days	43	45

These times could also have been worked out by analysis as shown in Table 3.

Calculating latest finishing times

The times for each path have been shown in circles as before, but this time the *lowest figures* have been used in each case (Figure 15).

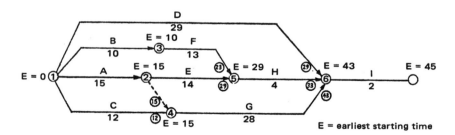

Figure 14

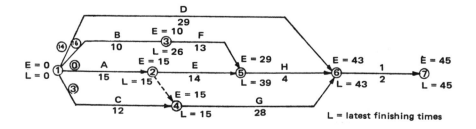

Figure 15

Table 4

	Activity	Duration	Latest		
			Start	Finish	
A	1–2	15 days	0	15	
B	1–3	10 days	16	26	
C	1–4	12 days	3	15	
D	1–6	29 days	14	43	
	2–4	dummy	15	15	
E	2–5	14 days	25	39	
F	3–5	13 days	26	39	
G	4–6	28 days	15	43	
H	5–6	4 days	39	43	
I	6–7	2 days	43	45	start here

Table 5

	Activity	Duration	Earliest		Latest	
			Start	Finish	Start	Finish
A	1–2	15 days	0	15	0	15
B	1–3	10 days	0	10	16	26
C	1–4	12 days	0	12	3	15
D	1–6	29 days	0	29	14	43
	2–4	dummy	15	15	15	15
E	2–5	14 days	15	29	25	39
F	3–5	13 days	10	23	26	39
G	4–6	28 days	15	43	15	43
H	5–6	4 days	29	33	39	43
I	6–7	2 days	43	45	43	45

It is most important that the dummy activity is taken into account when calculating the earliest starting and latest finishing times. These times could have been analysed as before, but in this case the calculating is started at the bottom of the table, and the durations are deducted from the latest finishing times, as shown in Table 4.

The two tables can now be combined, as shown in Table 5.

Floating times

From the diagrams and the analyses it will be seen that, if the earliest starting times are deducted from the latest finishing times, some activities have a greater length of time available for carrying out the activity than the work content requires. The spare time in each case is called the *total float*.

The total float for each activity is calculated as follows:

latest finishing time – earliest starting time – duration of the activity

Table 5 can now be used to calculate the total float for each activity, as shown in Table 6.

Critical path

Where there is a zero float against an activity, this activity will be a *critical* item. This means that such an item *must not* be delayed otherwise it will delay the whole project. These activities will form a continuous chain through the network, and this chain is called the *critical path*. There may well be more than one critical path in a network.

Table 6

	Activity	Duration	Earliest		Latest		Total float
			Start	Finish	Start	Finish	
A	1–2	15 days	0	15	0	15	0
B	1–3	10 days	0	10	16	26	16
C	1–4	12 days	0	12	3	15	3
D	1–6	29 days	0	29	14	43	14
	2–4	dummy	15	15	15	15	0
E	2–5	14 days	15	29	25	39	10
F	3–5	13 days	10	23	26	39	16
G	4–6	28 days	15	43	15	43	0
H	5–6	4 days	29	33	39	43	10
I	6–7	2 days	43	45	43	45	0

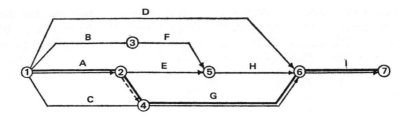

Figure 16

Table 6 shows that the critical path is composed of the following activities: 1–2, 2–4, 4–6, and 6–7 which are A, dummy, G and I which are shown in Figure 16.

The critical path includes the dummy activity.

All of the other activities have longer times than the durations need.

Bar charts

The activities which have been illustrated in Figures 14 and 16 can also be presented in another form of charting, as shown in Figure 17. The times for starting and finishing can be taken from the analysis.

Figure 18 shows a network of all of the activities for the erection of a house, and the analysis for this network should be set out as shown in Table 7.

The activities marked with an asterisk (*) in Table 7 are the critical path items, and are 1–2, 2–4, 4–5, 5–6, 6–7, 7–12, 12–14, 14–16, 16–19, 19–24, 19–25, 24–26, 25–26, 26–27, 27–28, 28–29, 29–33, 33–34. Activities 19–24, 19–25, 24–26 and 25–26 form two critical paths. This is quite in order, as it is possible to have more than one critical path in a network.

The sequence of operations outlined above can be shown in bar chart form as illustrated in Figure

Activity	Duration	Days
A 1–2	15 days	XXXXXXXXXXXXXXXXXXXXXXXXXXX critical activity
B 1–3	10 days	XXXXXXXXXXXXXXX[float]
C 1–4	12 days	XXXXXXXXXXXXXXXXXXXX [float]
D 1–6	29 days	XXXXXXXXXXXXXXXXXXXXXXXXXXXXXXXXXXXXXXXXXXXXXXXXXXXXXXXXXX[float]
E 2–5	14 days	XXXXXXXXXXXXXXXXXXXXXXXXXXXXXX[float]
F 3–5	13 days	XXXXXXXXXXXXXXXXXXXXXXXXXXX[float]
G 4–6	28 days	critical activity XXXXXXXXXXXXXXXXXXXXXXXXXXXXXXXXXXXXXXXXXXXXXXXXXXXXXXXX
H 5–6	4 days	XXXXXXXXXX[float]
I 6–7	2 days	critical activity XXXXXX

Figure 17

19. The floating time is indicated by dashes but the operations can be carried out at any period within the total time; that is, operational time plus floating time depending upon the sequence of work and the availability of resources.

Programming of work

Bar charts are most useful for plotting the progress of the various operations on the site, and can be used for indicating:

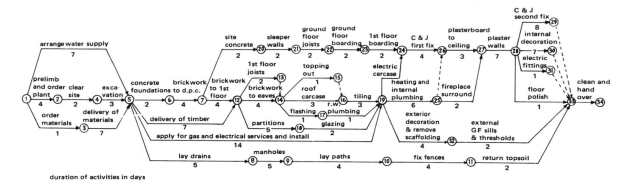

Figure 18 *A detailed network for the construction of a house*

Activity	Number	Duration in days	Days
Preliminaries	1–2	4	
Order material	1–3	1	
Water supply	1–5	7	
Clear site	2–4	2	
Del. of material	3–5	7	
Excavation	4–5	3	
Conc. Founds	5–6	2	
Lay drains	5–8	5	
Del. of timber	5–12	7	
Services	5–19	14	
Bwk up to dpc	6–7	4	
Bwk. to 1st fl.	7–12	4	
Site concrete	7–20	2	
Manholes	8–9	5	
Lay paths	9–10	4	
Fix fences	10–11	4	
Return topsoil	11–33	2	
1st F. joists	12–13	2	
Bwk to eaves	12–14	4	
Partitions	12–18	2	
Topping out	14–15	1	
Roof carcase	14–16	3	
Flashings	14–17	1	
Tiling	16–19	3	
R.W. plumbing	17–19	1	
Glazing	18–19	2	
Elec. Carcase	19–24	2	
Heating & Pl.	19–25	6	
Ext. decorate	19–32	4	
Sleeper walls	20–21	2	
G.F. joists	21–22	2	
G.F. floor bds	22–23	2	
1st F. fl. bds	23–24	2	
C. & J. 1st fix	24–26	4	
Fireplace sur.	25–27	2	
Plast. to Ceil.	26–27	3	
Plast. to wall	27–28	7	
C. & J. 2nd fix	28–29	8	
Int Decoration	28–30	7	
Elect. fitt.	28–31	1	
Polish floors	28–33	1	
Ext. sills etc.	32–34	2	
Clean & H.O.	33–34	2	

xxxx Duration of activity
—— Total float

Figure 19 *Bar chart showing the sequence of operations for a house*

Table 7

Activity	Number	Duration	Earliest		Latest		Total float
			Start	Finish	Start	Finish	
Prelims and order plant	1–2	4 days	0	4	0	4	0*
Order material	1–3	1 day	0	1	1	2	1
Arrange water supply	1–5	7 days	0	7	2	9	2
Clear site	2–4	2 days	4	6	4	6	0*
Delivery of materials	3–5	7 days	1	8	2	9	1
Excavation	4–5	3 days	6	9	6	9	0*
Concrete foundations	5–6	2 days	9	11	9	11	0*
Lay drains	5–8	5 days	9	14	33	38	24
Delivery of timber	5–12	7 days	9	16	12	19	3
Gas and electrical services	5–19	14 days	9	23	15	29	6
Bwk up to d.p.c.	6–7	4 days	11	15	11	15	0*
Bwk to 1st floor level	7–12	4 days	15	19	15	19	0*
Site concrete	7–20	2 days	15	17	21	23	6
Manholes	8–9	5 days	14	19	38	43	24
Lay paths	9–10	4 days	19	23	43	47	24
Fix fences	10–11	4 days	23	27	47	51	24
Return topsoil	11–33	2 days	27	29	51	53	24
1st floor joists	12–13	2 days	19	21	21	23	2
Bwk to eaves	12–14	4 days	19	23	19	23	0*
Partitions	12–18	5 days	19	24	22	27	3
Dummy	13–14		21	21	23	23	2
Topping out	14–15	1 day	23	24	25	26	2
Roof carcase	14–16	3 days	23	26	23	26	0*
Flashings	14–17	1 day	23	24	27	28	4
Dummy	15–16		24	24	26	26	2
Tiling	16–19	3 days	26	29	26	29	0*
R.w. plumbing	17–19	1 day	24	25	28	29	4
Glazing	18–19	2 days	24	26	27	29	3
Electrical carcase	19–24	2 days	29	31	29	31	0*
Heating and internal plumbing	19–25	6 days	29	35	29	35	0*
External decorate, etc.	19–32	4 days	29	33	47	51	18
Sleeper walls	20–21	2 days	17	19	23	25	6
G.f. floor joists	21–22	2 days	19	21	25	27	6
G.f. floorboards	22–23	2 days	21	23	27	29	6
1st f. floorboards	23–24	2 days	23	25	29	31	6
C & J 1st fixing	24–26	4 days	31	35	31	35	0*
Dummy	25–26		35	35	35	35	0*
Fireplace surround	25–27	2 days	35	37	36	38	1
Plasterboard to ceilings	26–27	3 days	35	38	35	38	0*
Plaster to walls	27–28	7 days	38	45	38	45	0*
C & J 2nd fixing and fittings	28–29	8 days	45	53	45	53	0*
Internal decoration	28–30	7 days	45	52	46	53	1
Electrical fittings	28–31	1 day	45	46	52	53	7
Polish floors	28–33	1 day	45	46	52	53	7
Dummy	29–33		53	53	53	53	0*
Dummy	30–33		52	52	53	53	1
Dummy	31–33		46	46	53	53	7
Ext. g.f. sills and thresholds	32–33	2 days	33	35	51	53	18
Clean and hand over	33–34	2 days	53	55	53	55	0*

1   The time spent on each activity.
2   The quantity of work done on each activity to date.
3   The percentage of work done to date.

In the following example, six activities have been selected from the bar chart of a project and show the amount of work completed and the time spent on each activity up to the end of week 9.

Figure 20 shows the level site, excavations and concrete foundations are all complete. The quantities for each week are clearly indicated and the percentage is shown by hatching in the planning line. The brickwork below ground level shows that $4\frac{1}{2}$ weeks have been spent on this activity, and 40,000 bricks have been laid. This is 55 per cent of the total and has been indicated on the planning line. The hardcore has had three weeks spent on it and 50 per cent of the work is completed. This has also been shown by hatching in the planning line. One week has been spent on the concrete slab with 10 per cent of the work being completed.

Incentives

Although it is often said that a fair day's work deserves a fair day's pay, human nature will usually produce extra work for extra money. Therefore, a well-designed incentive scheme can be very useful in increasing productivity on site. It is in this field that another useful application of work study can be made to set realistic targets for various operations.

If an incentive scheme is to be successful, it is important that both the employers and the operatives agree to the details of the scheme. In fact, the Terms of Settlement agreed in 1947 by the National Joint Committee for the Building Industry provide for the basic features of an incentive scheme to be discussed and jointly agreed. It is

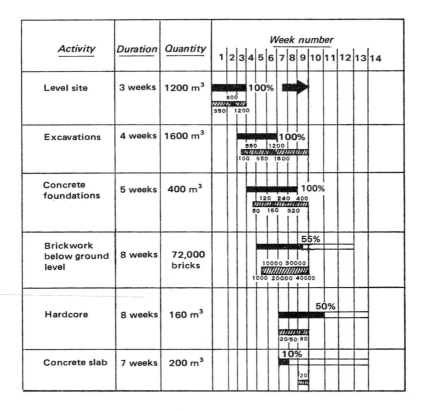

Figure 20

equally important that a successful scheme should also be designed so that both employer and employee stand to gain from it.

The essential features of any incentive scheme are that it must be:

1 Operated with honesty by all concerned.
2 Accepted by the representatives of the various craftsmen on site.
3 Easily understood and operated.
4 Possible for targets to be attainable by the average person.
5 Operated so that the bonus is paid weekly.

It will be fully appreciated that good planning is essential to a well operated incentive scheme.

Targets

Targets are not easily determined, and care must be taken in reaching reasonable figures for targets. Work study is a great help with their determination, but experience and a knowledge of site work and conditions can also play a most important part in reaching target rates. It is also vital that accurate information is fed back from the site to head office to show whether the estimates of targets are reasonable.

It is generally better to set the targets in terms of hours rather than in terms of money, so that each person, or gang, has a reasonable idea of how much bonus has been earned each week. It may create suspicion if people are paid a bonus and have no idea of how it has been earned. At first the extra money is readily accepted, but after a short while each person will ask if it is the right amount, and productivity will not necessarily be maintained at a good standard. In such cases it would be far better to pay a fixed rate of extra money each week; at least it would be an *honest* incentive.

The amount of bonus that it should be possible for craftsmen to earn above their weekly wages varies from firm to firm, and ranges from 10–35 per cent per week. Some firms pay as a bonus the full value of the hours saved, whereas others introduce a factor into the calculation paying 50–80 per cent of the time saved.

The following information is necessary when setting targets:

1 Full particulars of the type of work to be done.
2 The quantity of work.
3 The method to be used.
4 The men/hours per unit of work.

Method of calculating a bonus

Example 1

Assume that the full value of the hours saved is paid as a bonus.

Total weekly hours per person
$$= 44$$
Number of workers in the gang
$$= 2 \text{ bricklayers and 1 labourer}$$
Target hours for the completed job
$$= 78 \text{ bricklayers/hours}$$
$$39 \text{ labourers/hours}$$
Hours booked to complete job
$$= 64 \text{ for the bricklayers}$$
$$32 \text{ for the labourers}$$
Total hours saved = 21
Bonus hours per person
$$= 7$$
Therefore, the total payable hours for the completed job
$$= 32 + 7$$
$$= 39$$
If 12 hours are spent on another job which is not completed at the end of the week, then the weekly wage should be: $39 + 12 = 51$ hours per person (for working a 44 hour week)

Example 2

To raise the height of a 275 mm cavity wall through one scaffold lift (25 m² of walling).

A factor of 75 per cent is used in calculating the bonus.

Target for the bricklayers
$$= 60 \text{ hours}$$
Number of bricklayers
$$= 2$$
Total number of hours booked for the job
$$= 50 (25 \text{ per bricklayer})$$
Hours saved   = 10

Number of hours per man
$$= 5$$

Bonus payable $= \dfrac{\text{hours saved}}{\text{hours worked}} \times \text{factor}$

$$= \frac{5}{25} \times 75 \text{ per cent}$$

$$= 15 \text{ per cent}$$

Therefore, the bonus payable
$$= 15 \text{ per cent of 25 hours}$$
$$= 3\tfrac{3}{4} \text{ hours}$$
Total hours payable for the work done
$$= 25 + 3\tfrac{3}{4}$$
$$= 28\tfrac{3}{4} \text{ hours per bricklayer}$$

Self-assessment questions

1 Why is it important for the programme of the work on a site to be known by everybody concerned?

2 What is meant by the term *resources* in relation to site work?

3 Calculate the time required to build a 275 mm cavity external wall consisting of 1500 m² of walling. (Face bricks on the outer leaf and 100 mm lightweight blocks on the inner.)

4 If a gang of eight bricklayers is available to carry out the job in question 3, calculate how long it will take them to build the walling. How many bricklayers would be needed if the work has to be completed within 7 weeks.

5 Explain the meaning of the terms *work study* and *method study*, and state the advantages of their use in the building industry.

6 What is meant by the term *work measurement*?

7 What are the objectives of good work measurement?

8 What types of charts are used for the programming of site work?

9 Define the following terms
   (a) activities
   (b) events
   (c) dummies
   (d) total float

10 Seven operations – A, B, C, D, E, F and G – are to be programmed in a network diagram. From the following information construct a network showing their sequence:
   Activity E relies on A
   Activity B relies on A
   Activity C relies on B
   Activity F relies on E
   Activity D relies on E and C
   Activity G relies on D and F

11 If the times for the activities in question 10 are A = 3 weeks, B = 4 weeks, C = 4 weeks, D = 3 weeks, E = 10 weeks, F = 1 week and G = 2 weeks, analyse the times, calculate the total floats and determine the critical path.

12 Draw a bar chart showing the activities in question 10.

13 Explain how useful incentives can be on site.

14 What are meant by *targets* and what information should be available when setting them?

15 Calculate the hours payable to a gang of four bricklayers and two labourers for the construction of walling if the target hours are 150 for the bricklayers and 75 for labourers. If a factor of 80 per cent is payable, calculate the bonus payable when 125 hours have been booked.

Chapter 3

Drawings and bills of quantities

After reading this chapter you should be able to:

1 Have a good knowledge of the preparation and use of drawings and bills of quantities on site.
2 Understand the terms first, third and combined first and third angle projections and their uses.
3 Have an appreciation of the terms used in bills of quantities and their application to descriptions of work and materials.
4 Have a good knowledge of the scope of a bill of quantities and appreciate the importance of a site supervisor being familiar with the conditions and requirements contained within the bill.

Before work on a site is actually started it is most important that the contract supervisor is given full details of the construction which is to be built. This will enable the supervisor to carry out the work in the most efficient and economical way. With this information available, the supervisor will be able to maintain full control of:

1 The planning of the work and various processes.
2 The organization and economical employment of the labour force.
3 The ordering of materials and equipment to be installed.
4 The ordering and utilization of plant to be used in the construction of the buildings.

All the detailed information is usually provided in the form of drawings and a bill of quantities.

Drawings

These should be drawn in accordance with the requirements of BS 1192: Drawing Office Practice for Architects and Builders.

The requirements of this standard include the following points:

1 Centre lines should be indicated by a chain dotted line, that is: –·–·–·–· these should never be used to indicate dimensions.
2 Lines of hidden work or overhead lines should be indicated by a dotted line, that is: ··········.
3 Break lines are indicated by straight lines with short zigzags.
4 Section lines should be drawn as shown in Figure 21.
5 Dimension lines should be:
   (a) full lines, but thin in relation to outline;
   (b) continuous and not interrupted for the insertion of figures;
   (c) terminated at the lines to which they refer with either a dot or with sharp arrow heads.
6 The figures should always be placed parallel to the line and not at right angles (Figure 22).

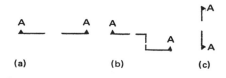

(a)   (b)   (c)

Figure 21

7 All dimensions should be so arranged that they can be read from the bottom or right edge of the drawing (Figure 23).
8 Where the structure is framed, all dimensions should be related to the column or stanchion centres.
9 Where the structure is of wall-bearing construction, dimensions should be related to the rough unfinished wall faces.

Building drawing practice requires the use of graphic symbols, which include the following:

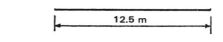

Figure 22

Figure 23

Description	Symbol
Centre to centre	C/C
Centre line	℄
Direction of view	⟶
External	ext
Internal	int
North point	⊕
Bench mark	BM
Existing level on plan	X 0.000
Existing level on section	V 0.000
Finished floor level	FFL
Ground level	GL
Required level on plan	X 0.000
Required level on section	V 0.000
Temporary bench mark	TBM

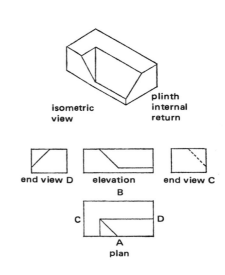

Figure 24 *First angle projection*

Finished floor levels

A suitable point on the main ground floor should be taken as a local datum, and all other floors should be related to it.

It is recommended that for building drawings first angle orthographic projection should be used.

Figure 25

Types of projection

First angle projection

With this method each view is so placed that it represents the side of the object remote from it in the adjacent view. Figure 24 shows the first angle projection of an internal angle return plinth brick.

The distinctive symbol of this method is shown in Figure 25. This symbol on a drawing indicates that the drawing is in first angle projection.

In this method of projection each view is so placed that it represents the side of the object next to it in the adjacent view.

Third angle projection

Figure 26 shows a third angle projection of the same plinth internal angle return.

The distinctive symbol of this method is shown in Figure 27.

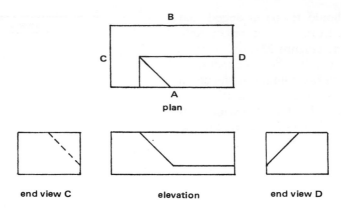

B

C   D

A
plan

end view C   elevation   end view D

Figure 26   *Third angle projection*

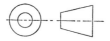

Figure 27

Combination of first and third angle projection

In relation to the elevation, end views are so placed that they are in third angle projection and plans are in first angle projection (Figure 28).

BS 1192 also shows recommended standard symbols, and site supervisors would be well advised to familiarize themselves with these and the drawing symbols, so that the drawings on site are well understood.

Representation of materials

Hatching for sectional brickwork, special bricks, existing brickwork, mass, reinforced and existing concrete, partitions, unwrot and wrot wood, earth and hardcore are all shown in Figure 29.

For efficient planning and construction, a complete set of drawings of the work to be executed should be available on the site before the work is actually begun. If these drawings are not ready, the contractor can be seriously handicapped by the lack of special details. A pictorial view of the work should be given, with the situations of the various buildings, roads, etc. The drawings will be drawn to scale but figured dimensions should

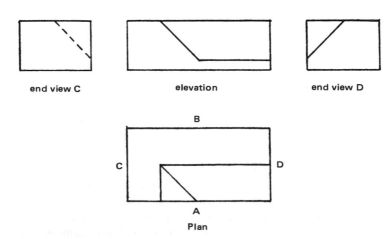

end view C   elevation   end view D

B

C   D

A
Plan

Figure 28   *Combined first and third angle projection*

always be taken in preference to those which are scaled. Any serious discrepancies, however, should be brought to the architect's notice as soon as possible.

Typical scales commonly used for different types of drawings in the metric system are:

Location drawings	1:2500	(0.4 mm to 1 m)
Block plan	1:1250	(0.8 mm to 1 m)
Site plan	1:500	(2 mm to 1 m)
	1:200	(5 mm to 1 m)
General location	1:200	(5 mm to 1 m)
	1:100	(10 mm to 1 m)
	1:50	(20 mm to 1 m)
Component drawings	1:100	(10 mm to 1 m)
	1:50	(20 mm to 1 m)
	1:20	(50 mm to 1 m)
Details	1:10	(100 mm to 1 m)
	1:5	(200 mm to 1 m)
	1:1	(full-size)
Assembly	1:20	(50 mm to 1 m)
	1:10	(100 mm to 1 m)
	1:5	(200 mm to 1 m)

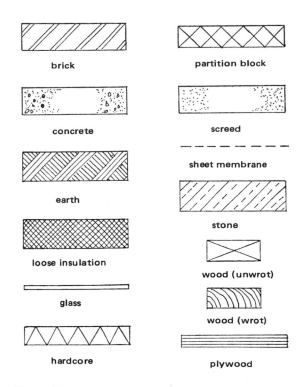

Figure 29

The drawings on site should be carefully filed in a plan chest and listed in a record book or on record sheets. All amended drawings which are sent to the site when the work is in progress, must also be carefully recorded together with the date of receipt. The superseded drawings must be clearly marked to indicate that they are outdated and to prevent them from being accidentally used by supervisory staff. A simple register of all drawings received on site should show the following information:

Drawing number	Date received	Title of sheet	Whether original or an amendment	Remarks

Bill of quantities

This states the quantities of materials and labours for the various sections of the work. The contractor will price work from the *bill*, although the site copy is generally a plain one with no prices indicated for the various items. The general conditions under which the work is to be conducted are stated and the works to be executed will be accurately represented by giving a full description of the quality of materials to be used and the standard of workmanship required.

When taking over a new site, the site supervisor must be absolutely familiar with the drawings and the bill of quantities, which must be read through thoroughly. The supervisor should take checks on the quantities of materials required, particularly any special items, and reconcile the bill with the drawings; and should also make a check on any *prime cost* items or any special items of equipment which have to be installed in the new structure, particularly if they have to be specifically ordered for that job. These should be ordered well in advance to allow time for making and assembling. On the other hand, special items should not be ordered and delivered to the site long before they are actually wanted for fixing, as there is a possibility of the items being lost or damaged while they are being stored.

The site supervisor must, therefore, have a sound knowledge of the method of *taking off quantities*, and the ambitious craftsman, who wishes to take up supervisory duties, must be prepared to include the subject of quantities when studying and to become familiar with the work of the quantity surveyor.

The bill of quantities is divided into sections, which includes the general conditions and preliminaries, and all the trades which would be applicable to the work to which the bill refers.

General conditions and preliminaries
This is a most important section which lays down the conditions of the contract, and gives many instructions with which the contractor must comply.

The description of the site stating where it is situated, its access and any special conditions, such as keeping access roads free from mud, hutment areas.

The description of the works giving a broad outline of the work to be carried out, with any special architect's instructions.

The examination of the contract documents by the contractor emphasizing the importance of inspecting the documents, and also the site, to determine the full extent of the works to be done, particularly to any works where special difficulties may be encountered. Money is easily lost on items which have been overlooked when making the preliminary examination of the site.

Insurances and holidays with pay stating that the contractor must insure against injury to persons and property, fire, payments for the National Insurance Act, National Insurance (Industrial Injuries) Act and holidays with pay for workmen.

Welfare and safety provisions. The requirements of the Construction Regulations regarding safety must be observed when carrying out site operations. These would include:

No. 1439 Health and Safety at Work etc. Act.
Trade Union and Labour Relations Act.

Notices and fees to local authorities. All fees and charges for services must be paid by the contractor. These will include such items as water supply, public services, and all other fees which may be demandable by the local authority.

Watching and lighting. The contractor must provide for all requisite day and night watching and lighting.

Maintenance of public and private roads. The site supervisor must ensure that roadways, footpaths and all other property of every kind and description are not damaged. If such damage accidentally happens, it must be made good to the satisfaction of the architect.

Water for works. The contractor must provide for the supply of water for the works on site; and is also responsible for the protection of any meters and cocks on the site.

Lighting and power. Artificial lighting and power must be provided on the site for all personnel, including subcontractors and nominated subcontractors (those who are nominated by the architect). The site supervisor is responsible for sufficient temporary leads and proper industrial sockets and plugs for general use on site.

Dayworks. This is payment for works which are either not part of the contract or which are a part but which are difficult to measure, for example, alterations or excavating under buildings, such as underpinning. In such cases authority can be given to carry out the works by daywork. The site supervisor must submit sheets describing the work involved, and give the workmen's names, trades, daily time and the materials used. These sheets are usually prepared in duplicate or triplicate and submitted to the clerk of works at the end of each week for verification. The clerk of works retains only one copy and the others are returned to the contractor. The duplicate copy is sent to the costing department. If three copies are used, one copy can be retained by the site supervisor on site.

Materials and workmanship. This should indicate the quality of the material and workmanship to be used; British Standards can be quoted. It may also require that samples of materials should be submitted to the architect before they are used on site. Samples of work may also be needed by the architect, for example brick panels with specimens of pointing.

Provisional sums. These are sums of money which are provided to cover the cost of an operation or special work on site, which at the time of estimating the actual cost cannot be accurately determined. The sum of money may be adjusted by the architect when the actual costs are known after the work has been executed.

Prime cost sums. These are sums of money which are provided for the provision of special items of equipment which are to be installed in the structure. These sums may also be adjusted when the items have been installed and the final accounts are being prepared.

Fix only. This term refers to items where the contractor is required to fix equipment which is supplied. It can also include taking delivery of the equipment or goods supplied by nominated suppliers, unloading, storing, assembling and fixing, which the site supervisor should ensure are included in the contract.

Attendance facilities. Each trade shall attend upon, cutaway for, and make good after all other trades. In the case of nominated subcontractors this item can also mean providing the use of scaffolding and plant, storage accommodation, free use of water, artificial light and power, assistance in unloading and hoisting materials.

Temporary buildings. Temporary buildings include hutments for the clerk of works, foreman, and workmen, which must have the necessary attendance, as well as adequate heating, lighting, furniture, washing facilities and telephones for the clerk of works and foreman. Storage space must also be provided for materials and small equipment. Adequate temporary latrines must be provided for the use of all workmen on site and these must be kept clean and disinfected daily. On the completion of the works, all temporary hutments must be removed and the area made good.

Temporary hoarding and gantries. The contract may require that the necessary hoardings, gantries or temporary footways are installed on the site. The supervisor should ensure that the work complies with the contractual and local authority requirements, but also that it is executed as economically as possible.

Protection, clearing and drying of works. The site supervisor should ensure that the works are protected against damage through adverse weather conditions and accidental or thoughtless actions by workmen. Therefore, sufficient covers, hessian and temporary casings must be provided. (It is much more economical to provide temporary casings to expensive items such as dressed stone or hardwood frames, than to replace or even repair the damaged items.) Contracts often require the structure to have been dried out before it is handed over to the client or before decoration work is begun. Therefore, sufficient drying equipment should be provided. The structure must also be thoroughly cleaned and all surplus materials removed before handing over to the client. A good supervisor who maintains a clean and tidy site can save a lot of money by preventing wastage of materials. This will also keep the cost of cleaning to a minimum.

Most bills of quantities list these items, although there is a certain amount of variation in the wording and requirements to suit different sites. A study of these will show the importance of this section, and it will be readily seen that an efficient supervisor can be very valuable to a company and will produce good site organization.

After the general conditions and preliminaries section, the bill is then divided into *trade* sections, giving specific descriptions for work on the particular site to which the bill refers. It is, therefore, only possible to give broad outlines of the items to which reference can be made in a bill of quantities, and these are as follows:

Demolitions and alterations

Description. The description should state the location of the demolitions and its precise nature.

Materials arising from demolitions. The contract will state whether the salvaged materials remain the property of the client or become the property of the contractor, and the supervisor should be quite certain as to which the case may be. The contract will also state whether or not old materials can be re-used in the case of work which is to be altered.

Adequate shoring. Adequate shoring must be provided to satisfy the requirements of the contract and the building regulations.

Excavation and earthworks

The description. This shall require that accurate levelling must be carried out in conjunction with all excavation work.

Nature of the subsoil. It is essential that the nature of the soil is determined as well as the water table level before the excavations begin. Allowance should also be made for pumping surface water out of trenches (see *Brickwork 2*, Chapter 1).

Levels. Great care should be taken to ensure that all excavations are taken down to their correct levels. If any excavation is taken down to a greater depth than necessary, the filling-in should be made with concrete and not earth. All other filling-in should be made with the best of the excavated material, and should be well-compacted in layers not exceeding 225 mm in thickness.

Bottoming up. All excavated surfaces shall be cleanly bottomed up, levelled or bottomed to falls and gradients as required, and well-compacted.

Hardcore. Hardcore shall be clean, hard, dry, broken brick. Alternatively stone ballast rejects, or old Portland cement concrete can be used. The hardcore must be deposited, watered and compacted in layers to the required depths, and not exceeding 225 mm layers. The blinding should be either approved hoggin, which is free from all vegetable and organic matter, or hard, fine gravel, compacted to receive concrete.

Concrete

Description. The description should give the required quality of the materials, such as cement, sand and coarse aggregate, and the quality of the water (see *Brickwork 2*, Chapter 16).

Mix proportions. Some contracts will specify actual mix proportions while others will state the minimum strengths of concrete required. They can also quote whether the concrete materials are to be batched by volume or by weight. Specified mixes may also be stated (see Chapter 15).

Quality of concretes and testing. The bill will usually state the minimum standard of quality of the various mixes of concrete, in addition to the tests that may have to be carried out to verify such quality (see *Brickwork 2*, Chapter 16).

Protection and curing. This section emphasizes the need for protecting the freshly laid concrete against sunshine, drying winds and rain. Concrete should also be prevented from drying too rapidly; curing should be carried out over a period of at least seven days for mass concrete and fourteen days for reinforced concrete.

Reinforcement. This should comply with the British Standard requirements for structural steel or for hard drawn steel wire, whichever is applicable. All steel should be free from loose mill scale, loose rust, oil, grease or dirt.

Brickwork

Description. This section should describe the types and qualities of the materials to be used in the walling, such as the lime, cement, sand, and various types of bricks (see *Brickwork 1*, Chapters 1 and 2). It may also require samples to be submitted to the architect for approval before being used on the site.

Gauging of mortars. These should be gauged in their correct proportions so that they are of uniform colour, and thoroughly mixed together on a properly constructed platform. Anti-freeze liquids or plasticizers are not usually used except when expressly approved by the architect. (The site supervisor should be careful not to introduce work aids of this type without first obtaining approval from either the clerk of works or the architect.)

Construction. A typical clause is: 'The brickwork shall be laid four courses to 300 mm, frog up, carried up level and plumb with each course well-filled and flushed-up with mortar as the work proceeds. No portion of the work shall be built more than 900 mm higher than the adjoining work and shall be racked back and not toothed. Both skins of cavity walls shall be carried up together, the ties being built in solid as the work proceeds. The bond to walls 1-brick thick or over shall be Flemish bond (or any other bond) and to ½-brick walls shall be stretcher bond.'

All cavities and wall ties should be kept clear of mortar droppings and rubbish by means of battens or straw bands raised with the work. Temporary openings for the purpose of cleaning out bottoms of cavities and over openings should be left, and made good to match the surrounding work. No cleaning hole should be made good before inspection by the clerk of works.

Face work. All bricks used for facings should be carefully handled to prevent broken arrises. No chipped or dirty bricks should be used on face brickwork, which should be protected in wet weather from splashes and stains, especially at scaffold levels. The whole should be cleaned down and putlog holes made good in mortar and gauged to match the remainder of the brickwork.

Rubble walling

Description. The kind of stone needed should be stated, for example, sandstone, limestone, granite, flint, and any requirements regarding the stone or the quarry.

Type of walling. Whether it is to be squared, random, or coursed. If it is to be coursed the average heights of the courses should be stated. If diminishing courses are to be used, the maximum and minimum heights of courses must be stated.

Finish of walling. The texture and finish of the walling should be described; that is, whether it is to be natural, rough-dressed or hammer-dressed.

Mortars. The composition and mixes of mortars should be described for bedding, jointing and pointing the stones. The method of pointing should also be clearly described.

Masonry: natural stone

Description. The type of stone to be used should be clearly described, for example, granite, slate, sandstone, limestone or marble, and any requirements as to the stone and the quarry.

Finish. The finish to the exposed face of the stonework should be stated, for example, sawn, rubbed, tooled, vermiculated, reticulated or polished.

Mortar. The composition and mix of mortar for bedding jointing, and pointing, should be described.

Pointing. Any requirements for the pointing of the stonework should be stated, as well as any requirements for the coating of the surface of the finished work and cleaning on completion of the work.

Masonry: cast stone

Description. The description should include the kind and quality of cast stone, and any special requirements as to the thickness, mix and colour of the facing material.

Finish. The texture and finish of the blocks should be described, which may include rough, smooth, rubbed, vermiculated, reticulated or polished.

Mortar. The materials and composition of mortars should be stated.

Pointing. The method of pointing should be stated, as well as the materials to be used. Any requirements regarding the cleaning of works on completion will also be described in this section.

Asphalt work

Description. Asphalt work is usually kept under three separate headings: (1) damp-proofing and tanking; (2) paving; (3) roofing, and described as such. The kind and quality of asphalt should be given.

Application. The number of coats to be applied should be stated, as well as the required thickness.

Surface treatment. The method of treating the surface of the asphalt should be described.

Roofing

Description. The description should state the kind of slate or tile to be used, for example, asbestos-cement, slates, natural slates, stone slabs, clayware tiles, concrete tiles or shingles.

Quality of materials. The size, type and quality of the tiles or slates should be given.

Fixing. This should clearly describe the method of fixing, the required lap, and the number and kind of nails or pegs per slate or tile, together with the size and type of laths or battens. Similarly, for other types of roof coverings, such as corrugated or troughed sheet, roofing, roof-decking, bitumen-felt, sheet metal, the description should include their quality, extent of laps, method of fixing, and any surface treatment.

Carpentry

Description. The timber should be the best of its respective kind, sawn die square out of suitable logs, and free from all defects such as improper seasoning, large loose or dead knots, radial heart, cross shakes, warp, wane, sapwood or deadwood. All timber should be inspected by the architect or representative before it is fixed.

The carcassing timber. This must be of Douglas fir.

Fixing. All carpentry should be executed in a workmanlike manner and jointed to the satisfaction of the architect.

Impregnated timbers. Timber described as treated with wood preservative must be vacuum/pressure impregnated with the specified ingredient to the dry salt retention specified by the manufacturer. All timber should be machined to its final dimension as far as possible before treatment. Where subsequent cross-cutting or boring of the treated timber is unavoidable, all exposed surfaces must be liberally swabbed with a suitable preservative.

Joinery

Description. This should include the quality and type of timber to be used, and any preliminary treatment that may be required, such as kiln drying, or impregnation.

Joinery. All joinery should be wrought on all faces, 3 mm should be allowed from the nominal size to allow for each wrought face. All joinery should be adequately protected from the weather and should be delivered to site unprimed, sanded smooth for painting. All sharp edges and machine marks removed. Any disfiguring marks and defects should be removed at the contractor's expense. External work should be put together with hardwood dowels and a mixture of white lead and glue, unless otherwise described. All joinery work must be adequately protected from any damage that may arise from other trades which are being carried out.

Plumbing and engineering installations

This section is generally under several headings which include the following: *rainwater*; *sanitary installation*; *cold water*; *hot water*; *heating*; *ventilating* and *air conditioning*; *fire-fighting equipment*; *hydraulic installations*; *gas* and *compressed air*. Reference should be made to any rules, regulations, bye-laws, etc., with which the installation has to comply. The kind and quality of all materials should be stated and all tests to be carried out should be fully described.

Plasterwork

The description can include full details of the materials to be used and references to the British Standards which apply. The work which is to be executed should also be classified under separate headings.

The plasterwork should not be carried out in unsuitable weather and must also be protected from frost and strong sun.

The plasterboard used throughout should be 10 mm thick gypsum wallboard in sheets complying with BS 1230. Fixing should be by means of No. 12 s.w.g. galvanized countersunk head nails at 150 mm centres to softwood. Sheets should be fixed to break bond, leaving a slight gap which should be filled with neat board finish plaster and covered with reinforcing jute scrim cloth. Jute scrim should also be fixed at the joint between the ceiling and the wall and at external angles.

The finish on the plasterboard should be Class B retarded hemi-hydrate board finish and mixed and used within the period recommended by the manufacturers. Any material which has started to set must not be retempered. Mixes containing cement should be used within two hours of mixing and any material which has not been used after this time must be discarded.

The wall finishes are to be carried out in Class C anhydrous gypsum plaster with a backing coat of one part plaster to two parts of clean, washed sand and a neat finishing coat. The backing coats should be mixed and applied in accordance with the manufacturer's instructions.

All surfaces to be plastered should be thoroughly clean and free from loose material, mould oil, grease or anything that might interfere with the adhesion of the rendering coat. No plastering should take place until the key of the surface has been inspected and approved.

Glazed earthenware wall tiles should comply with the requirements of BS 1281, and be well-soaked before bedding. Tiles should be bedded in cement mortar (1:3). fixed with continuous vertical and horizontal joints and pointed with white cement. Alternatively the wall tiles can be bedded on an approved adhesive which should be applied in accordance with the manufacturer's instructions.

Granolithic paving should consist of two parts of Portland cement to five parts of granite chippings to BS 1201 from 6 mm down to No. 100 sieve waterproofed with an approved cement waterproofing powder and sprinkled with carborundum powder 1 kg/m^2.

Granolithic surfaces should be trowelled immediately upon laying to give a level surface, and further trowelled when the mix has stiffened to a point where a hard compact surface can be obtained without bringing up laitance. Dusting with cement before final trowelling must not be allowed.

The paving should be kept damp for a minimum period of seven days after laying.

Glazing

The general description should include the various kinds and quality of glasses to be used. They should be in accordance with the requirements of BS 952.

All glass should be puttied and back puttied with the appropriate putty or mastic and sprigged where required as follows:

To wood with beads – linseed oil putty to BS 544.
To metal without beads – arbolite.
To wood or metal with arbomast 500 with butyl rubber beads.

All scratched glass must be replaced at the contractor's expense.

680 g glass must be used when glazing to wood panes not exceeding approximately 0.4 m^2.

1 kg should be used for glazing to metal in panes over 0.4 m^2 but not exceeding 0.8 m^2.

Painting and decorating

The work in this section should be divided into internal and external work.

Knotting should comply with the requirements of BS 1336.

Priming paint should comply with the requirements of BS 2521 and 2523.

Washable distemper should comply with the requirements of BS 1053(b).

Mordant solution to be composed of 50 g of copper acetate to 1 litre of water.

Where galvanized surfaces are damaged prior to painting, one coat of cold galvanizing compound must be applied in accordance with the manufacturer's instructions.

Paint should be delivered to the site in manufacturers' sealed containers and used without dilution or adulteration.

Before being painted, all ironwork must be scraped and wire brushed to remove all grease, rust and scale, and all galvanized surfaces coated with a mordant solution, unless previously treated by the supplier.

The prices include covering up and protecting floors and all other work and fittings.

Drainage

Drainage trenches should be constructed under the same rules which apply to earthwork trenches.

The kind and quality of the pipes should be stated also their appropriate British Standard, viz. salt-glazed ware pipes and fittings BS 65, pitch fibre BS 2760.

Pipes should be laid in straight lines from point to point and in even falls.

Trenches should be excavated at least 300 mm wider than the diameter of the pipe, and all bottoms well-consolidated and graded to falls as required. Backfilling should be executed in 150 mm layers well-consolidated, the first 300 mm being free from stones and rubble.

Drains, except where otherwise stated, are to be laid direct on the concrete bed, grooves being formed or cut for the collars so that the pipes are bedded or supported during their whole length. Any other suitable method of laying salt-glazed ware pipes (see *Brickwork 2*, Chapter 13) can be used.

Soil and surface water drains which are laid to a slope exceeding 45 degrees or with less than 300 mm cover to finished ground level or which are laid on made up ground are to be completely encased in concrete 100 mm thick. Soil drains laid to a slope between 30 and 45 degrees or with less than 1 m cover to ground level are to be bedded on concrete 100 mm thick and haunched half-way up the sides.

The surface water drains should be subjected to a smoke test and the soil drains should be subjected to a water test and a ball test in sections to the satisfaction of the architect. These tests are usually carried out before any haunching or backfilling has begun.

Note: The Building Regulations state that a test should be carried out after the completion of the haunching and backfilling (see *Brickwork 2*, Chapter 13).

Methods of constructing manholes, catchpits and soakaways should also be described.

A bill of quantities is therefore a comprehensive document, and, to understand the requirements of a bill of quantities, a site supervisor must have a good knowledge of all trades.

Although it is essential for craftsmen to make a full study of their own trade, it is equally important to observe the associated crafts and to study how they fit in with each other, and the methods of co-ordinating the work as a whole.

Self-assessment questions

1 Explain why it is so important for the site supervisor to have full information of the work which is to be carried out, before the work is begun.

2 Illustrate the methods of showing centre lines, break lines, dimension lines and section lines on a drawing.

3 From where should datum lines be taken?

4 What is meant by first angle and third angle projection?

5 To a scale of a quarter full-size draw a plan, elevation and two end elevations in first angle and third angle projection of the squint brick shown in Figure 30. The brick is 75 mm thick.

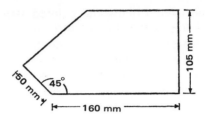

Figure 30

6 Illustrate the hatching, in accordance with BS 1192, for special bricks, existing bricks, concrete, existing partitions, earth and wrought wood.

7 Why is it so important for the site supervisor to understand a bill of quantities?

8 Explain the meaning of *dayworks*.

9 What are meant by *prime cost* and *provisional sums*?

10 What facilities should the site supervisor have to provide for *fix only* items?

11 What methods should be adopted for the protection, cleaning and drying of works?

12 When demolition work is being carried out on site, is it permissible for the salvaged materials to be used in the new structure?

13 What particulars regarding earthworks should be included in the *earthworks* section of the bill?

14 How can the quality of concrete be specified in the bill?

15 Outline a typical clause for the construction of brickwork.

16 State the typical requirements for face work.

17 State the finishes that can be found in rubble walling and masonry.

18   What points should be included when specifying timber for carpentry?

19   Explain the definition of *impregnated timbers* and any special precautions that should be taken when cutting and fixing.

20   How should the supervisor expect to receive joinery on site?

21   Describe a method of fixing and finishing a plasterboard ceiling.

22   Describe the laying of granolithic paving.

23   State the composition of mordant solution and for what purpose it is used.

24   How should salt-glazed pipes be laid?

25   What special precautions should be taken when pipes are laid at a steep angle?

Chapter 4

Measurement of work

After reading this chapter you should be able to:

1 Have a good knowledge of the principles of measurement.

2 Be able to understand and apply abbreviations when taking-off.

3 Be able to take-off quantities for brickwork, partitions and drainage.

In Chapter 3 it was shown how the bill of quantities fully described and accurately represented the work to be executed. Work which could not be measured accurately was described as *provisional* or given in a bill of *approximate quantities*. Other work is measured from drawings in order to determine the quantity of materials and labour involved in the erection of the structure.

The principles of measurement

These measurements have to be taken systematically so that every item and operation essential to carry out the work is included in the measurement and accurately calculated.

When measuring walling, it is the usual practice to measure over all the work and deduct openings from that overall amount. This method allows the work to be measured without having a great number of small dimensions. This is clearly illustrated by the example shown in Figure 31.

The area of walling is calculated by multiplying the length of the wall by the height of the wall and then deducting the total area of the three windows. This method only requires two measuring operations, whereas six measuring operations would be necessary if each portion of walling were measured separately (Figure 32).

Therefore, it is obvious that the more measuring operations that are used in taking off quantities, the more chance of mistakes and the greater the difficulty in trying to reconcile the measurements with the drawings.

It is also most important that the measurements

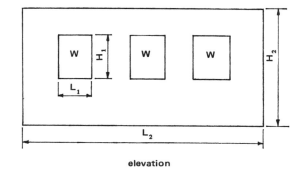

elevation

Figure 31

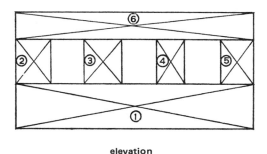

elevation

Figure 32

are recorded in a uniform and systematic way. The paper used for this work is called *taking-off* or *dimension paper*, and is ruled, for example:

Timesing	Dimensions	Quantities	Description

The dimensions are entered in the second column (marked *dimensions*, see above example) and these are always entered in their correct order. For example, if numbers of items or linear measurements are to be shown, single numbers are entered in the second column. If areas are to be measured then the length is always the first number and the height or depth is the second number. When volumes are measured, the figure indicating the length is entered first, the figure representing width or breadth second, and the figure representing height or depth last, for example:

20		Number
20.0		Linear measurement
10.0	length	} Area of superficial measurement
20.0	height	
15.0	length	} Volume
5.0	breadth	
20.0	height	

When the quantity for each item has been computed, the total is entered in the third column which is marked as *quantities*, for example:

Timesing	Dimensions	Quantities	Description
2/	20.0 10.0	400.0	= 2 × 20 × 10 = 400 m²
3/2/	20.0 10.0	1200.0	= 3 × 2 × 20 × 10 = 1200 m²
2/½/	20.0 10.0	200.0	= 2 × ½ × 20 × 10 = 200 m²

In order to identify each measurement, an accurate description must be written against each item. These descriptions can be abbreviated to save time and space but they must be clearly understandable to everyone who has to read the quantities.

Where there are a number of measurements relating to one item, these measurements can be listed under the one description. The best way of doing this is to bracket them together with a straight line drawn between the *quantities* and the *description* columns, as in *planking* and *strutting* in Example 1 on page 53.

The 'timesing' column is used when there are a number of items of the same dimensions to be taken off. Instead of entering a long list of measurements in the *dimensions* column, the number of times that the same item occurs is entered in the timesing column and a sloping line is drawn between the figure and the measurement (see above example).

To ensure complete accuracy when measuring work, extreme care must be taken at all times. Mistakes will always be costly. Dimensions are taken to the nearest 10 mm, that is, units 5 mm or over will be taken to the next unit of 10 and numbers under 5 will be ignored.

Booking dimensions
The following are general points to watch when booking dimensions:

1 Book dimensions in metres and correct to two places of decimals only.
2 Where dimensions are for less than one metre, place a nought before the decimal point.
3 Use millimetres in descriptions (except where the Standard Method of Measurement does otherwise).
4 'mm' to be written at the end only of a size sequence in a description where the normal order of dimensions applies. For example, 350 × 280 × 180 mm precast concrete slab.
5 Use metres in descriptions where figures are separated by words. For example, exceeding 1.50 m but not exceeding 3.00 m deep for trenches.
6 Give cubing in metres and add 'm' to avoid doubt.
7 Use two decimal places for cubings, as for other bookings. Occasionally three places may be used where the dimensions are very large.
8 Book side casts should be taken to three places of decimals when dimensions on drawings are in metres. Book side casts in millimetres to the nearest millimetre where dimensions on drawings are in millimetres.

9   When taking side casts in millimetres, the total should be taken to two decimal places and the last figure ignored if below 5, but, one should be added to the second figure if above 5.

10 Squaring dimensions should be carried out correct to two places of decimals.

Measuring perimeters

When taking-off quantities for brickwork, excavations and concrete for a building, it is essential to calculate the perimeter of the structure. Such calculations must be shown clearly in the *description* column of the *taking-off* sheets. Example 1 shows the method of calculating the perimeter for the rectangular building shown in Figure 33.

Example 1
Using the external dimensions:

The mean perimeter = 2/ 40 =   80.0
                      2/ 20 =   40.0
                              ───────
                               120.0
         less 4/1.0   4.0
                              ───────
                               116.0 m
                              ───────

Using the internal dimensions:

The mean perimeter = 2/ 38 =   76.0
                      2/ 18 =   36.0
                              ───────
                               112.0
         plus 4/1.0   4.0
                              ───────
                               116.0 m
                              ───────

Therefore, the area of the wall on plan is equal to $116.0 \times 1.0 = 116.0 \ \text{m}^2$

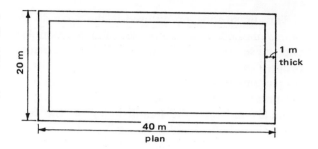

Figure 33

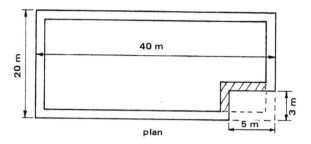

Figure 34

The mean perimeter = 2/40   =   80.0
                      2/20.0 =   40.0
                              ───────
                               120.0
         less 4/1.0   4.0
                              ───────
                               116.0 m
                              ───────

The area enclosed within the walls will be   38.0
                                              18.0
                                           ───────
                                             684.0
                    less 5 × 3   15.0
                                           ───────
                                             699.0 m²
                                           ───────

Example 2

This is calculated in a similar way to Example 1, and it will be seen from Figure 34 that the shaded portion will fit into the position shown by the dotted lines. Therefore, the mean perimeter will be exactly the same length in this instance as it was in Example 1.

Example 3

In this example, a recess is shown in Figure 35 on one wall, and the portion marked A will fit in between the walls of the recess. Therefore, the mean perimeter will be the same as it was in Examples 1 and 2, *plus* twice the depth of the recess.

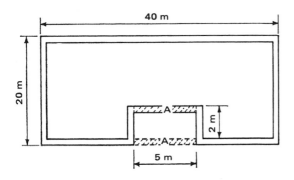

Figure 35

The mean perimeter = 2/ 40 = 80.0
2/ 20 = 40.0
___
120.0
less 4/1.0 4.0
___
116.0
plus 2/2.0 4.0
___
120.0 m
___

The area enclosed within the walls will therefore be

38.0
18.0
___
684.0
less 2/7 14.0
___
670.0 m²
___

The area of the walling on plan will be the mean perimeter multiplied by the width of the wall = 120.0 × 1.0 = 120.0 m².

Abbreviations

In order to make the most of the space in the dimension sheets and to save time in measuring the work, the descriptions of common items of work or materials are often abbreviated. These abbreviations must, however, be perfectly clear to any other person who may have to interpret them.

The following abbreviations are some of the more well-known abbreviations often used by those concerned with the measurement of work:

a.b.	as before
a.b.d.	as before described
av.	average
bk	brick
b/s	both sides
bwk	brickwork
c.a.	cartaway
c.l.m.	cement, lime, mortar
c.m.	cement mortar
ddt	deduct
EO	extra over
ext.	external
inc.	include
int.	internal
k.s. & p.	knot, stop and prime
lab.	labour
l.m.	lime mortar
m.g.	make good
m.h.	manhole
n.e.	not exceeding
p. & s.	planking and strutting
PC	prime cost
p.c.c.	Portland cement concrete
r.f. & r.	return, fill and ram
r.w.p.	rainwater pipe
s.p.	soil-pipe
t. & g.	tongued and grooved
wrot	wrought
1ce	once
2ce	twice
3ce	thrice
③ce	three coats of oil paint

Taking-off quantities

This must be done in a systematic way otherwise great difficulty will be encountered when trying to remember if items have been measured or not.

In the following examples (which all refer to Figure 36) the method of taking-off quantities is shown, and the various steps are clearly indicated by bracketed numbers. The measurements have been shown in metres and millimetres but the

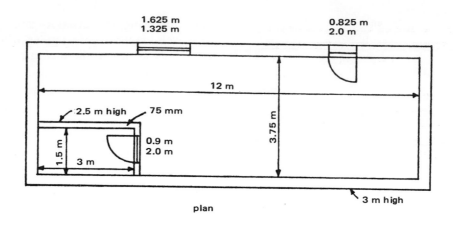

1.625 m
1.325 m

0.825 m
2.0 m

12 m

3.75 m

2.5 m high   75 mm

0.9 m
2.0 m

1.5 m

3 m

3 m high

plan

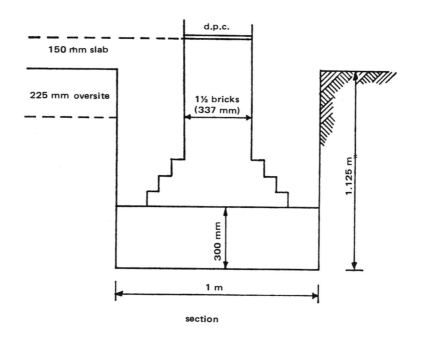

d.p.c.

150 mm slab

225 mm oversite

1½ bricks
(337 mm)

1.125 m

300 mm

1 m

section

Figure 36

dimensions have been entered in the 'dimensions column' in metres and centimetres.

Example 1: taking-off the quantities for the foundations

1 The extreme limits of the area of the ground covered by the building are calculated, and each dimension is determined by adding the internal dimension between the walls, two thicknesses of wall, six footing courses (three at each end) and two projections of foundation concrete.

2 This area is multiplied by the thickness of the excavation to cube the dimension.

3 The mean perimeter is calculated and used for taking off the quantities for excavation, level and ram, planking and strutting, foundation concrete, brickwork and damp-proof course.

4 Note that the trench is calculated for taking off the excavation, and that return, fill and ram is then immediately added.
5 Planking and strutting is also measured for one side of the trench to allow for the excavation of the topsoil.
6 When the foundation concrete and the brickwork is measured, the return, fill and ram is then deducted and the cartaway is added.

7 The brickwork is measured as a plain wall from the top of the foundation concrete up to the damp-proof course, and the footing courses are then averaged and multiplied by their height and added to the main wall.
8 The mean perimeter of the distance between the footing courses and the side of the excavation is calculated and multiplied by the height of the three courses, and the average width.

Example 1: taking-off the quantities in metric for the foundations of the building in Figure 36

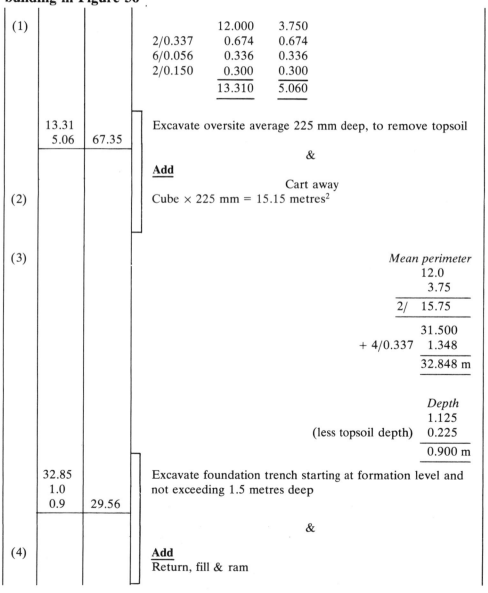

(1)

	12.000	3.750
2/0.337	0.674	0.674
6/0.056	0.336	0.336
2/0.150	0.300	0.300
	13.310	5.060

13.31
5.06   67.35

Excavate oversite average 225 mm deep, to remove topsoil

&

Add

Cart away

(2)   Cube × 225 mm = 15.15 metres²

(3)

Mean perimeter
12.0
3.75

2/   15.75

31.500
+ 4/0.337   1.348
32.848 m

Depth
1.125
(less topsoil depth)   0.225
0.900 m

32.85
1.0
0.9   29.56

Excavate foundation trench starting at formation level and not exceeding 1.5 metres deep

&

(4)   **Add**
Return, fill & ram

	32.85 1.0	32.85	Level & ram bottom of excavation

(5)

$$8/\tfrac{1}{2}/1.0 \quad \begin{array}{r} 32.848 \\ 4.0 \\ \hline 36.848 \end{array}$$

2/	32.85 0.90	59.13	Planking & strutting to sides of trench starting at formation level and not exceeding 1.5 metres deep
	36.85 0.23	8.48	
		67.61	

	32.85 1.0 0.3	9.85	Portland cement concrete (1 : 6) 0.37 mm aggregate exceeding 150 mm & not exceeding 300 mm thick in trenches

&

Deduct

r.f. & r.

&

Add

c.a.

(6)

(7)

$$\begin{array}{r} \tfrac{1}{2}\text{-bk} \\ 1\text{-bk} \\ 1\tfrac{1}{2}\text{-bk} \\ \hline \div\, 3 \quad 3\text{-bk} \\ \hline 1\text{-bk} \end{array}$$

	32.85 0.23	7.39	1-brick in common brickwork in hard-burnt bricks in cement mortar (1 : 3) in projections

$$\begin{array}{r} 1.125 \\ +\ 0.150 \\ \hline 1.275 \\ -\ 0.300 \\ \hline 0.975 \text{ m} \end{array}$$

	32.85 0.98	32.03	1½-brick wall

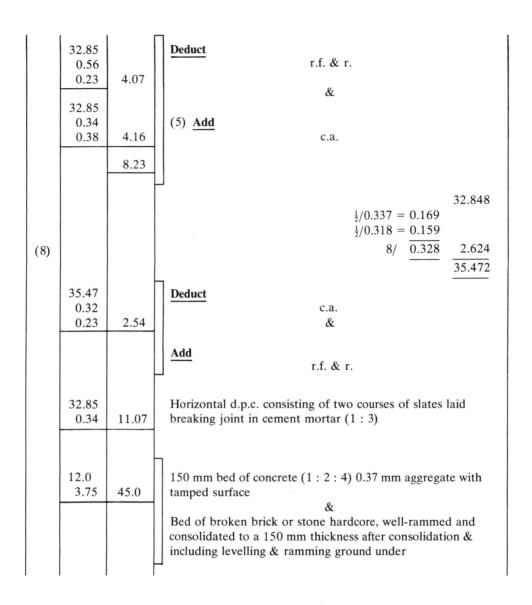

32.85			**Deduct** r.f. & r.
0.56			
0.23	4.07		&
32.85			
0.34			(5) **Add**
0.38	4.16		c.a.
	8.23		

$$32.848$$
$$\tfrac{1}{2}/0.337 = 0.169$$
$$\tfrac{1}{2}/0.318 = 0.159$$
$$8/\ \overline{0.328}\quad 2.624$$
$$\overline{35.472}$$

(8)

35.47		**Deduct** c.a.
0.32		&
0.23	2.54	**Add** r.f. & r.

32.85		Horizontal d.p.c. consisting of two courses of slates laid
0.34	11.07	breaking joint in cement mortar (1 : 3)

12.0		150 mm bed of concrete (1 : 2 : 4) 0.37 mm aggregate with
3.75	45.0	tamped surface
		&
		Bed of broken brick or stone hardcore, well-rammed and consolidated to a 150 mm thickness after consolidation & including levelling & ramming ground under

Example 2: taking-off quantities for brickwork and facings and adjusting for door and window openings

For the purpose of the exercise the thickness of walling is 1½-bricks. The height of the brickwork has been taken as 3 m, built with facing bricks on the face and finished with fair-faced brickwork on the internal face. The door and window openings are to be bridged with a soldier arch on face and a concrete lintel internally. The door frame is to be constructed from timber and the window frame is to be hot, dipped galvanized.

The various steps and adjustments made in the taking-off are shown by bracketed numbers and these are listed as follows:

1 The mean girth is calculated.
2 The outside perimeter of the wall is calculated and adjustment for the facing bricks is made as extra over common brickwork.

3 Similarly the internal perimeter is calculated and the adjustment for internal fair-faced finish is also measured as extra over common brickwork.
4 Adjustment for the door opening is made.
5 Adjustment for the lintel is shown. (Note the deduction of brickwork and fair-faced finish.)

6 A similar adjustment is made for the soldier arch.
7 Sketches should be shown on taking-off sheets where the construction may be difficult to describe briefly.
8 Adjustments are shown for the metal window frame including fixing, also the timber frame.

Example 2: taking-off quantities for brickwork and facings and adjusting for door and window openings

(1)			*Mean perimeter*
			12.0
			3.75
			2/ 15.75
			31.50
			4/0.337 1.348
			32.848 m
(2)	32.85		1½-brick wall in common bricks built in cement mortar (1 : 3)
	3.00	97.54	
			32.848
			4/0.337 1.348
			34.196 m
(3)	34.20		*Facings*
	3.0	102.59	Extra over common bricks built in cement mortar (1 : 3) for facing with multi-coloured bricks including pointing with a neat weather joint in English bond
			Internal
			32.848
			−4/0.337 1.348
			31.500 m
	31.5		Extra over common bricks a.b.d. for fair-faced finish including pointing with a neat struck joint
	3.0	94.5	

Adjust for door opening, soldier arch on face externally, and 225 × 225 mm reinforced concrete lintel internally

0.825 × 2.0 m door

50 × 100 mm wood frame

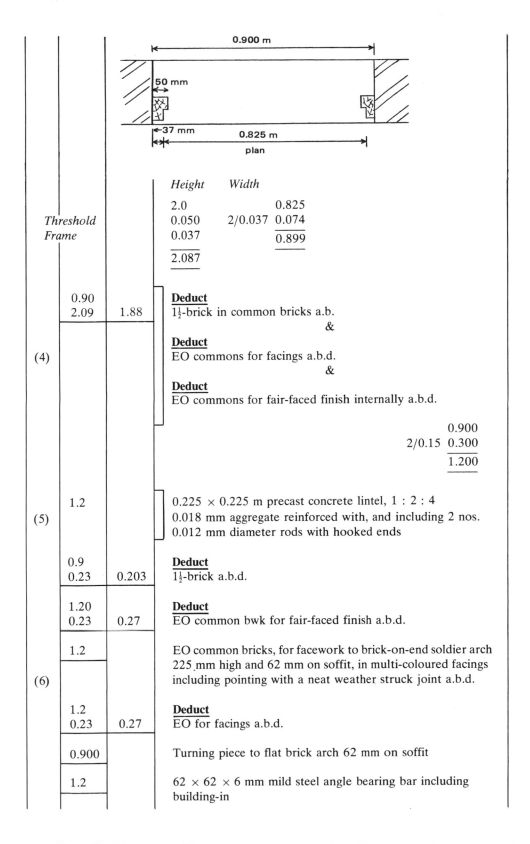

			0.900 m
			plan
			50 mm
			37 mm 0.825 m

			Height *Width*
			2.0 0.825
Threshold			0.050 2/0.037 0.074
Frame			0.037 ‾‾‾‾‾
			‾‾‾‾‾ 0.899
			2.087
	0.90		**Deduct**
	2.09	1.88	1½-brick in common bricks a.b.
			&
(4)			**Deduct**
			EO commons for facings a.b.d.
			&
			Deduct
			EO commons for fair-faced finish internally a.b.d.
			0.900
			2/0.15 0.300
			‾‾‾‾‾
			1.200
(5)	1.2		0.225 × 0.225 m precast concrete lintel, 1 : 2 : 4
			0.018 mm aggregate reinforced with, and including 2 nos.
			0.012 mm diameter rods with hooked ends
	0.9		**Deduct**
	0.23	0.203	1½-brick a.b.d.
	1.20		**Deduct**
	0.23	0.27	EO common bwk for fair-faced finish a.b.d.
	1.2		EO common bricks, for facework to brick-on-end soldier arch
(6)			225 mm high and 62 mm on soffit, in multi-coloured facings
			including pointing with a neat weather struck joint a.b.d.
	1.2		**Deduct**
	0.23	0.27	EO for facings a.b.d.
	0.900		Turning piece to flat brick arch 62 mm on soffit
	1.2		62 × 62 × 6 mm mild steel angle bearing bar including
			building-in

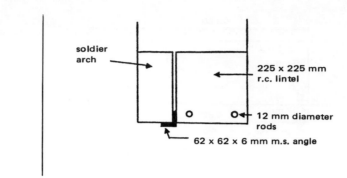

soldier arch

225 x 225 mm r.c. lintel

12 mm diameter rods

62 x 62 x 6 mm m.s. angle

Window opening

Hot, dipped galvanized metal frame 1.5 × 1.2 m type . . . , opening size 1.625 × 1.325 m in 75 × 100 mm softwood frame in 1½-brick wall

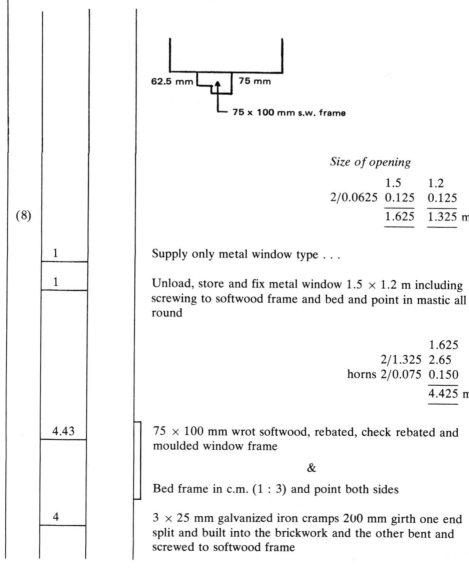

62.5 mm   75 mm

75 x 100 mm s.w. frame

Size of opening

	1.5	1.2
2/0.0625	0.125	0.125
	1.625	1.325 m

(8)

1 — Supply only metal window type . . .

1 — Unload, store and fix metal window 1.5 × 1.2 m including screwing to softwood frame and bed and point in mastic all round

	1.625
2/1.325	2.65
horns 2/0.075	0.150
	4.425 m

4.43 — 75 × 100 mm wrot softwood, rebated, check rebated and moulded window frame

&

Bed frame in c.m. (1 : 3) and point both sides

4 — 3 × 25 mm galvanized iron cramps 200 mm girth one end split and built into the brickwork and the other bent and screwed to softwood frame

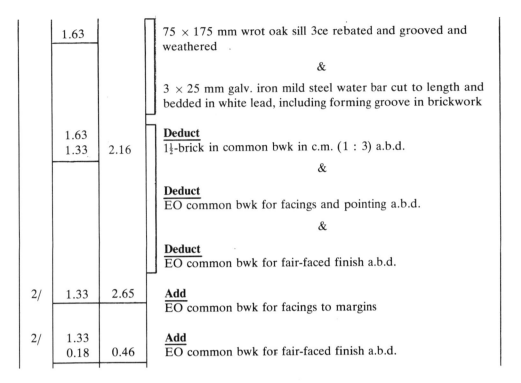

	1.63		75 × 175 mm wrot oak sill 3ce rebated and grooved and weathered & 3 × 25 mm galv. iron mild steel water bar cut to length and bedded in white lead, including forming groove in brickwork
	1.63 1.33	2.16	**Deduct** 1½-brick in common bwk in c.m. (1 : 3) a.b.d. & **Deduct** EO common bwk for facings and pointing a.b.d. & **Deduct** EO common bwk for fair-faced finish a.b.d.
2/	1.33	2.65	**Add** EO common bwk for facings to margins
2/	1.33 0.18	0.46	**Add** EO common bwk for fair-faced finish a.b.d.

Example 3: taking-off quantities for the partitions

For the purpose of Example 3, the height of the partitions has been taken as 2.5 m.

The various steps and adjustments are as follows:

1 The total length of partition is determined; allow one thickness of block where the partitions bond together.
2 Allow for cutting, toothing and bonding into the main wall at every junction.
3 Allow for d.p.c. under the partitions. (For upper floors this item would not be necessary.)
4 Allow for pinning the partition to the underside of the concrete slab.
5 Adjust the 75 mm breeze block partition for the door opening.
6 Adjust the breeze partition for the precast concrete lintel.

Example 3: taking-off the quantities for the partitions

			Partitions 2.5 m high Total length 3.0 1.5 0.075 ——— 4.575 m
(1)			
	4.58 2.50	11.44	75 mm breeze block partition in cement mortar (1 : 3)
2/ (2)	2.50	5.00	Cut, tooth and bond into brickwork including leaving pockets every other course

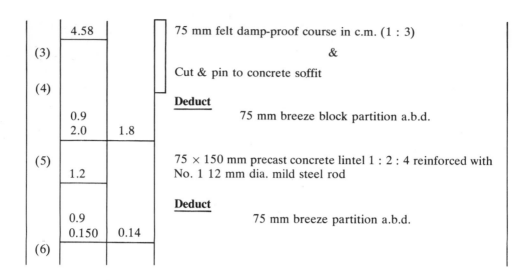

	4.58		75 mm felt damp-proof course in c.m. (1 : 3)
(3)			&
			Cut & pin to concrete soffit
(4)			
	0.9		**Deduct**
	2.0	1.8	75 mm breeze block partition a.b.d.
(5)			75 × 150 mm precast concrete lintel 1 : 2 : 4 reinforced with
	1.2		No. 1 12 mm dia. mild steel rod
			Deduct
	0.9		75 mm breeze partition a.b.d.
	0.150	0.14	
(6)			

Example 4: taking-off the quantities for soil drainage, including manholes

For this exercise the materials used have been assumed to be second-class engineering bricks for the manholes, and 100 mm diameter B S tested salt-glazed pipes for the drains. The pipes to the w.c.s are passed through a concrete slab and mastic asphalt floor. The portion of the drain which passes under the roadway is to be encased in concrete at least 150 mm thick. The various steps and adjustments to be made are ringed on the taking-off sheets and these are listed as follows:

1 The external dimensions of the excavations for the manholes are calculated. (Note that two thicknesses of walling and two projections of the concrete foundation are added to the internal dimensions of the manholes.)

2 The depths are also calculated. (Note that the depth of a manhole is taken from the invert level. Therefore, 50 mm is allowed for the distance from the invert to the top of the foundation concrete.)

3 The excavation is measured in two stages. The first stage does not exceed 1.5 m and the next stage exceeds 1.5 m but is not more than 3 m in depth. (Note the adjustment for this.)

4 The perimeters of the shafts are calculated for the planking and strutting.

5 The mean perimeters of the manhole walls are then calculated.

6 The length and the amount of the projections are calculated. (Note that the measurement is taken as the total length for two courses of brickwork and is given as ¼-brick walling.)

7 Adjustment is now made for the return, fill and ram of the space between the walls of the manholes and the sides of the excavations. The mean perimeter is again used.

8 Note that the standard method of measurement is calculated by numbers in the dimensions column with the sizes given in the description column.

9 Each pipe that is passed through the side of the manhole is measured and numbered.

10 The rendering is taken from the top of the benching up to the underside of the corbels. (Note that this item also includes for raking out the brickwork joints.)

11 The excavation of the drains is calculated. The depth of the concrete under the drains is 50 mm less than that under the manholes. Therefore adjustment has to be made for this. The average depth is also calculated.

12 The length of the trench is adjusted to allow for the thickness of manhole wall and the projection of foundation concrete, as this has

already been measured with the manhole excavation. Therefore, two measurements of 375 mm have been deducted from the total measurement because there are two manholes and allowance has been made for the excavation at each end.

13 The average depth of the tributary drains is calculated.

14 The total length of the tributary drains has been added because they are practically the same depth. If they varied, they would be measured separately. Four deductions have been made, one for each drain.

15 The adjustment for the casing of the pipe under the roadway is made, deducting benching to pipes and adding encasing.

16 Note that the drains are measured overall and extra over is made for bends. This saves the problem of measuring small lengths of pipes between bends.

17 An item is included for testing of the drains to the architect's approval.

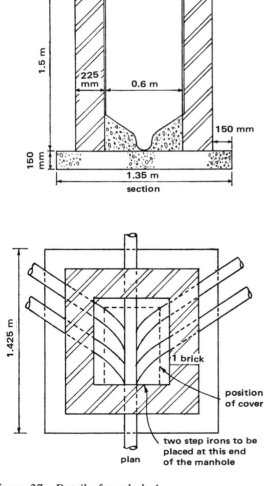

Figure 37 *Detail of manhole 1*

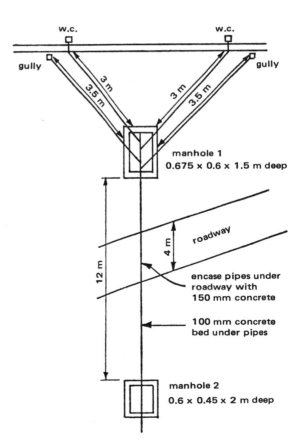

Figure 38 *Detail of drainage layout*

Example 4: taking-off the quantities for soil drainage, including manholes

Soil drainage

(1)

The following in No. 2 manholes

2/225 mm	0.6	0.675	0.45	
	0.45	0.45	0.45	
2/150 mm	0.3	0.3	0.3	
	1.35	1.425	1.2	m

(2)

2.0	1.5	
0.050	0.05	
0.15	0.15	
2.2	1.7	m

1.43		Excavate to form manhole n.e. 1.5 metres deep & get out
1.35		
1.70	3.27	
		&
1.35		
1.2		
2.2	3.56	
	6.83	c.a.
1.43		**Deduct**
1.35		Excavate as last
0.20	0.39	
		&
1.35		
1.2		
0.7	1.13	
		Add
	1.52	Ditto exceeding 1.5 metres but n.e. 3 metres deep and get out

(3)

(4)

	1.425		1.35	
	1.35		1.2	
2/	2.775	2/	2.55	
	5.55		5.1	

	5.55		Planking and strutting to sides of manholes n.e. 3 metres deep
	1.7	9.44	
	5.1		
	2.2	11.22	
		20.66	
	1.43		150 mm concrete (37 mm aggregate) bottom, including level
	1.35	1.92	and ram ground
	1.35		
	1.2	1.62	
		3.54	

(5)

$$\begin{array}{cc} 0.675 & 0.6 \\ 0.6 & 0.45 \\ \hline 2/\ 1.275\ \text{m} & 2/\ 1.05\ \text{m} \\ \hline 2.55 & 2.1 \\ +4/0.225\ 0.90 & 0.90 \\ \hline 3.45\ \ \text{m} & 3.0\ \ \text{m} \end{array}$$

	3.45		1-brick in sides to manholes in 2nd class engineering bricks in
	1.5	5.18	c.m. (1 : 3)
	3.0		
	2.0	6.0	
		11.18	

$$\begin{array}{cc} 2/0.675 & 1.35 \\ & +0.60 \\ \hline & 2.95\ \text{m} \end{array}$$

(6)

$$\begin{array}{r} 75\ \text{mm} \\ 37\ \text{mm} \\ \div 2\ \overline{112}\ \text{mm} \\ \hline 56\ \text{mm} = \tfrac{1}{4}\text{-bk} \end{array}$$

	2.95		$\frac{1}{4}$-brick in projections
	0.15	0.44	

(7)

$$
\begin{array}{rr}
 & 5.55 \quad 5.1 \\
-4/0.15 & 0.6 \quad\;\; 0.6 \\
\hline
 & 4.95\ \text{m} \quad 4.5\ \text{m}
\end{array}
$$

4.95
0.15
1.5
	1.11	**Deduct**
		
		    c.a.
		    &	

4.5 0.15 2.0	1.35	**Add** r.f. & r.	
	2.46		

1 — 100 mm dia. salt-glazed stoneware half-round, straight, main channel 0.6 metre long & pointed in c.m. (1 : 1)

1 — Ditto 0.675 m long do.

4 — 100 mm dia $\frac{3}{4}$-section salt-glazed stoneware branch channel bends bedded and pointed as last

1 — Concrete 1 : 2 : 4 (37 mm agg.) benching to manhole 0.675 × 0.6 m average 225 mm deep including forming slopes to channel and branch channels & trowelling smooth

(8)   &

Ditto to m/hole 0.6 × 0.45 m av. 225 mm deep inc. forming slopes to channel & trowelling smooth

(9) 6
  2 — Build in 225 mm sides, 100 mm dia. drainpipe and make good rendering one side

$$
\begin{array}{lrr}
 & & 1.5\ \text{m} \\
\text{less corbel} & 0.15 & \\
\text{benching} & 0.225 & 0.375 \\
\hline
 & & 1.125\ \text{m}
\end{array}
$$

(10)

$$
\begin{array}{lr}
 & 2.0 \\
\text{less benching}\quad & 0.225 \\
\hline
 & 1.775\ \text{m}
\end{array}
$$

2.55 1.78	4.53		
2.1 1.125	2.36	Cement rendering (1 : 2) to sides of manholes &	
	6.89	Rake out joints of bwk as key for rendering	

	2		0.6 × 0.45 m coated cast iron m/hole cover & frame (weight about 25 kilogrammes) & inc. bed frame in c.m. (1:2) and bedding cover in grease and sand
2/	2	4	Galv. iron step iron & build in to side of m/hole inc. make good rendering

Drains

	Depth at m/h No. 1	1.70 m
	less 50 mm concrete	0.05
		1.65 m

(11)

	Depth at m/h No. 2		2.2 m
		less 50 mm concrete	0.05
			2.15 m

	Average depth	1.65
		2.15
	÷2	3.8
		1.9 m

(12)

		12.0 m
	less 2/0.375	0.75
		11.25 m

	11.25		Excavate trench for 100 mm dia. pipe average 1.9 m deep, exceeding 1.5 m but n.e. 3 m deep, inc. planking & strutting to sides, levelling and grading bottom, part r.f. & r. & remainder c.a.

	Average depth	0.3
		1.5
	÷2	1.8
		0.9 m

(13)

	3.0
	3.0
	3.5
	3.5
	13.0

	less 4/0.375	1.5
		11.5 m

(14)

	11.5		Excavate trench for 100 mm drain as last but average depth of 0.9 metres and not exceeding 1.5 metres deep

	11.25	11.25	100 mm bed of concrete (1 : 6) 37 mm agg. under
	11.5	11.5	
		22.75	100 mm drain and inc. benching up on both sides of pipe
	4.0		**Deduct**
(15)			last
			&
			Add
			Ditto but completely surrounding pipe in concrete 150 mm thick
	12.0		100 mm dia. BS tested salt-glazed pipes jointed with gaskin &
	13.0	25.00	c.m. (1 : 1) laid to falls on concrete bed
2/	2	4	Extra for bends
(16)	2		Surround vertical drainpipe with concrete at least 150 mm thick height of about 0.6 m
			&
			Make good concrete bed around large pipe
			&
			Make good mastic asphalt flooring
			&
			Hole through 275 mm cavity wall & make good
	2		150 × 150 mm salt-glazed stoneware reversible gully with galv. iron grating & 100 mm outlet, bed on, & surround with concrete at least 150 mm thick & including excavation & joint to drain
(17)			Test drains with water to architect's approval

Self-assessment questions

1 Briefly describe how walling is measured.

2 Calculate the mean perimeter of the building shown in Figure 39.

3 Take-off the dimensions and calculate the quantities for the following items from the plan and section shown in Figure 39. Enter the dimensions on taking-off paper
   (a) the excavation of the trenches
   (b) the foundation concrete
   (c) the brickwork up to d.p.c. level
   (d) the 150 mm slab to cover the area within the walls

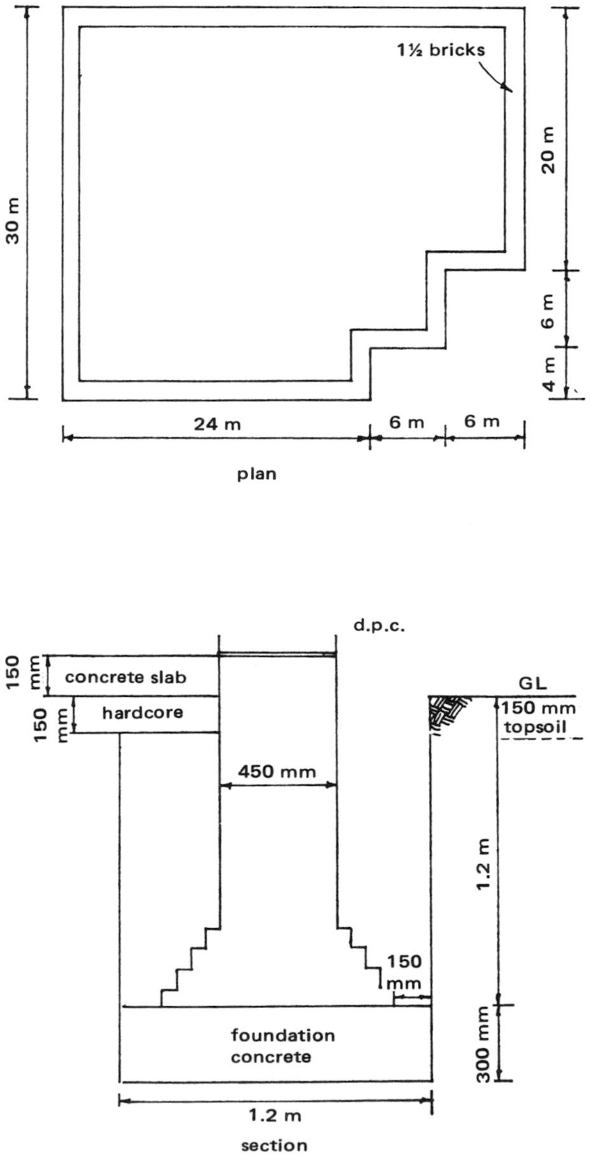

Figure 39

Chapter 5

Commence-ment of site work

After reading this chapter you should be able to:

1   Have a good understanding of the importance of planning the site layout before operational work begins.

2   Have a good knowledge of the layout and construction of temporary roads in order to provide access to the site.

3   Know what temporary hutments are required on a site and the importance of their strategic placing on the site.

4   Be able to plan the positions of stationary plant and the storage of materials.

Planning the site layout

When work is about to start on the site it is most important that the layout is planned so that items such as hutments, stationary plant, stores, latrines and materials are placed in the most strategic and convenient positions. They should be kept clear of the space where the building is to be erected, although this may well be difficult on some congested sites particularly in urban areas. They should also be erected in such a position that will not necessitate their later being taken down and re-erected in another position on the site. Extra costs are incurred on a site every time hutments are moved, without any corresponding payments as compensation.

It is always a good idea to draw up a site plan which will show the outline and position of every intended construction. All the items which are to be kept on the site can then be superimposed. These items may include the following:

Access to the site
Temporary roads (if required)
Hutments
Stationary plant
Materials

Access to the site

On some sites, such as housing estates or factory sites, roads may be an integral part of the contract. Therefore, no special requirement will be necessary for the provision of access to the site. On other sites, however, where no permanent roads are to be constructed, it is quite usual for a temporary access to be provided to allow lorries to enter the site and unload materials. If such access has to be made across an existing footway, it is essential to apply to the local authority for permission for this to be done. In some cases the local authority will carry out the temporary work, while in other cases the builder will be allowed to carry out the temporary work subject to the approval of the authority's engineer and the re-instatement of the footway when the work is finished. A standard fee is usually charged by the local authority for a temporary access.

Temporary roads

If lorries have to be driven on to the site it is important to lay a temporary road surface. It may well be possible to drive lorries over the ground when it is dry and hard, but as soon as rain falls, the ground will become soft and turn into a quagmire. Any money which may originally have been saved by not laying a temporary surface will probably be spent by extricating lorries from the mud, and by generally slowing up the work on the site. Filthy conditions can slow up dumpers or other methods of transporting materials and make site conditions most unpleasant for everybody. This will, of course, lower the morale of the personnel. It could also be expensive because of the extra wear and tear on the lorries. Therefore, in most cases, it is more economical to provide a reasonable surface for vehicles to travel over than to risk the site turning into a quagmire. This surface can be provided in several ways.

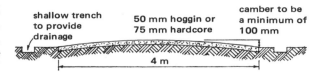

Figure 40 *Section through a road surfaced with hoggin or face gravel*

1 Ballast, hoggin or hardcore can be laid and rolled into a hard surface. If good drainage is provided, this type of road can be most efficient as well as economical, provided it is laid on a hard dry surface. It is of little use laying such a surface on top of mud, as it will quickly break up and form large potholes which will cause more wear and tear on lorries. Figure 40 shows a typical section of temporary road constructed in this way.

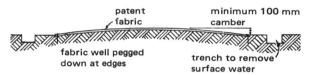

Figure 41 *Section through a temporary road surfaced with patent fabric*

2 Patent fabric of welded steel will provide an excellent riding surface even over ground which may have been a little soft before it was laid. This is a method that has been used to advantage for many years by military forces. This type of material will also allow heavy vehicles to move safely over ground which may tend to be on the soft side. When laying this fabric the ground should first be prepared by shaping and providing a camber to shed the water. The edges of the fabric should then be thoroughly pinned down to prevent the edges from curling up, which could cause damage to lorry tyres, and create a hazard for site personnel who may trip over the steel. Figure 41 shows a typical section through this type of road.

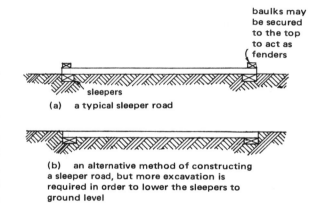

Figure 42 *Sleeper roads*

3 Timber sleepers may be used to great advantage but are not in plentiful supply. A useful riding surface is given, provided sufficient care is taken when the sleepers are first laid. The ground should be prepared by levelling off and cutting two channels, one on each side of the road (Figure 42). The sleeper road can then be laid on the top and spiked to the lower members. This will help to prevent the sleepers from being dislodged when lorries ride over them.

It is important to remember that the cost of laying a temporary road surface can easily be off-set by materials being unloaded near where they are to be used. This will reduce the overall cost of handling and transporting.

Hutments
These may include the following:

1 Site agent's office
2 Timekeeper and other office staff (dependent on the size of the site)
3 Clerk of work's office
4 Office for the trade foremen

5 Canteen for site personnel
6 Latrines
7 Stores for materials and equipment
8 Hutments for subcontractors

These offices should be conveniently situated so that they are readily accessible to visitors on the site who want to meet the supervisors. The timekeeper should be adjacent to the entrance of the site to check on lorries and personnel arriving and leaving the site.

Both the agent's and clerk of work's offices should be furnished with a telephone, plan chest, office desk, facilities for washing and some form of heating. Both offices should be large enough to hold site meetings. There should be sufficient space adjacent to the offices for samples of work to be erected for inspection by the architect. These specimens often include small units of walling built with different makes of brick and various types and colours of pointing. These are built at the early stage of the work on site. This gives a good opportunity to see how the samples can *weather* while all of the preliminaries and ground work are under way.

The stores huts should be substantial and fitted with strong doors and locks for security. They should also be provided with shelves and racks for storing items of equipment and materials. A well-conducted and secure store on site can prove an economy, as it is quite surprising how many items disappear if proper supervision is not maintained. Small items such as screws, handbasin and bath plugs, and lavatory chains are very commonly *lost*. Although these items are not expensive in themselves, a great deal of time is wasted in looking for them when they are lost, or in ordering new stock and obtaining replacement items.

The canteen should be suitably furnished with tables, chairs or stools, adequately heated, and with facilities for drying clothes. The size of the site will usually determine the standard of the canteen facilities. A larger project may have a kitchen attached to the canteen and hot meals provided each day; a smaller site may have just a tea-boy who will look after the provision of hot drinks and a fire for drying clothes.

The latrines should be under cover, kept clean, disinfected daily, and maintained in a sanitary condition. It is most important that they are out of sight of neighbouring properties and do not cause any offence to adjoining property owners. A great deal of time can be spent in dealing with complaints from neighbours, or even the local authority, if the neighbours have complained about unpleasant smells or offensive sights. It is also important to remember that even temporary latrines have to conform to the rules laid down by the Public Health Act concerning hygienic conditions. Neighbouring owners or occupiers have the right to complain about offensive lavatories, and the authorities are bound to investigate these complaints. A little forethought on the type and situation of latrines can save time and effort. On most sites the chemical closet is the most suitable, but on larger sites it is quite common to erect a flush water closet suite. Although it is more expensive to install a flush water closet suite on site than a chemical closet, it can be cheaper in the long run because it is always more economical to keep clean. Extra costs will be inevitably incurred in disposing of the effluent from a chemical closet.

The provision of hutments for subcontractors can be included in the bill of quantities; alternatively, some subcontractors will provide their own temporary accommodation. In either case, convenient space for the hutments, clear of structural work but convenient to the subcontractor's, should be allotted.

Stationary plant

All stationary plant must be strategically placed on the site so that maximum use of the machines can be made. Careful planning of the siting of this type of plant is essential to ensure that it does not have to be moved once it has been installed. It is important to remember that every time a machine is moved, it is a costly operation which causes loss of production and wastes a lot of time.

Stationary plant would include tower cranes, derricks, hoists, concrete mixers or batching plants and concrete pumps, as well as mortar pans, cement silos, wood-cutting machinery, and brick saws. To achieve the most efficient results from this stationary plant the following points should be kept in mind:

1 Machines should be set up truly horizontal.
2 They should be securely fixed to solid bases.
3 Hoisting equipment must be capable of safely lifting the heaviest loads that may have to be hoisted on site. Their maximum load must be clearly marked and safety cut-outs properly installed.
4 Cranes should be so placed that they are able to reach all of the materials which are stored in the stacking bay, and capable of reaching all the points of deposit.
5 Mixers and mortar pans should be specially situated to keep the distance for wheeling the concrete or mortar as short as possible; for example, adjacent to hoists or even to discharge direct into a skip hoist. Remember that the wheeling of materials is a costly operation.
6 Batching plants should be set up in a central position on the site to be readily accessible for dumpers or lorries throughout the contractual period.
7 Mixers and mortar pans should be easily accessible for lorries to discharge sand and shingle immediately behind each one.
8 Cement silos must be immediately adjacent to the mixer so that the mixer can discharge the cement directly into the mixer hopper.
9 Concrete pumps must also be situated immediately underneath the mixer hopper so that the concrete can be discharged directly from the mixer into the pump hopper.
10 Wood-cutting machinery and brick saws, if used on site, should be placed on level bases and under cover. The working space around the machines must be of a non-slip nature, and kept well clear of debris.

It is beyond the scope of this book to describe every possible type of plant that may be encountered on site. Nevertheless, it is quite apparent that careful planning of the type and siting of stationary plant results in efficient and economic operation. The following are some of the questions that a site manager should be asking when considering the installation of plant:

Is it situated in the most convenient position?
Is the capacity of the plant sufficient to produce the work that will be required?
How far will the material have to be transported from the plant to the place of deposit? Is it the shortest possible route?
How will the material be raised? Is this the most economic method?
Is the capacity of the hoisting equipment sufficient to lift the greatest unit of weight of material or equipment on site?
Is the method of transporting the mortar or concrete adequate and the most economical? Will the wheelbarrow, dumper or lorry carry all the output of a mixer at each mixing cycle?

Materials
A wide variety of materials, in many cases expensive, are used in structures, and there is a lot of waste because of bad handling and storage. It is also a fact that the cost of a material increases every time it is handled or carried. Therefore, the following points should be kept in mind when storing materials:

1 The distance for carrying the materials should be kept to an absolute minimum.
2 The materials should not be liable to damage by weather conditions nor placed in direct contact with the ground.
3 The materials should never be damaged by bad stacking and must be protected from pilfering.

Bricks
Bricks should be stacked either close to the site where they are to be laid, near to the hoist, or within the range of the jib of the tower crane. Facing bricks should be stacked on platforms, to prevent them from having contact with the ground. Stacking in direct contact with the ground is liable to cause bad staining or, with some types, very bad spalling. This will render useless most of the bricks at the bottom of the stack, which will result in considerable wastage of expensive items. Brick stacks should also be covered over with polythene sheets or similar material to prevent them from becoming saturated. This will also pre-

vent excessive shrinkage in the constructed walling and keep cracking to a minimum. It will also reduce the possibility of the bricks becoming badly damaged through being spalled by frost in winter. Dry bricks will readily withstand cold weather.

The bricks should be placed tidily, and arranged so that the stacks do not easily collapse. Such a collapse could be very wasteful because the bricks will probably be damaged by being broken or chipped, especially if the facing bricks are soft.

Many bricks are now banded together before being delivered to the site, which makes stacking far easier. If, however, the bricks are to be raised to upper floors, their weights must come within the capacity of the hoisting equipment.

Sand

Sand should be stored on a hard base to prevent contamination from the soil. It is also wise to keep the sand heaps away from trees, as falling leaves, or pine needles can spoil the sand. In winter months, the sand should be covered over with polythene or similar sheeting to keep out frost.

Shingle and concreting sand

These should be stored in bays which are kept separate by thin walling to prevent the sand and shingle from becoming mixed together while still in the heaps. The heaps should be situated immediately behind the mixer and so arranged that the lorries can easily discharge their loads on to the respective piles.

Cement and lime sheds

Bags of cement and lime should be stored in sheds which can be opened at both ends to allow continuous use of the bags. If a single opening shed were used, there may be a tendency to use the freshly stored cement, while the first consignment remains at the back of the shed until the contract has been completed. The bags of cement should not be stacked too high; six or seven rows high is plenty, and they should be placed on a raised platform to be clear of the ground. The sheds must be completely watertight to prevent wastage of the cement or lime through premature hydration.

Drainpipes and accessories

These should be stored in a place free from traffic, and preferably in an area which can be barricaded off to prevent damage to the fittings and pipes. The pipes may be stacked on top of one another, provided the ends of the stacks are well-raised or stopped. This will prevent damage to the pipes by rolling. The stacks should be kept separate, that is, tested, firsts, seconds, and so on.

Accessories need a considerable amount of space as they are not stacked easily. Items like three-quarter section channels should be laid out so that the various shapes can readily be seen. The drainlayer is then able to select the channels which he needs without having to turn over the stack, thereby avoiding the possibility of the pipes, channels or fittings becoming badly chipped or broken, which, of course, would mean wastage.

Pitch-fibre pipes should be stacked in a pyramid, ensuring that the first row of pipes is placed on a hard, even surface, and well-pegged at the outside to prevent the pipes from rolling. The maximum height of these stacks should not exceed 1.5 m. Pitch-fibre fittings should be stored under cover so that they are kept frost free.

Roofing tiles

Roofing tiles should be stacked carefully because they are so brittle. Any major collapse in the stack can result in a considerable amount of breakage and waste. The tiles at the end of the stack should be laid flatwise and those in the remainder of the stack laid on edge. The stacks should not be too high; four layers is usually about the maximum number for safe stacking. The tiles should be stacked on planks to keep them free from ground contamination. They should also be kept well clear of scaffolds or other working platforms to prevent the tiles from becoming damaged by falling objects.

Wall tiles

These are generally supplied in boxes and it is usually wise to store them under lock and key to prevent excessive handling and risk of being broken, chipped or stolen.

Reinforcing rods

Reinforcing rods should be stacked either on timbers to keep the rods raised off the ground, or in racks built with scaffolding, like the storage of scaffold poles (see *Brickwork 1*, Chapter 16).

The various diameters of rods should be kept separate for ease of selection, and also for ease of checking the stocks of the various sizes of rods which are in hand. It is also wise to keep reinforcement under some form of cover to keep off the weather, unless the rods are going to be used very quickly. Slight rust on reinforcing rods is not detrimental but, if rust scales are formed, it is most likely that the reinforcement would be condemned, resulting in more waste of a material on site.

Timber

Timber for carcassing should be stored under cover and stacked flat in a well-ventilated place. The timbers should be raised off the floor to prevent any possibility of its becoming contaminated with water. The stacks should also be so arranged that timbers can be taken from them, without men having to clamber over the stack in order to select the timber they need. This can damage the timbers and could cause the stack to collapse.

Therefore, always remember that reasonable care must be taken of every material on site. The material must be stored or stacked in an efficient way to prevent unnecessary waste through damage. The materials must be placed in the most convenient position to allow for ease of handling and to keep transportation and handling to an absolute minimum.

Self-assessment questions

1 Describe a method of planning the layout of equipment and materials on a site, and state the main points that would be kept in mind with this operation.

2 What facilities should be provided to allow lorries to be driven on site? State any major points concerning the provision of these facilities.

3 Why is it so important to provide temporary roads where permanent roads are not available on a site? Describe various methods of constructing these roads.

4 Make a list of the offices that may be needed on a fairly large building site. State how they should be furnished, and explain why they should be furnished in the way you suggest.

5 Make a sketch showing a suitable layout for a large stores-hut on a building site.

6 State the main points that should be kept in mind regarding lavatories on site.

7 What points should be considered when selecting plant for lifting materials on site?

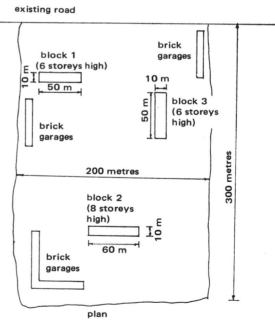

plan

Construction of the blocks:

reinforced concrete frame brick panel in-filling fly ash blocks for the inner leaf of the cavity wall and for the partitions

Figure 43

8   Describe the main points that should be kept
     in mind when selecting and placing a con-
     crete mixer on site. How should a mixer be
     set into position?

9   When wood-cutting machinery or brick-
     cutting saws are installed on a site, what are
     the main factors to be considered?

10   State the manner in which materials in gen-
     eral should be stored on site, and state the
     particular requirements for the storage of
     (a)   bricks
     (b)   drainpipes and accessories
     (c)   tiles of all types
     (d)   reinforcement
     (e)   timber

11   Sketch an outline of the site shown in Figure
     43 and indicate the positions of the follow-
     ing: site roads, temporary hutments, stores,
     stationary plant, and materials.

Chapter 6

Site surveying

After reading this chapter you should be able to:

1 Have a good understanding of the use of ranging poles, chains and arrows and surveying equipment.

2 Know how to use a sitesquare and Cowley level.

3 Have a good understanding of the use of dumpy levels; precision levels; and autoset levels.

4 Know how to set out gradients with the aid of surveying instruments.

5 Know how to book readings using the rise and fall method; and the collimation method.

6 Know how to read simple verniers.

Surveying equipment

Before construction work on a site can begin, it is essential to carry out a comprehensive survey of the site and set out the construction work. To achieve the necessary accuracy, precision instruments, commonly called *surveying equipment*, must be used. There is a wide variety of these instruments and each one is designed for a special purpose. The ambitious craftsman and student who wishes to become a site manager must make themselves completely familiar with the various types of instruments used on building sites.

This equipment is expensive and, although it is not fragile, it must be handled with care and well-maintained to give accurate readings constantly for many years. The following points can be a useful guide for the care of equipment:

1 Always grasp the instrument tightly when removing it from its box or case and replacing it to ensure that it is not dropped.

2 When putting the instrument away in its box, be certain that it is placed in its correct position in the box. Never slam the lid on the top of the instrument, as this is likely to cause damage if the instrument has not been correctly put away.

3 When the protective screw cap is removed from the tripod, place it in the instrument box to safeguard it from becoming lost or dropped in the mud or dirt. This dirt could be transferred to the screw thread on the tripod which would create undue wear and tear when the instrument is screwed and unscrewed from the tripod.

4 Always set up the tripod so that the instrument is approximately level before adjusting the levelling screws. This will ensure that the amount of adjustment needed to level the instrument will be kept to the minimum, which will in turn save excessive wear on the screw threads.

5 Never over-tighten clamping screws; this causes unnecessary strain on the clamping device and consequently excessive wear.

6 Always protect the instrument from rain. A polythene bag kept in the instrument box is a useful accessory if it suddenly rains while the instrument is being used.

7 If the instrument should inadvertently

become wet, let it dry thoroughly before putting it into the box. If this cannot be done, remove if from the box as soon as possible and wipe all wet parts with a clean cloth. A thin coat of a very fine oil can be put on the screw threads; this will allow ease of movement. But *never* put a lot of oil on an instrument and never oil on the telescope casing as this will make the instrument slippery. Excessive oil will make the instrument messy and dirty; therefore, remember to be *very miserly* with the oil.

8 Never let the instrument become caked in mud or dirt as this will cause extra wear on the screw threads. The instrument should always be kept clean.

9 When screwing the instrument on to the tripod always ensure that it is firmly set before you let go. Never wrench the instrument on to the top of the tripod; just tighten it gently.

10 Care is essential when taking the instrument from one place to another. If the instrument has to be taken over a long distance, it should be removed from the tripod and carried on its box. If, however, it just has to be carried a short distance, it can be carried by putting the shoulder between two legs of the tripod and lifting the tripod with the instrument on the top of the shoulder and at the side of the head.

11 Never carry out any adjustments to the instrument unless you know exactly what to do and how it should be done.

Most of the surveying equipment used on building sites is mainly needed for setting out straight lines, angles and levels. This equipment includes the following:

Ranging poles
Chains
Chaining arrows
Sitesquare
Cowley automatic level
Cowley 'slope attachment'
Engineer's dumpy level
Engineer's precision level
Levelling staff

Ranging poles

Ranging poles are obtainable in lengths from 2 to 4 m. They are usually painted in alternate red and white bands, but are sometimes red, white and black bands at decimetre intervals. The variation in the colours is deliberate so that the ranging pole can be easily seen a long distance away. The poles are usually fitted with a metal shoe so that the pole can be pushed into the ground. They are set up at predetermined points and other poles can be sighted through at intervals, which will produce a very simple method of setting out a straight line. They can also be used with chains for contouring the ground on a site, and with a sitesquare for setting out angles.

Chains

Chains are generally used for surveying large areas and are not usually needed for the smaller site. A chain is a most simple piece of equipment and, provided it is not abused, it is an extremely useful method of measuring distances or plotting areas. Chains are available in 20 m lengths. The metre lengths are divided into 100 links with tallies at every 10 links, that is, each link will be 0.2 m and tallies will be spaced at 2 m intervals (Figure 44).

Chaining arrows

Chaining arrows are used with the chain. They are pointed lengths of steel each about 300 mm long, with a loop at the top. They are usually used in sets of ten, and often red tape is tied on the loop at the top so that they are easily found during a survey if concealed in long grass. These arrows also form a simple method of counting the number of chain lengths that may have been used to measure a distance.

10 links or 90 links   20 links or 80 links   30 links or 70 links   40 links or 60 links   50 links

Figure 44 *Metal marking tags for chains*

The sitesquare

The sitesquare is used for setting out right angles accurately on building sites. The two fixed focus telescopes are precision set at exactly 90 degrees, each with its own hair lines. They swivel independently up and down through a wide angle while still maintaining their right angle. This enables sighting to be made either uphill or downhill, which in turn will enable right angles to be set out on any land that may be encountered on a building site. If there is a built-in circular spirit level on top of the instrument, the extending datum rod can be plumbed over a peg. Provided the bubble is centred carefully, by sighting the *hairline* of the intersection of one telescope and swivelling the other telescope up and down, vertical work can be set plumb.

The range of the sitesquare is from 2 to 100 m with an accuracy of 6 mm in 30 m. Figure 45 shows a sitesquare.

When a right angle is to be set out, the position of the corner of the angle and one side of the angle is always known; the instrument can assist in determining the second side of the angle in a simple, quick and reliable way.

The instrument is erected on the corner A (Figure 46). One of the two telescopes is set along the first side of the angle; sighting through the second telescope gives the exact right angle.

The method of setting up the sitesquare is as follows:

1 Unfold the tripod so that the steel pin points upwards. Make sure that the bolts joining the pin and the legs of the tripod are always tight. This avoids any *shake* when the instrument is in use (Figure 47).
2 Slip the clamp of the datum arm over the tripod pin and position the arm so that it is roughly horizontal, with the clamp approximately mid-way along the arm.
3 Place the tripod in a position so that the datum rod is approximately over the peg or mark that is set at the corner point or vertex of the angle. Make sure that the legs are firmly on the ground. The extending spike of the rod has a point on one end; this should be placed on the corner mark. The opposite end of this

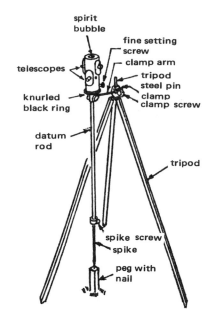

Figure 45

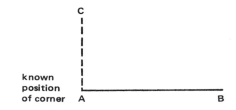

Figure 46

Figure 47 *Setting up the tripod for a sitesquare*

rod has a hollow which should be used if the instrument is being placed over a nail driven into a peg at the corner point. The head of this nail should *not* be too large otherwise it will not fit into the hollow (Figure 48).

4   Release the spike screw and extend the spike so that it sits firmly on the nail or mark. Now tighten the spike screw.

5   Remove the sitesquare from its case and screw it on to the datum rod. Secure the instrument by turning the knurled black ring at the base of the instrument in a clockwise direction. This will lock the instrument on to the datum rod, but will allow rotation.

6   The instrument should now be adjusted so that it is in a truly vertical position. This is carried out by holding the instrument in one hand and releasing the clamp screw. The instrument should now be moved until the bubble in the top of the instrument shows exactly in the centre of the back circle. When this is done, tighten the clamp screw firmly and recheck the bubble. The sitesquare is now ready for use. Ensure that you do not lean on the tripod or instrument when viewing, as this will tend to vibrate the telescope which will result in incorrect readings.

Using the sitesquare

After the base or building line has been set out with pegs or marks at the required distance (A B) erect the sitesquare at one end and sight through to the other end of the line through the lower telescope. Obtain the *dead on* position by means of the fine-setting screw which moves the telescope to the right or left, and by tilting the telescope up or down (Figure 49).

When the instrument is set accurately into position, measure the distance to the peg C at the extremity of the line being set out perpendicularly to the base line. By sighting through the upper telescope, and keeping the instrument absolutely steady, an assistant can be signalled to move the peg either to the right or left. When it is *dead on* (Figure 49) the new line will be at right angles to the base line.

This operation can now be repeated at peg C

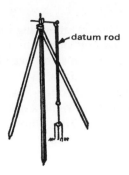

Figure 48   *Setting the datum rod over the peg*

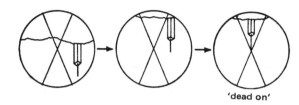

Figure 49   *Sighting through the instrument on to the peg*

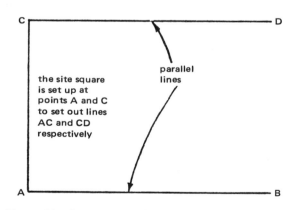

Figure 50   *Setting out a rectangle with a sitesquare*

and the third line set out perpendicular to line A C and parallel to the base line A B (Figure 50). If profiles are used, the positions of the lines can be easily marked on the top of them.

Optical plumb line

If the sitesquare is erected carefully, by means of the optical plumb line within the instrument, it is possible to check the verticality of any upright line, such as a corner or profile, by tilting the telescope up and down along the line to be checked. Any deviation of that line can be noted from the centre of the cross-lines (Figure 51).

Testing the sitesquare

The sitesquare can be tested for accuracy of performance very simply as follows:

1　Erect the sitesquare over the point A and sight one telescope to a point B 15 m away.
2　Set out a third point, C, at right angles to line AB by looking through the second telescope.
3　Turn the instrument through 90 degrees so that the first telescope is directed towards peg C and then set out a fourth point, D.
4　Repeat this procedure at point E. There are now four points, B, C, D and E, all at 15 m from point A (Figure 52).
5　Take a reading at B. If the instrument is correct, the second reading will coincide with the first reading at B. If the two readings do not coincide, there is a fault in the instrument.

It is important to remember that any fault would have to be divided by four. For example, if there was an error of 24 mm the error at each reading would be 6 mm. If an excessive error were discovered, the instrument should be returned to the manufacturers for adjustment.

Cowley level

The Cowley level is an automatic level which can be used by builders. It has no spirit level and has an accuracy of 6 mm in 30 m.

The tripod should be set up with the pin pointing upwards (Figure 53). The instrument is mounted on the tripod so that the pin goes full length into the hole on the underside of the instrument.

The staff is held vertically with the target on the spot which is to be levelled, with the hollow front towards the instrument.

The reading of the level is taken by looking into the aperture at the top of the instrument. The instrument is then swivelled so that the target can be seen in two halves through the aperture (Figure 54). The field of view can appear as a whole circle (A, B or D) or it can be split, as at C. The

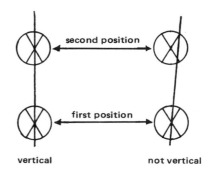

Figure 51　*Using the sitesquare as an optical plumb line*

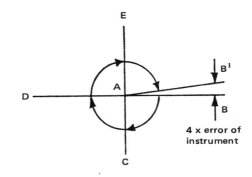

Figure 52　*Testing the sitesquare for accuracy*

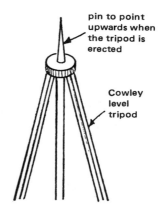

Figure 53　*Setting up a Cowley tripod*

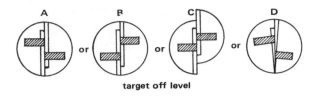

Figure 54 *Sighting through the aperture of a Cowley level*

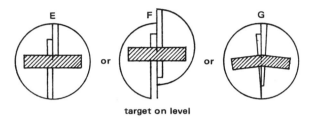

Figure 55 *Different views of a correct level*

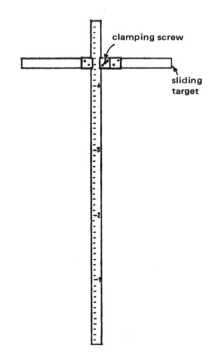

Figure 56 *The Cowley staff*

target can appear horizontal as at A, B or C or tilted as at D.

The target is then either raised or lowered until the two halves on the target are brought into coincidence with each other, as shown at E, F and G in Figure 55. It does not matter if the two halves are not level (as at G), because the target will be exactly level with the instrument.

The height of the target can be read on the back of the staff (Figure 56). Other levels can be taken from the same position of the instrument by swivelling it around to face different positions at which the target may be placed. The level will still be correct as long as the tripod has not been disturbed.

Where it is impractical to erect the tripod, the bricklayer's stand can be used to great advantage on the top of the walling. When the instrument is removed from the tripod the mechanism of the instrument is locked.

Always remove the instrument from the tripod or stand when carrying it.

An aluminium distance target painted yellow and approximately 1 m long can be clipped on to the standard target. This will extend the range of the Cowley level by approximately 30 m.

Cowley level sliding staff
The Cowley level sliding staff levels to a height or depth of nearly 3 m and can be taken with this unit (Figure 57). The target is fitted to the staff in the closed position. Readings are taken in the same way as they are with the sight staff and target. To take readings over 1.5 m, the target is set with the arrow pointing at zero. The staff is slid and the reading is taken from the top of the fixed staff.

Testing the Cowley level
If the level should, at any time, be dropped or badly knocked, it is most important that it should be checked for accuracy, before being used for taking levels. The procedure is as follows:

1 Mark two positions (A and B) along the ground at equal distances from a centre point C. About 6 m apart is sufficient (Figure 58).

2 Set up the level at the exact centre point, place the staff at A and take a reading.
3 Turn the instrument around without moving the tripod, place the staff at B and take a second reading. Note the difference in level between A and B.
4 Remove the level to a position D which should be in line with the other two pegs and about 9 m away from one of the pegs. Take readings on the staff A and B and again note the difference of level between them.

If these instructions are carried out correctly, and if the Cowley level is in good condition, the difference of readings taken from position C should agree with the difference between the readings taken at D to within 3 mm. If the differences are greater than this, the instrument should be returned to the supplier for examination and any necessary correction.

Cowley slope attachment
The Cowley slope attachment is an attachment which fits over the front window of the Cowley level and is secured by stretching a black strap over the back of the instrument (Figure 59). It is fitted with four projections at the rear of the attachment to prevent the attachment from rotating.

With this attachment, predetermined falls can be set out, as well as pegs between *high* and *low* levels, without having to adjust the staff or to use calculations.

The attachment can be used to advantage under two conditions: where the fall is given; and where the distance and gradient are unknown.

Where the fall is given
1 Erect the Cowley level as usual, and position it in front of the slope.
2 Preset the required fall on the *slope* attachment dial.
3 Fit the *slope* attachment in the *fall* position.
4 Take the staff and target to the extreme point of the fall. The assistant can do this.
5 Set the target for coincidence while looking through the instrument.
6 Move the staff towards the instrument to set

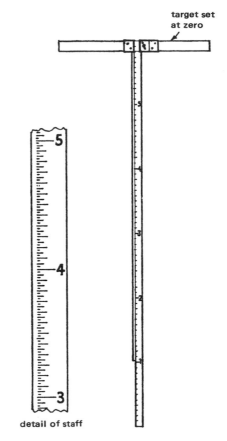

detail of staff

Figure 57   *The Cowley level sliding staff*

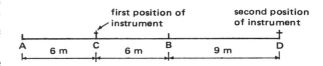

Figure 58   *Testing a Cowley level*

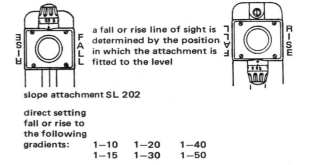

Figure 59   *Slope attachment*

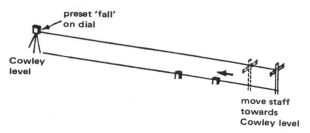

Figure 60a   *Setting out a gradient where the fall is given*

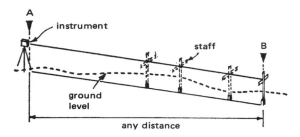

Important note: Do not remove tripod or target throughout operation

Figure 60b   *Setting out a gradient where distance and fall are unknown*

Figure 61   *Carl Zeiss Automatic Level*

out the slope. At regular spaces drive pegs into the ground, the heights of which are adjusted, so that the target is coincident with the line of sight at each point (Figure 60a).

Where the distance and gradient are unknown

1 Erect the instrument in front of point A as shown in Figure 60b.
2 Fix the *slope* attachment in the *fall* position.
3 Stand staff and target on point A.
4 Set target level with *slope* attachment.
5 Move staff and target to point B.
6 Adjust 'slope' attachment to bring target into coincidence.
7 Drive pegs into the ground at regular intervals and adjust their heights while the assistant moves the staff towards the instrument. The target should now be coincident with the line of sight at each point.

It is most important to remember that the tripod must not be disturbed during the whole of the setting out process, nor must the target height be re-adjusted. If the slope has to be set out from the bottom of the gradient instead of from the top, the same procedure is used, but the attachment must be set in the *rise* position.

There are two types of attachments each with its own direct settings for rise or fall. The following gradients may be set out directly with these instruments:

Attachment no. SL202: 1–10; 1–15; 1–20; 1–30; 1–40; 1–50.
Attachment no. SL203: 1–60; 1–80; 1–100; 1–120; 1–180; 1–200; 1–250.

The Carl Zeiss Automatic Level
This is a very efficient surveying instrument (Fig. 61) which is compact and easy to use.

It has a minimum site distance of 0.4 metres.

It is provided with a quick acting device for levelling the instrument. The prelevelling of the instrument is carried out by means of the wedge formed disks at the base of the instrument and is achieved in two simple steps:

(a) Turn the diametrically opposed handles of the pair of wedges at the right-angle position to the bubble deflection.

(b) Turn the handles to move together in the direction of the required bubble runout.

Alternatively the instrument may be available with a ball joint base. This is particularly useful where steep terrain makes the setting up of this instrument difficult.

Prelevelling is checked with the aid of the circular bubble located just beside the eyepiece.

This type of instrument may also be provided with a horizontal circle for setting out angles. This circle is set out in 1 degree divisions. Alternatively it may be provided with a right angle sight for setting out right angles.

The accessories which are available for use in conjunction with these instruments include the following:

(a) *Swivel eyepiece* for measuring in a restricted space.

(b) *Inclination reticule* which may be fitted in the instrument instead of the standard recticle and serves in connection with a target on the levelling staff for setting out inclined lines within the range of 0.8%.

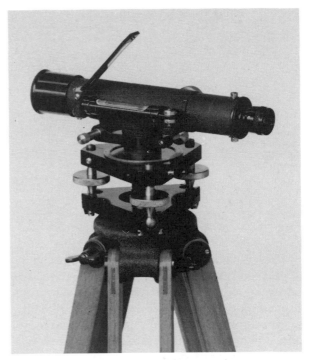

Figure 62 *Stanley builder's dumpy level*

Engineer's dumpy level

The term engineer's dumpy level is applied to a level which has its telescope permanently fixed parallel to the horizontal axis of the body of the instrument. This means that the telescope cannot be tilted either up or down to set out gradients. Figure 62 shows an example of a Stanley dumpy level. The design of this type of level is simple and robust, giving great strength in construction which ensures maximum stability, durability and resistance to rough handling.

As the instrument is used with the axis set up vertically, any maladjustment of the bubble can be immediately seen, allowed for, or corrected. This type of instrument is eminently suitable for spot levelling.

The dumpy level is adjusted by means of the three screws at the base of the instrument (Figure 62).

The telescope is rotated so that it is parallel to the two screws A and B (Figure 63). These screws are contra-rotated, which means that both can be turned inwards or outwards, until the bubble on

the top or side of the instrument registers in the middle of the spirit tube.

The instrument is then rotated through 90 degrees so that the telescope is directly over the third screw, C (Figure 64). The third screw is then adjusted until the bubble shows the instrument truly level.

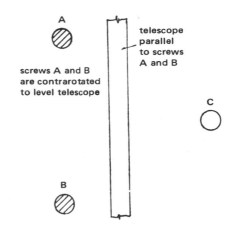

Figure 63 *The first position of the telescope when setting up a dumpy level*

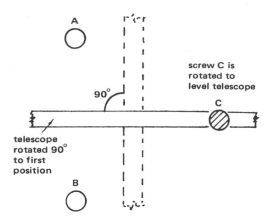

Figure 64 *The second position of the telescope*

Figure 65 *Stanley optical mean reading level*

The instrument is again rotated through 90 degrees so that it is once again parallel to the two adjusting screws A and B; these are again contra-rotated to level the telescope. (If the instrument is in good order then only a small amount of adjustment will be necessary at this stage.)

Finally the instrument is rotated so that it is again directly over the third screw, C, which is adjusted, if necessary, though no further adjustment should be necessary at this point. The instrument is now ready for use and the telescope can be rotated in any position and a reading can be taken.

A Stanley Optical Mean Reading Level is shown in Figure 65. This is a first-class instrument which permits highly accurate levelling even when there may be slight bubble inaccuracies.

Engineer's precision level

The engineer's precision level is sometimes called a *quick-set* precision level. Figure 66 shows a Stanley instrument of this type.

This type of instrument can be supplied with or without footscrews for adjusting the level, but as the previous section dealt with the adjustment of footscrews, this section will describe the types of instrument that are without footscrews. The instrument is adjusted for level with the aid of the ball joint situated at the base of the instrument. The instrument is screwed on to the top of the tripod. The locking-ring on the top of the ball joint is then loosened and the telescope is ad-

Figure 66 *Stanley engineer quick-setting precision level*

justed by hand until the bubble registers in the centre of a circular spirit tube situated at the side of the instrument. The telescope is then sighted on to the staff. The telescope must be levelled by means of the gradient screw situated at the underside of the telescope.

Each time the instrument is rotated to take a reading, the gradient screw *must* be adjusted to level the telescope. This operation is vital if accurate readings are to be made.

Therefore the dumpy level telescope is level in all positions, and readings can be readily taken at every point, whereas with the precision instrument the gradient screw *must* be adjusted to level the telescope each time it is rotated.

Watts Precise 'Autoset' Levels

Figures 67 and 68 show the two types of Watts Precise Autoset Levels. One is fitted with a ball joint as described for the precision level and the other has three footscrews similar to the dumpy level. Both these instruments, however, have the added refinement of being fitted with optical stabilizers.

The optical stabilizer is comprised of a fixed prism above two swinging prisms, the suspended prisms being supported on four metallic tapes forming a cross-spring, flexure pivot. The fixed roof prism is a reflector for securing an erect image. The suspended prisms form a double reflector which changes its angular relation to the optical axis at the same rate as the telescope is

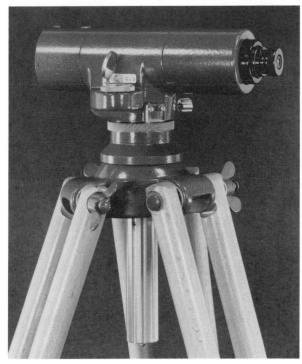

Figure 68   *Watts precise autoset level 2*

tilted, and so maintains the line of sight truly horizontal.

Figure 69 shows how the compensator will ensure that the line of sight is truly level even though the telescope itself may be out of level.

A Watts Precise 'Autoset' Level is mounted on the tripod and adjusted so that the bubble is in the centre of a circular spirit tube. The instrument is fixed, and is then ready for use without needing any further adjustment for levelling. It is also possible to take readings from this instrument at

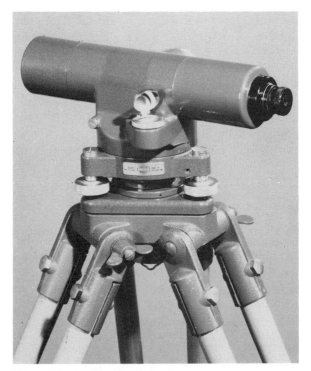

Figure 67   *Watts autoset level*

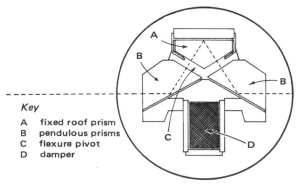

Key
A   fixed roof prism
B   pendulous prisms
C   flexure pivot
D   damper

Figure 69

any position of the telescope, as there is no need for any further adjustment whatever. This allows for rapid setting up of the instrument and for quick readings to be taken.

Temporary adjustments
Certain temporary adjustments are needed when a dumpy level is set up. The following adjustments should be made before taking readings:

To check the accuracy of the spirit tube on the dumpy level. When the telescope has been levelled by adjusting the three footscrews, the telescope should be rotated through 180 degrees. If the bubble still shows in the centre of the spirit tube, it is correct. If, however, the bubble shows in the centre of the tube in one direction and off centre when the telescope is rotated through 180 degrees, the spirit tube should be adjusted. This is carried out by turning the locking capstan screws situated at one end of the spirit tube (Figure 62).

When the adjustment has been made the instrument should be re-levelled and again checked for accuracy. This sort of adjustment should only have to be carried out on rare occasions, but going through the motion of the checking of the bubble should become an automatic habit, so that an error can be found before taking any readings.

Adjusting for parallax. When the instrument is set up and ready for taking readings, the eyepiece must be rotated to the right or left so that the diaphragm lines stand out very clearly. This *must* be done before any readings are taken. This is called *adjusting for parallax* and is really setting the eyepiece to suit the eyesight of the person who is taking the readings.

Taking readings
When a reading is to be taken, the telescope should be sighted in the direction of the levelling staff and the clamping screw should be turned to lock the telescope into position. The telescope can now be finally sighted on to the staff by means of the tangent screw.

Diaphragm lines
Diaphragm lines are obtainable with web lines, that is, spider web being used for the actual lines

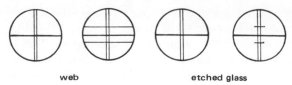

web   etched glass

Figure 70

on the diaphragm, or with the more common method of etched glass. Figure 70 shows both types of diaphragms which are available.

The vertical line or lines are used to ensure the exact position of the staff in the centre of the telescope. If a reading is taken when the staff is off centre, it may result in an inaccurate reading due to parallax. The centre line is intended for levelling, and is the line at which levels are read.

The upper and lower lines are called *stadia* lines and these are used for measuring distances together with a staff. When the instrument has been set up, the staff man holds the levelling staff at the point which is to be measured in feet from the instrument. Readings are taken on the staff at the upper and lower stadia lines, the lower reading is subtracted from the upper and the result is multiplied by 100. This gives the distance from the instrument to the staff. Therefore if the upper stadia reading were 4.57 ft and the lower stadia reading were 3.31 ft, the distance from the instrument to the staff, in feet, would be $(4.57 - 3.31) \times 100 = 1.26 \times 100 = 126$ ft.

For readings in metric the method will be exactly the same as described for feet; for example, if the upper reading were 2.15 m and the lower reading 1.67 m, the distance from the instrument to the staff would be $(2.15 - 1.67) \times 100 = 0.48 \times 100 = 48$ m.

The levelling staff
The levelling staff is used together with the levelling instrument to determine levels. Levelling staffs are available in mahogany or light alloy, and are constructed in sections which are easily joined together.

The handling of the staff is important and the following points should be kept in mind:

1 The staff must be held in an upright position. The staff operator should stand immediately

behind the staff with one hand on each side of it. This enables the operator to have the greatest control over the staff by keeping it still and upright.

2   The sections must be pushed firmly home when being joined together.

3   The underside of the staff must be kept clean from mud or dirt, especially when taking spot levels on ground surfaces and transferring them on to pegs. A small lump of dirt or mud can result in an inaccurate reading.

There are a variety of levelling staffs available and each one has a specific use. Figure 71 shows two examples of these.

Taking levels

All levels which are read are always assumed to be in relation to a *fixed* level. For example, whenever the heights of hills or mountains are calculated, the height is determined by its distance in metres above sea level. Similarly, the depth of a mine would be calculated by its distance in metres below sea level.

The fixed level is called a *datum*. On the site it is quite usual to set a datum level and all other levels are reckoned in relation to that level. This datum will generally be predetermined by the architect or engineer responsible for the site. It is often given from a local bench mark, which is an Ordnance Survey point at a known height above sea level. These bench marks (Figure 72) are frequently seen on the sides of buildings. The level is taken from the centre line of the horizontal groove.

For convenience on site a datum peg is usually set so that it can be readily seen from most parts of the site. It should preferably be placed somewhere near the site office so that it can be easily checked if it is knocked out of position by a machine. The datum peg should be bedded in concrete and a timber framework should be built around it to prevent it, so far as possible, from becoming disturbed (Figure 73). Quite often the datum on site is the ground floor or damp-proof course, but any similar fixed point could just as easily be used.

Reduced level

This is a convenient way of maintaining the relationship between levels without having to resort to minus signs. For example, if a building were being built at the sea shore, the site datum could

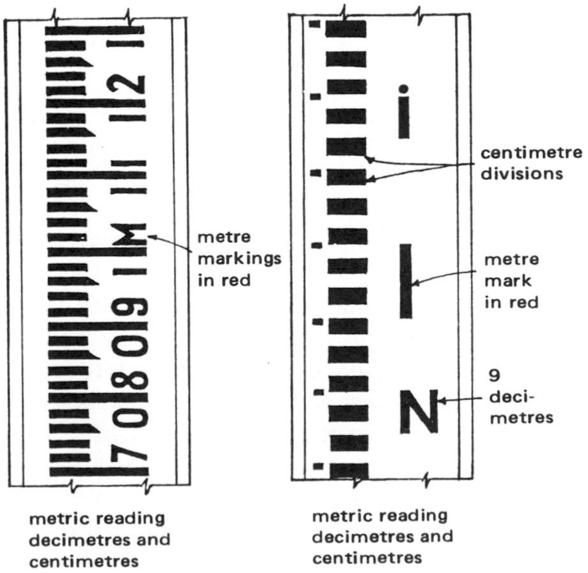

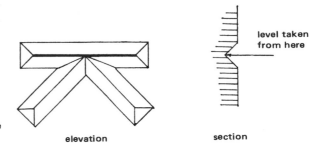

elevation   section

Figure 72   *Ordnance Survey bench mark*

centimetre
divisions

metre
markings
in red

metre
mark
in red

9
deci-
metres

metric reading
decimetres and
centimetres

metric reading
decimetres and
centimetres

Figure 71   *Levelling staff*

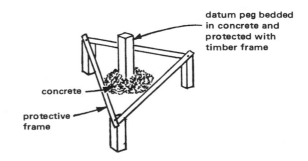

datum peg bedded
in concrete and
protected with
timber frame

concrete

protective
frame

Figure 73

be zero; if a basement 5 m deep had to be constructed, the depth of the basement must be registered as a minus quantity, or stated as being 5 m below zero or datum. Both these methods are cumbersome. Therefore, if the datum is given a *reduced* level of, say, 25 m, the bottom of the basement will be 25 less 5 m which will be 20 m. Therefore, all the figures are positive numbers. The reduced level of the datum can be given any number which is large enough to accommodate the greatest depth on the site.

Recording levels

It is most important to keep a record of all levels which are taken on site for three reasons:

1 To keep a record of all levels for future reference.
2 To carry out a check on the accuracy of the levels taken.
3 To predetermine the readings for given levels.

There are two methods of booking levels:

1 The collimation or height of instrument method.
2 The rise and fall method.

The collimation method of booking

The first method is the more convenient to use, as each reduced level can be calculated in one simple calculation. Two operations are needed with the second method of booking.

Typical headings for the form used for the collimation method are:

Back-sight	Inter-mediate sight	Fore-sight	Height of instrument	Reduced level	Station

Typical headings for the form used for the rise and fall method are:

Back-sight	Inter-mediate sight	Fore-sight	Rise	Fall	Reduced level	Station

Backsight is the *first* reading that is taken on a series of levels. For example, when starting a series of levels from a datum, the first reading taken at the datum would be entered in the backsight column.

Foresight is the *last* reading that is taken in a series of levels.

Intermediate sights are *all* the readings that are taken between the backsight and foresight.

A *series of levels* is the number of readings that are taken while the instrument remains in one spot. As soon as the instrument is moved, a new series is started. Every series of levels must start with a backsight and end with a foresight.

Station is the term given to the spot from where the level is being taken.

Collimation method of booking levels. In this method the backsight reading is added to the reduced level of the station at which the staff is placed, for example, the datum. The reduced level plus the reading on the staff represent the reduced height of the instrument, as shown in Table 8. If all the other readings taken in that series of levels are subtracted from the height of the instrument, these will give the reduced levels of the stations.

When a new series of levels are to be taken, a new backsight is taken on one of the stations in the previous series. This reading is now added to the reduced level of *that* station. Therefore, a new height of instrument is obtained (Table 8). The rest of the readings in the new series are deducted from this new height of instrument. Table 8 also shows two series of levels taken and booked with the collimation method. The readings are in metres, decimetres and centimetres.

The entries in booking must be checked for accuracy by adding all the backsights and all the foresights, and deducting the smaller total from the larger total. This figure should equal the difference between the first and the last reduced level in the booking. Here again, the smaller figure should be taken from the larger figure. This method of checking only ensures that the booking has been carried out correctly. It does not prove that your readings on site are accurate; this can only be ensured by the skill of the operator and the accuracy of the instrument.

Table 8

Backsight	Intermediate sight	Foresight	Height of instrument	Reduced level	Station	Remarks
1.63			21.63	20.00*	Datum	(The backsight is added to the level)
	1.41		21.63	20.22		(The intermediate sights and the foresight
	1.36		21.63	20.27		are all deducted from the height of
	1.24		21.63	20.39		instrument)
2.12		1.38	22.37	20.25		(The new backsight is added to the last
	2.38		22.37	19.99		reduced level of the first series, that is,
	2.25		22.37	20.12		20.25 + 2.12 to give the new height of
	2.45		22.37	19.92		the instrument)
	2.61		22.37	19.76		
		2.74	22.37	19.63*		
3.75		4.12				
		3.75				
	Difference	0.37				

* The difference between the first and last reduced levels should be equal to the difference between the sum of the backsights and the sum of the foresights. In this instance it would be 20.00 − 19.63 = 0.37.

This method of booking can also be used to great advantage when a number of levels at various predetermined heights have to be set out (Table 9). With the aid of this method of booking, the reduced levels can be worked out in the office. As soon as the instrument is set up ready to read the levels, and the first backsight is taken, the height of instrument can be entered and the rest of the *readings* can be calculated by deducting the reduced levels from the height of instrument. The following example shows how this can be done:

Peg A   the datum, 20.00 m
Peg B   0.25 above the datum

Peg C   0.50 above the datum
Peg D   1.15 above peg C
Peg E   0.75 below peg B
Peg F   same as the datum
Peg G   0.55 below peg D

The first operation would be to enter these figures on the booking sheet and calculate the reduced levels, as shown in Table 9.

Although this set of figures would be unlikely on a site, they clearly show that any combination of figures can be computed in this way.

Once the reduced levels have been calculated,

Table 9

Backsight	Intermediate sight	Fore-sight	Height of instrument	Reduced level	Station	Remarks
				20.00	Peg A	The datum
				20.25	Peg B	0.25 above the datum
				20.50	Peg C	0.50 above the datum
				21.65	Peg D	1.15 above peg C
				19.50	Peg E	0.75 below peg B
				20.00	Peg F	Same as datum
				21.10	Peg G	0.55 below peg D

the instrument can now be set up and the reading on the first backsight taken. It can be assumed that this reading is 0.184 m. The height of the instrument can now be entered on the sheet as 20.00 + 1.84 = 21.84 and the rest of the readings can be calculated by deducting the reduced level in each case from the height of instrument, as shown in Table 10.

By using this method for setting pegs at predetermined levels, it is clear that the pegs must be at their correct heights once the reduced levels

have been obtained and the readings taken on the staff. In addition to this, the operator has a complete record of his working.

The rise and fall method of booking

This is not such a versatile method of recording levels, and the rise (or fall) of each level is calculated and entered in the appropriate column. The same figures used in the example in Table 8 are booked using the rise and fall method.

Table 11 shows that, where a reading is a smal-

Table 10

Backsight	Intermediate sight	Fore-sight	Height of instrument	Reduced level	Station	Remarks
1.84			21.84	20.00	Peg A	
	1.59		21.84	20.25	Peg B	
	1.34		21.84	20.50	Peg C	
	0.19		21.84	21.65	Peg D	
	2.34		21.84	19.50	Peg E	
	1.84		21.84	20.00	Peg F	
		0.74	21.84	21.10	Peg G	
Check		0.74				
1.84						
0.74						
1.10						1.10 difference between first and last reading

Table 11

Backsight	Intermediate sight	Foresight	Rise	Fall	Reduced level	Station	Remarks
1.63					20.00	Datum	
	1.41		0.22		20.22		
	1.36		0.05		20.27		
	1.24		0.12		20.39		
2.12		1.38		0.14	20.25		
	2.38			0.26	19.99		(The RL in this case is the
	2.25		0.13		20.12		difference between the
	2.45			0.20	19.92		backsight and the inter-
	2.61			0.16	19.76		mediate sight)
		2.74		0.13	19.63		
3.75		4.12	0.52	0.89			
		3.75		0.52			
		0.37		0.37			

0.37 = the difference between the first and last reduced readings

ler number than the previous reading, it is a *rise*, and where the figure is greater than the previous reading it is a *fall*. When calculating the reduced levels the rises must be added, and the falls deducted.

If the bookings are correct the following sums must all be equal:

1 The difference between the sum of the back-sights and the sum of the foresights.
2 The sum of the rises and the sum of the falls.
3 The difference between the first and last reduced level.

The reduced levels are the same with both methods of booking.

Setting out angles

On many modern levelling instruments, horizontal circles are fitted for setting out angles. These are generally divided every 1 degree, and each degree is read by a simple microscope direct to ten minutes and by calculation to one minute. Figure 74 shows two examples of readings on typical horizontal circles. The readings are clearly indicated in both cases.

Other types of horizontal circles are read by means of a vernier. In this type of instrument the

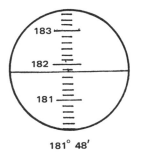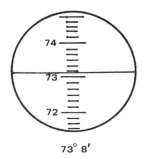

Figure 74

angle can be read to the nearest five minutes. The divisions are set out in degrees and the vernier is used to read off the number of minutes. This is done by looking closely at the vernier to determine the two lines (one on the horizontal circle and the other on the vernier) which coincide with each other. There will only be two lines coinciding at any position where the vernier is placed. Figure 75 shows two examples of this type of vernier.

The method of setting out an angle with the aid of a horizontal circle is as follows:

1 The instrument is set up over the point A from which the angle is to be set out. This is usually done by suspending a plumb-bob from the centre of the instrument and driving a peg into the ground at vertex of the angle.

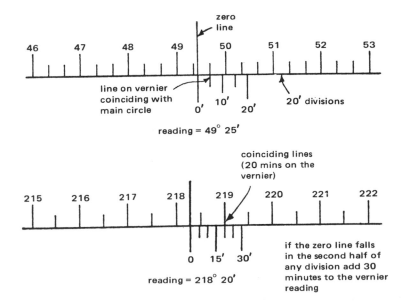

Figure 75 *Simple types of vernier*

2 A ranging pole is placed at one end of the line forming one side of the angle B.

3 The telescope is sighted on to the ranging pole.

4 The zero on the horizontal circle is set immediately under the zero on the vernier.

5 The telescope is now rotated until the required angle is read on the horizontal circle under the zero of the vernier.

6 A ranging pole is then placed at the end of the other side of the angle at C, and adjusted until it is sighted in its correct position by means of the telescope.

7 Angle ABC now forms the required angle.

When carrying out this type of operation it is most important to check the work carefully at each stage to ensure accuracy.

Self-assessment questions

1 Why is it so important for surveying instruments to be handled with care?

2 State the various ways in which instruments can be protected from damage.

3 Describe a typical chain used for surveys.

4 Describe a simple method of counting chain lengths.

5 Describe the method of setting out a right angle with the aid of a sitesquare.

6 For what other purpose can a sitesquare be used?

7 Describe the method of testing a sitesquare for accuracy.

8 How is a Cowley level set up for reading levels?

9 How are the levels taken?

10 Does it make any difference to the readings if the appearance through the aperture of a Cowley level appears to be bent?

11 How are levels taken with a Cowley level at a depth greater than the target?

12 Describe the method of testing a Cowley level for accuracy.

13 Describe how a Cowley level can be used for setting out slopes.

14 What is the difference between a *dumpy* and a *precision level*?

15 Describe the method of setting up a dumpy level.

16 Describe the method of setting up a quick-set precision level.

17 State the advantages of the *autoset level* over the precision level.

18 Describe the *temporary* adjustments that should be carried out before taking readings with a dumpy level.

19 Describe the use of stadia lines on a diaphragm.

20 How should a staff be held by the staff operator?

21 What points should be observed by the staff operator to ensure that no errors are created by the staff?

22 State the meaning of
(a) datum
(b) backsight
(c) intermediate sight
(d) foresight
(e) reduced level
(f) station

23 What are the two methods of booking levels? Why is it so important to record all levels taken on a site?

24 Enter the following levels and determine
their reduced levels if the datum has a
reduced level of 20.00
BS 2.14; Int.S 1.98, 1.76, 1.58, 1.78;
FS 1.57; BS 1.98; Int.S 2.04, 2.14, 1.97;
FS 2.10.

25 The following predetermined levels have to
be set out on the site. Calculate their reduced
levels and enter them on a booking sheet
Peg A (the datum) 30.00 m
Peg B to be 1.25 below the datum
Peg C to be 0.75 above peg B
Peg D to be 1.15 below the datum
Peg E to be 0.50 above peg C
Peg F to be the same as peg D
Peg G to be 0.70 above peg D
When the entries for the above levels are
recorded on the booking sheet and their
reduced levels are obtained, assume that the
instrument is now set up and that the backsight on to the datum is 2.90. Calculate the
readings that will be needed for all the
remaining levels.

26 Describe the method of setting out an angle
with a horizontal circle.

27 Sketch a reading on a horizontal circle of 25
degrees 45 minutes.

28 Sketch a vernier which will read to 5
minutes. Show by means of a sketch a reading of 45 degrees 35 minutes.

Chapter 7

Excavations: ground work

After reading this chapter you should be able to:

1 Have a good understanding of the need for trial holes on a site and how the information gained from them may be used to advantage.
2 Know how to control subsoil water.
3 Know how to seal a sump hole.
4 Have a good understanding of a de-watering system.
5 Have a good knowledge of the various methods of excavating and the types of equipment that may be used.
6 Know the methods of transporting spoil and to be able to compare their costs.

Trial holes

Before the foundations of a site can be designed or the work begun, it is essential to find out the nature of the subsoil below the surface level of the ground. The information that is needed from this preliminary work would include the following:

1 The thickness of each stratum, or layer, of every subsoil.
2 The composition of each stratum.
3 The size of the various particles of which the subsoil is composed in each stratum.
4 The condition of each stratum (see *Brickwork 2*, Chapter 3).
5 The water table level.
6 The quantity of water below ground level.

All these items will have an affect upon the general design of the foundation and upon the method which may have to be used to carry out the work.

In many cases, the trial holes will be dug before tenders are called for, so that the designer can determine the type and size of the foundation work needed for the project. The contractor must also ensure that notice is taken of all the informa-tion available from the details of trial holes. The cost of installing the foundations will be greatly affected by the amount of temporary work that will have to be carried out, such as the amount of timbering necessary to ensure the safety of the workmen; the stability of the sides of the excavation; the amount of pumping necessary to keep the water table level down; and the type of plant that may be needed to carry out the work.

The necessary information about the subsoil can be found either by digging a bore hole with an earth auger (see *Brickwork 2*, Chapter 3) or by digging a trial hole.

The size of the trial hole will depend upon the depth the hole has to be taken, as enough room must be allowed for a person to work inside the hole. As the hole is being dug, a careful record must be made of the subsoil and water level. The water level, and also the rate at which water will fill the trial hole as it is being dug, should also be noted, as this will determine the number of pumps that may be needed when the foundation work is under way, and possibly the type of pump that may be necessary.

As the hole is excavated, the workman must be safeguarded by timbering the sides of the hole.

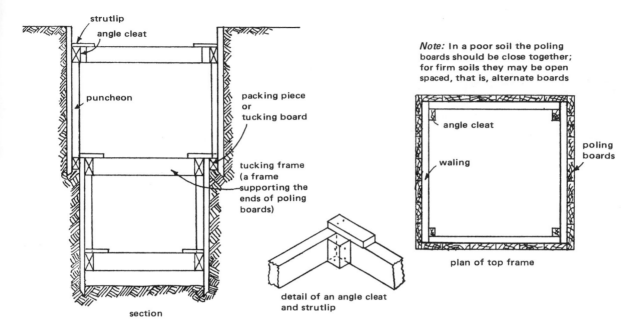

Figure 76 *Typical timbering for a shaft or trial hole*

Figure 76 shows a typical method of timbering the sides of a shaft of this type.

The number of trial holes which must be dug on a site will depend upon the size and mass of the structure that is to be erected and upon the area of the site. A sufficient number of trial holes should always be excavated. This will not only determine a good cross-section through the sub-soil but will also determine the nature of the soil.

Control of subsoil water

The subsoil water in excavations on most sites can usually be readily controlled by centrifugal or diaphragm pumps (see *Brickwork 2*, Chapter 2, which gives outputs of various types of pumps). On sites, however, where the volume of water is quite large and the foundations can be strengthened by drainage, the subsoil water can be collected by one of the following methods:

1   Using a sump hole.
2   Digging a perimeter trench.
3   De-watering the subsoil.

When the soil is saturated it has a low angle of repose, whereas if the water is extracted and the moisture content of the soil is reduced, this will ensure greater stability in the soil.

Sump hole

Where the excavation cannot have a perimeter trench around the outside such as on a confined site where no space would be available, provision must be made for the extraction of water within the excavation. This can be done by means of a sump hole, the bottom of which is kept about half a metre below the bottom of the main excavation. This sump hole must be maintained continuously while the construction work on the foundations within the main excavation is being done. This often means that the sump hole must be left in the basement floor while the structural work is being completed. Therefore, great care must be taken when finally sealing the floor after the work is finished. This may be carried out by stepping back the asphalt at each layer around the sump (Figure 77). When the work is completed an asphalt plug is made up so that it will fit snugly into the space left by the asphalters (Figure 78). When everything is ready, the sump hole is filled up to the

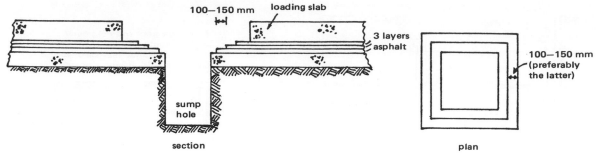

Figure 77   *A sump hole*

Figure 78   *Asphalt plug cast ready to fit into the sump hole*

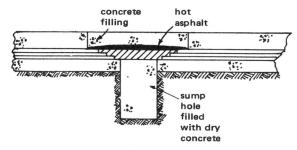

Figure 79   *Section showing the method of filling in a sump hole*

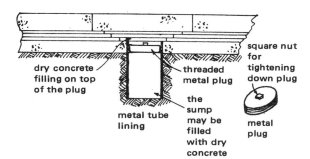

Figure 80   *Filling in a sump hole with the aid of a metal liner and plug*

underside of the asphalt with a very dry mix of well-rammed concrete. The asphalt plug is dropped into place and immediately a mound of hot asphalt is poured over the top and smoothed off by the asphalter (Figure 79). Concrete is then poured over the top to the height of the loading slab. Speed is the main factor in this operation. All the materials must be to hand and the concrete mix must be rich and dry. If the operation is not done quickly, the water is likely to build up a pressure and lift up all the new sealing round the sump hole before it is properly set.

An alternative method of sealing the floor is by building a tube fitted with an internal thread at the top into the concrete floor. When the work is finished and the sump hole is ready to be filled in, the tube is built in and concrete is poured around it and allowed to set hard. While this is being done, the water is still being pumped out from the inside of the tube. This will ensure that no pressure is built up by the water. When the surrounding concrete has hardened sufficiently to resist the pressure of the water, a plug is screwed tightly into the top of the tube. Hot asphalt is then poured over the top and smoothed off, and, finally, concrete is poured over the top up to the height of the loading slab (Figure 80).

When working in deep excavation, the amount of pressure that can be exerted by subsoil water should never be underestimated. The material used to fill in a sump hole can often be forced right out again. The whole process has then to be repeated, which is a costly operation.

Perimeter trenches

When a large excavation has to be dug in a waterlogged or unstable soil, it is often difficult to keep the level of the surface water down. Under these circumstances, a perimeter trench can be dug all round the main excavation. This trench should be kept about half a metre below the main excavation to enable the water to drain into it from the main work. Water can then be pumped from the trench with very little difficulty (Figure 81). The trench need only be narrow in width, with just enough room for a person to work. It is essential, however, that it is well-timbered to prevent any possible collapse of the sides. When the main excavation is completed and the basement constructed, the timber can be extracted and the perimeter trench filled in.

Another type of perimeter trench can be used. This is done by excavating the trench within the main excavation, laying the foundation and part of the floor of the basement, and then building the walls and asphalting the sides (Figure 82). The earth is refilled at the back of the walls and the dumpling of earth in the centre of the main excavation is then excavated. Extreme care must be taken to ensure that there is a good joint between the concrete floor and the asphalt. The layers of the asphalt must each have about a 150 mm lap.

If the basement floor is to be constructed of reinforced concrete, it is most important that the reinforcement is correctly lapped or linked together at the construction joint in the concrete. Any soil which may have fallen on the rods while the dumpling was being excavated must be cleaned off. If the rods are not cleaned there is a great possibility of bad adhesion between the reinforcement and the concrete, which could result in the floor caving in at the construction joints.

De-watering system
This is another very efficient way of extracting the water from a saturated subsoil. It allows the excavations on site to be carried out under dry and safe conditions.

Well points
Well points are tubes fitted with filters, which are jetted into the ground by means of high pressure

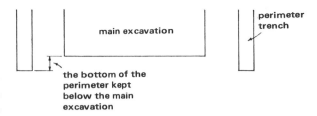

Figure 81 *Section through the main excavation and perimeter trenches*

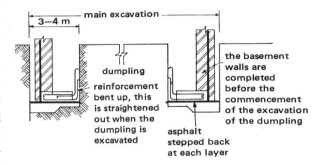

Figure 82 *Section showing a method of excavating for a large basement with a perimeter trench being dug all round the inside of the excavation*

from a jetting pump. The water is forced out of the bottom of the tube, removing the soil and causing the well point to sink by its own weight into the ground.

When the well points have reached the required depth (for a single stage work the maximum depth would usually be about 7 m) each one is connected to a header pipe, which in turn is connected to a suction pump. The water is then sucked out and discharged far enough away from the excavation to keep the immediate ground dry. The distance between the well points will depend upon the amount of water that is to be extracted from the ground.

If the excavation has to be taken to a depth greater than 7 m, two-stage work must be adopted. This means that another set of well points is jetted into the ground at the base of the first set.

There are two basic systems that can be used for de-watering:

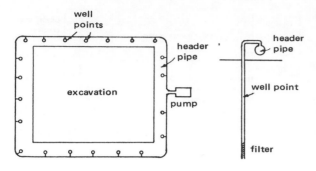

Figure 83   *Plan showing a typical layout for a ring system of well points*

1   A *ring system*, which is used for excavations for basements. In this, the well points are jetted at intervals all round the excavation (Figure 83) and connected to a header pipe.
2   A *progressive system*, used for long trenches, often needed for laying a new sewer scheme. In this system the well points are placed along the side of the trench, and as the work progresses forward, the well points are correspondingly jetted ahead of the excavations. As the work is completed, the well points are extracted from the ground, ensuring continuity of operation (Figure 84).

Both of these systems provide extremely efficient methods of lowering the table level of the water contained in the subsoil, and allow the work to continue under dry and safe conditions.

Excavating

There are a number of types of machine which can be used for excavating soil, and each one has special advantages for various conditions of working. These types include the following:

Back actor
Face shovel (or crowd shovel)
Dragline
Grab
Skimmer
Continuous bucket trencher

Descriptions of all these types are given in *Brickwork 2*, Chapter 1. Their uses are outlined below:

Back actor or drag shovel
This is a machine which is used from the top of the excavation which therefore means that it is necessary for the excavation always to be *bottomed up* (Figure 85), which means that it has to be levelled off *by hand* and then thoroughly rammed. This is essential because the machine cannot do it, as the movement of the arm, which works in a circular motion, cannot make a clean level cut at the bottom of the excavation. The machine should work sufficiently far back from the edge of the excavation; alternatively, a stop board should be provided to prevent the machine from falling in, especially where the soil is not very stable. Problems may arise with this type of excavator on a site where the basement extends over the whole

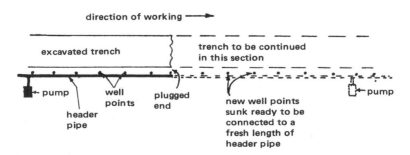

Figure 84   *Plan of a trench showing a progressive system of sinking well points*

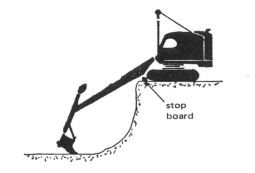

Figure 85 *Back actor*

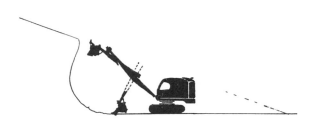

Figure 86 *Face shovel*

of the site. This often occurs on work in urban areas. In such a case, it is essential for the machine to work its way out of the site, which means that the last stages may have to be carried out from a road adjacent to the site, provided permission has first been obtained from the local authority and the police.

The use of this type of machine does allow for ease of access for the dumpers or lorries to remove the spoil from the excavation, as they can travel on the ground surface level.

The time cycle for loading a lorry with a back actor is rather slower than it is with a face shovel or skimmer, but this may be relatively unimportant on a site where there is difficulty of access and where no other method of excavating can be used. This type of machine usually has a bucket capacity of between 0.25 and 0.75 m^3 and is particularly useful in trenches which are 1–2 m wide and 5 m deep.

Face shovel

This machine is used in the bottom of the excavation. The work is carried out by sliding the bucket up the face of the sides of the work. The lorries or dumpers have to have access to the bottom of the excavation by means of a ramp in order to allow them to be loaded. This method of working is ideal on a job situated on a sloping site, as shown in Figure 86. In such cases no ramp is needed as the lorries can travel along the bottom of the excavation while the machine is working. Where a ramp has to be constructed, extra costs are incurred for its erection. These may, however, be offset by the more rapid machine excavation of the soil. In any case, on confined sites it is most difficult, and sometimes impossible, to use a back actor. The ramp should not be too steep and should be kept clear of soil so that it does not become slippery in wet weather. The use of a ramp does have the tendency to impede the other operations which are being carried out within the excavation.

A face shovel will dig soft or reasonably hard materials, including soft chalk, shale and marl. It will also produce a fairly clean bottom in most materials.

Dragline

This type of machine is suitable for a wide range of reasonably soft or loose soil materials. It will not leave a clean bottom, which means that this operation has to be carried out by hand after the bulk of the excavation has been dug. This type of machine works from the upper surface of the excavation, digging below itself (Figure 87). Where it is difficult to provide an access to the bottom of the excavation for transport, the dragline working from the top is preferred to a face shovel working from the bottom of the excavation. It is particularly useful when working in waterlogged soils or narrow cuts, and when depositing alongside the excavation. For most construction work, this type of machine usually has a bucket capacity of between 0.25–2 m^3, although buckets of far greater capacity are available for special types of work, such as opencast coaling.

Grab

A grab bucket can be used with a dragline or crane (Figure 88). It is particularly useful for excavating in waterlogged soils, foundation

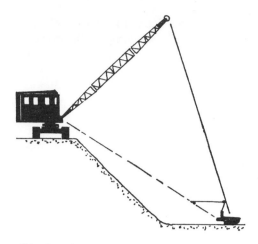

Figure 87   *Dragline*

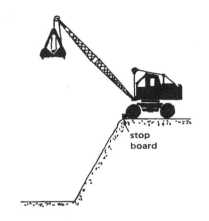

stop
board

Figure 88   *Grab*

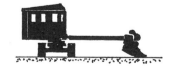

Figure 89   *Skimmer*

trenches or pits where a dragline cannot be used. The capacity of the grab is usually between 0.25–1 m³.

It is also invaluable for excavating soil from within a coffer dam.

Skimmer

This machine is designed mainly for surface excavation, and will provide a very clean bottom to the excavation (Figure 89). It is especially useful when clearing sites or removing the topsoil. It can also be used for loading spoil heaps into dumpers or lorries.

Continuous bucket trencher

A continuous bucket trencher is fitted with an endless chain of buckets which scrape up the face of the trench and deposit the excavated material on the side of the trench. Usually various widths of bucket can be fitted to the machine to suit the width of trench that is needed. This can range from about 0.5 to 1.5 m in width; the depth can also vary from about 1 to 5 m. The soil should be free of large stones, as these can reduce the output of the machine by causing jamming of the buckets.

The continuous bucket trencher is capable of high outputs and can also produce a reasonably level bottom as the boom can be raised or lowered to suit or take up any irregularities in the surface of the ground over which the machine is operating. The earth is usually deposited by the machine at a safe distance from the edge of the trench so that the weight of the soil will not make the trench sides collapse. When using this type of machine, it is possible to work very close to the machine with the trench sheeting or timbering. With all the other types of machine, sufficient room must be allowed for the machine to operate freely within the excavation. Therefore, it is very often difficult, if not impossible, to timber the sides of a trench close to where the machine is operating.

Transporting the soil

When the soil from an excavation has to be transported to a storage space on site or taken to another site altogether, it is extremely important that the type and quantity of transport equipment is carefully planned. Excavators are expensive items of machinery either to buy or hire, and to operate. Therefore, when they are working on site they should have as much continuity of operation as possible. It is equally important to remember that the transportation costs add to the cost of excavation but add nothing to the value of the soil being transported. Close investigation into the most economical method should always be made before assuming that any well-known traditional method will be used.

Typical methods of transportation include the following:

Barrows
Powered barrows
Dumpers
Lorries
Monorail
Skips
Belt conveyors

Barrows

Barrows are generally only used on smaller sites where the rate of excavation is slow and the length of barrow run is short, or where the conditions on the site make it extremely difficult to use any form of mechanical equipment.

This is a very expensive method of transporting material, as it is slow and one person can only move 0.1 m³ of material at a time (0.05 m³ of concrete). Therefore, it is comparatively simple to calculate the cost of transportation per cubic metre of soil by the following example.

Assume that a barrowman makes 15 journeys per hour. Then the total amount of earth that is moved would be $0.1 \times 15 = 1.5$ m³. Assume also that the total cost of the worker's time, including wages, insurance, holidays with pay and all other incidental costs, is £4.00 per hour. Then the cost per cubic metre of soil for transport only is

$$\frac{£4.00}{1.5} = 273 \text{ pence.}$$

The number of journeys made by the barrowman will, of course, depend upon the length of the barrow run and the speed of loading the barrow. This will also have an effect on the cost per cubic metre of soil; the *fewer* journeys made, the greater the cost and, on the other hand, the *more* journeys made, the less cost per cubic metre. It is

also important to remember that the hourly rate of the barrowman should include all expenses, not just net wages.

Powered barrow

There are a number of different types of powered barrow machines available and each one has its own special advantages. Some are controlled by the operator who walks behind the machine while others have a seat provided for the driver which would allow more journeys, as the machine would be able to travel faster than the walking pace. The general advantage of all these machines, however, is that they are capable of carrying heavier loads and more material can be shifted per hour. A method of calculating the cost of transporting a cubic metre of soil is shown in the following example.

Assume the total cost of a powered barrow is £300 per week including operator and running costs. Then the cost (for a 40 hour week) is £5.00 per hour. Assume that the number of journeys per hour is 15 and the capacity of the machine is 0.5 m³. Then the amount of soil carried per hour is $0.5 \times 15 = 7.5$ m³.

Therefore, the cost is $\dfrac{£5.00}{7.5} = 66$ pence per cubic metre.

Although these figures are hypothetical, they will give the reader an idea of the importance of computing transport charges carefully.

Dumpers

These are popular machines on most sites, as they are very manoeuvrable, robust and capable of carrying from 2 to 5 m³ at a time. Although there are models capable of carrying larger loads, they would normally be found only on very large sites. Dumpers are motorized and are therefore capable of more journeys per hour than barrows or power barrows. They are also easily unloaded by tipping the skip.

Assume that the number of journeys made per hour is 20 and the dumper is of 3 m³ capacity. Assume also that the total cost per week is £400 including operator, fuel and oil, insurances and hire. The number of cubic metres of soil carried $= 3 \times 20 = 60$ m³ per hour.

$$\text{Cost per hour} = \frac{£400}{40}$$
$$= £10.00$$

$$\text{Cost per cubic metre of soil} = \frac{£10.00}{60}$$
$$= 16.6 \text{ pence}$$

Lorries

These would not normally be used where the soil is being stored on the site (unless the site was a very large one) as the dumper would usually be of greater use under most site conditions. On the other hand, if the soil is to be removed from the site, lorries would usually give the better service. Their capacities vary from about 5–10 m³. All lorries should have tipping bodies so that the material is easily unloaded.

Monorail

This is a popular form of transportation as it is easily erected on site and does not need an operator for each mechanical unit, as it can operate automatically. While it is most useful for transporting concrete, it can also be used efficiently for any material which is to be transported within the site. The skips run on a single rail and, if the ground is fairly level, each skip is capable of pulling another one behind it. Therefore, a total load of about 2 m³ can be carried. Junctions can be provided which will allow two skip trains to be used. The skips can be started by the banksman working at the excavator and they will automatically stop at their destination, where they can be tipped by another operator who is controlling the spread of the soil. Therefore, by using two skips a regular constant supply of material can be maintained.

Skips

Although this is a similar method to the monorail, the skips are pulled by a locomotive on a narrow-gauge track. This method has to a great extent been replaced by more mobile forms of transportation but it still has its uses in special circumstances, such as removing the spoil from headings or tunnels, or transporting material on an extensive site. It is quite common to use side-tipping wagons with capacities of up to 10 m³ each.

Belt conveyors

Although this method of conveying excavated material has not yet been fully investigated by many firms, it is finding increasing use on many sites for both short and long hauls. For a number of years brickyards have found this a most economical method of transporting materials. Suitable loading hoppers must be provided to allow an even flow of material. Conveyors are extremely useful when large quantities of material must be excavated and transported over long distances. This justifies the considerable expense of installation. It can also be an economical method, when considerable amounts of sand and gravel, or similar materials, have to be conveyed for fairly short distances.

Selection of method of transportation

Therefore, the main factors to be considered in determining the method of transporting material on site include:

1 The quantity of material to be handled.
2 The type of material.
3 The length of the haul.
4 Where the material is to be tipped.
5 Excavating plant available.
6 Ground conditions.
7 The availability of labour for operating plant or track maintenance.

Plant maintenance

Details of replacement of working parts and extensive overhauls are beyond the scope of this book as this would be the work of a mechanic expert in machinery. However, everybody on site who has the control of plant operations must ensure that the machines are treated with proper care and attention.

Good maintenance plays a most important part in the operating of machinery and will:

1 Extend the working life of the machine.
2 Keep the replacement of worn parts to a minimum.
3 Ensure that extensive overhauls are not required at too frequent intervals.
4 Play an important part in preventing breakdowns, which only too often occur at the most inopportune moment on site, and are always costly in time, money and production.
5 Ensure more effective production or output, particularly in the case of mixers and mortar pans, where *caked* drums or pans have an adverse effect on the mixing of concrete and mortars.

Therefore a simple daily check on plant is important and will reduce costs, and the manufacturer's instructions should be carefully read and understood. Once a regular habit of plant maintenance is adopted by an operator it will very often become a routine matter each day. These routine checks should include the following:

1 Oil in the sump must be kept at the correct level and changed at regular intervals.
2 If the engine is water-cooled the radiator should be 'topped up' every day.
3 A clean can and funnel should always be used when filling the machine with petrol or diesel oil.
4 Grease should be kept in a clean, airtight tin, so that dirt cannot contaminate the grease and eventually find its way into the machine.
5 Petrol and oil caps should be properly fitted on the filler tubes.
6 Air filters should not be removed from the air intakes and never left off while the machine is operating.
7 The filtering media on the air filter should be changed at frequent intervals.
8 The cooling system of a water-cooled engine should be drained off every night during cold weather unless anti-freeze agents have been added to the water.
9 All moving parts should be kept well-greased or oiled.

10 Greasing nipples should be wiped clean before applying the grease gun to ensure that dirt is not injected into any bearings.
11 Tyres on dumpers and lorries should be kept at their correct pressures.
12 Stationary plant, such as mixers and hoists, should be placed on firm bases to prevent excessive vibration.
13 Wire ropes which have become frayed or badly worn should not be used on plant, but should be replaced immediately.
14 In general, plant should be kept clean, particularly items which are used for the mixing and transporting of concrete and mortars.

All these points are important for the efficient operation of mechanical plant, and the cost of these maintenance operations should be regarded as a portion of the operating costs rather than an overhead. This should ensure an adequate amount of time for this work, and the care of machinery should not be considered as an on-cost job.

Self-assessment questions

1 What information can be obtained from a trial hole and for what purposes would this be required?

2 How can the subsoil water be kept under control?

3 How can a sump hole be filled in when the work is complete?

4 For what purposes are perimeter trenches used?

5 Describe the installation of a de-watering system and its method of working.

6 Describe six different types of machines that can be used for excavating, and state their particular advantages.

7 Describe seven various ways in which excavated spoil can be transported.

8   Why is plant maintenance so important?

9   State the various ways in which maintenance of plant can be carried out.

10 Compare the costs of operating hand and powered units for transporting soil on a site.

Chapter 8

Excavations: timbering

After reading this chapter you should be able to:

1 Have a good knowledge of the methods of timbering for deep excavations.
2 Know how to use runners in connection with timbering.
3 Have a good understanding of sheet piling.
4 Appreciate the need for careful backfilling of excavations.
5 Know how to set out headings.
6 Understand the method of excavating a heading and the methods of timbering.
7 Have a sound knowledge of piling.

Timbering deep excavations

The selection of the method of timbering which is to be used in an excavation will largely depend upon the following points:

1 The type of ground in which the trench or basement is to be excavated
2 The amount of water in the soil
3 The type of soil
4 The depth to which the excavation is to be taken

Although timbering is both expensive and non-productive, there is a statutory obligation on the part of every person employed on site to ensure the safety of all personnel engaged in this work (see *Brickwork 2*, Chapter 1).

The following types of timbering are commonly used:

Poling boards
Horizontal sheeting
Runners
Sheet piling

Whatever method is decided upon there are several points which should be considered with all of them:

1 An allowance must be made for the thickness of timbering when setting out the trench. In the case of poling boards and tucking frames the number of frames that will be used must be considered, as well as the reduction in size at each staging.
2 Cost allowance must be made for the extraction of timbers when the work is finished.
3 Working space inside the excavation must be provided after the walling is completed, if other trades, such as asphalters or bricklayers, are to work on the face of the wall.
4 Struts should be spaced far enough apart to allow for ample working space and the removal of spoil, with the aid of skips, if necessary.

Poling boards

When digging in a reasonably firm soil, each staging of about 1.5 m should be excavated and the sides should be timbered with poling boards about 50 mm thick. The sides of the excavation should be first dug roughly and then trimmed off. When this has been done, poling boards can be positioned against the trench sides. The walings are then strutted into position against the poling boards and wedged into place. Lipping pieces or lip blocks are fixed to the struts to prevent them from sliding into the trench. As each frame is

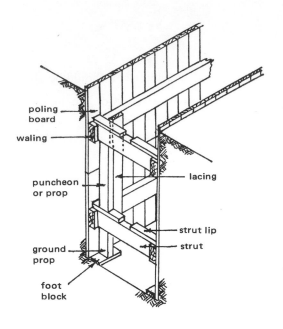

Figure 90   *Single or centre waling poling frame*

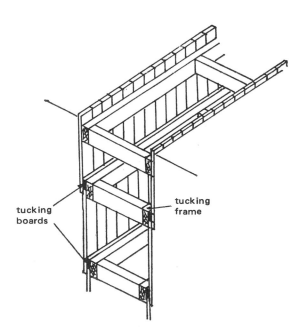

Figure 91   *Close boarding with tucking frame*

finished it is ground propped, puncheoned and laced to the frames above (see Figure 90).

A variation of the single or centre waling poling frame is the use of a 'tucking frame'. With this system each stage of the excavation is framed but tucking frames are used reducing in width at each stage. The amount of reduction in width is equal to the thickness of the waling, and the poling boards are supported at their tops by a *tucking board* or packing piece. The reason for reducing the width of the trench at each stage by the width of the walling is to allow for the driving of the poling boards into the soil should this be necessary, and the boards on one stage can slide by the walings in the upper stage (Figure 91). It also allows for ease of withdrawal of the boards if the soil is unstable, and allows for backfilling to be done in small heights.

When excavating in harder grounds which do not require to be timbered very closely, open poling boards, or poling boards and pinchers, may be used (Figure 92).

Horizontal sheeting

With this method of timbering the ground is excavated at small depths (about 0.3 m) and a sheeting board is placed horizontally against the earth face and held in place by a temporary strut. When a sufficient depth has been supported in this way the whole system is held back by soldiers which are secured by the permanent struts (Figure 93).

When the work is completed the sheeting is dismantled by removing one horizontal sheet at a time and holding the remainder of the sheets back by means of temporary struts (in reverse order from its installation). This method of sheeting has several advantages:

1   The trench can be excavated in a constant width throughout its depth.
2   It is a useful method to adopt in a poor-quality soil.
3   It is also a useful method where the ground is heavily weighted on its edges. This might happen if excavation is carried out in sloping ground, and a heavy surcharge is created on one side of the trench.

Runners

Runners are usually arranged to form close vertical sheeting which is driven down while the excavation is in progress. Runners are normally square-edged, but they can be vee-jointed in cases where the infiltration of silt or water has to be kept to a minimum. The lower ends of the runners are often sharpened to a chisel edge. In addition to this, they may also be splayed (Figure 94).

If runners are likely to be subjected to some hard driving, the lower edge should be iron shod and the head of the runners should be ringed or protected with hoop iron.

When starting to pitch runners, walings must be fixed at two levels. These walings must be held at a distance from the earth face equal to the thickness of the runner, plus the wedging space. This is done by fixing uprights behind the walings and against the excavated earth face. The runners are then slid down between the earth and the walings and held in position by page wedges.

In bad ground the runners are driven separately by digging away the earth at the foot of the runner, easing the pages and then tapping the runner down to the new level. Each runner is driven about 0.3 m at a time and the pages are tightened each time the runners are lowered. When there are struts which prevent runners being placed, the ground can be held back by cross-poling, as shown in Figure 95.

Sheet piling

These are usually rolled steel sections which interlock with each other. They can have many uses provided they are driven with care. Sheet piles can be driven by a drop hammer or by a single or double-acting hammer which can be steam or air-operated. The air-operated double-acting hammers are the most popular method, because the air supply can be readily produced by a mobile compressor which can be easily transported to various parts of the site.

The main advantage of sheet piling is that the piles can be driven into the ground before excavating is begun which will ensure complete safety during the operation.

Interlocking types of piles also provide a good

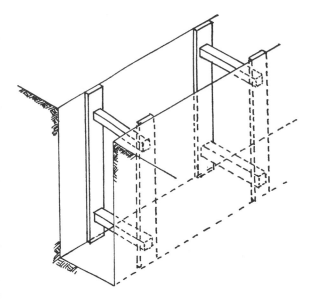

Figure 92 *Pinchers in firm ground*

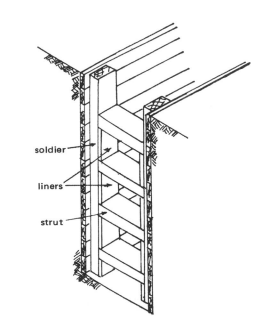

Figure 93 *Horizontal sheeting*

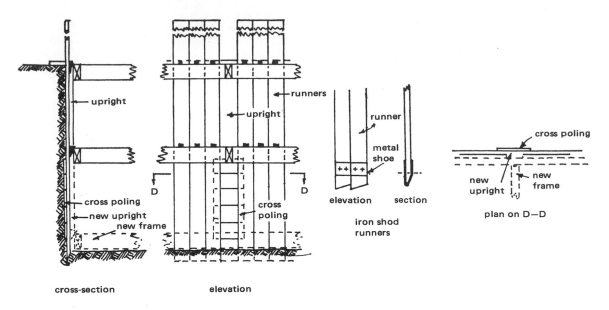

Figure 94   *Stage 3 – runners driven in and trench excavated ready for the next frame (which is shown by the dotted lines)*

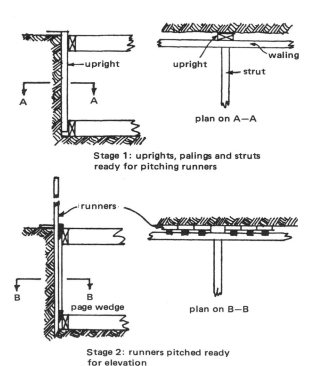

Figure 95   *Stage 2 – method of sheeting with runners*

resistance to the penetration of water and silt into the excavation.

When the work is completed, each pile is withdrawn by a special hammer which drives upwards instead of downwards, while both pile and hammer are being pulled upwards by a crane.

If concrete is to be poured against the sheet piles, felt should be placed between the concrete and the piles before pouring so that the piles can be withdrawn when the work is finished.

The piles can also be driven deep enough below the bottom of the excavation in water-bearing permeable soils such as sands to prevent a *boil* or *heave* taking place in the bottom of the excavation. This can occur when the upward pressure of water is greater than the weight of the overlying soil in the excavation.

Typical steel sections for sheet piling are shown in Figure 96.

Inspection of timbering

It is a statutory requirement that every part of an excavation should be examined at least once a day while workmen are employed there, and the

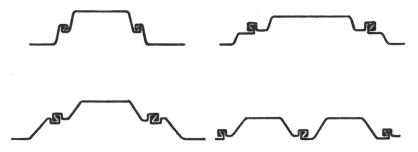

Figure 96   *Typical Larssen sheet piling sections*

working end of every trench more than 2 m deep should be inspected before the commencement of each shift.

This constant inspection is essential to ensure that all the components are in good working order and not in danger of being overloaded. Defects can arise from the following causes and should be the main points to observe when carrying out an inspection:

1 Shrinkage of the ground through drying out.
2 Expansion of the ground due to rain or ground water.
3 Shrinkage of the timbers due to drying.
4 Displacement of timber members by accidental blows during operations.
5 Leakage of soil from behind the sheeting.
6 Wedges becoming loose through drying or accidental dislodgement.
7 The possibility of rot which can occur in timbers which have been kept in a damp place for a long time.

Backfilling

Backfilling is important and needs the same care as other parts of the permanent works. Failure to do this can result in a great deal of trouble and expense.

The degree of compaction will depend on the

Figure 97   *Detail of interlock*

nature of the work and how much soil movement can be tolerated. In general, if the excavated material is being used for the backfill, the density and moisture content of the compacted fill should be equal to that of the undisturbed soil on each side of the excavation. Saturating the backfill is not a good practice, and can be a source of trouble after compaction by excessive shrinkage of the compacted fill. Typical plant that can be used for compacting backfilling are shown in *Brickwork 2*, Chapter 1.

Headings

When the excavation of a trench for pipes has to be taken to a depth which makes the operation uneconomical to carry out with an open trench, the work can be done in headings.

These should be dug in short lengths between shafts. An expert timberman should always be employed on this type of work as it can be very dangerous if carried out in wet or bad ground.

Timbering for shafts

Shafts are timbered in a similar way as trenches, except that the walings are used as struts (Figure 95), and angle cleats are used to prevent accidental displacement of the waling struts.

Setting out for a heading

1 The shafts are first dug to the required level.
2 A line is stretched across the two shafts or sighted through surveying instruments, and marked on profiles each side of the shafts (Figure 98).

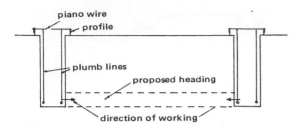

Figure 98   *Section through two shafts and a heading*

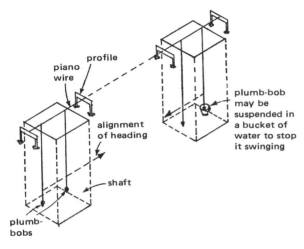

Figure 99   *A method of transferring the setting out line; from the surface to underground, for a heading*

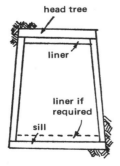

Figure 100   *Box setting*

3   A piano wire is stretched across the two profiles of one of the shafts and two plumb-bobs are then suspended from this wire. If there is a high wind or if it is difficult to prevent the plumb-bobs from swinging, the plumb-bobs can be suspended in a bucket of water (Figure 99).

4   The shaft can now be aligned from the two plumb lines and excavating can begin. It is better to excavate from both shafts at the same time which will keep the length of haulage of excavated soil to the minimum. Ideally, the heading should be started from each shaft and meet in the middle between the two shafts.

Typical methods of timbering headings in various types of soils are:

Box setting. This is only suitable for small headings in good ground; roof boards or side boards can be added where necessary (Figure 100).

Poling setting. This is used in ground which, after excavation, will stand long enough to allow a poling frame to be inserted. In good ground the poling boards can be open spaced instead of close boarded. In addition to this, if the bottom is hard, it may not be necessary to timber across the base of the frames (Figure 101).

Piling setting. This is used where the ground is soft and reasonably dry. This is a most difficult method of timbering and requires a high degree of skill. Therefore, it should only be carried out by a skilled timberman. The sheeting timbers are sharpened to chisel edges so that they can be driven into the ground ahead of the excavation. Figure 102 shows two frames in position with a third frame being prepared for driving.

Piling

Ground works very often involve the sinking of piles in order to stabilize the foundations of the new structure. These piles vary greatly in type and methods of sinking, and each type has its own special advantages and disadvantages. Structures vary greatly in size, shape and weight and, therefore, every piled foundation would be designed to suit each individual case.

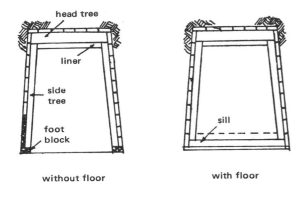

Figure 101 *Poling setting*

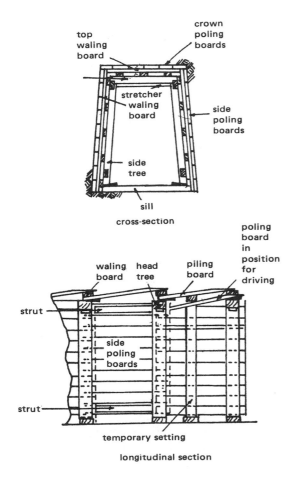

Figure 102 *Piling setting*

Piles can be divided broadly into two groups: *bearing piles*; and *friction piles*.

Bearing piles are driven down to a hard stratum and provide a direct support to the foundation from that stratum. Friction piles depend largely upon the frictional resistance between the ground and the surface area of the pile.

There are, however, certain distinct types of piles each with its own particular characteristics, and these would include the following:

Precast concrete piles (reinforced and pre-stressed)
Bored piles
Pressure piles
In situ piles (the concrete is hammered down)

Precast piles

Precast piles are piles which are cast, either in a factory or in a casting yard on site, and allowed to cure. They are then transported to the driving position, where they are hoisted in a vertical or raking position and driven into position by a drop-hammer and piling-frame. The drop-hammer can consist of a weight which is lifted and allowed to drop on the head of the pile, or it may be an air- or steam-operated single-acting hammer, composed of a heavy weight which operates on a shaft. The steam or air lifts the weight and then allows it to drop on to the head of the pile.

The foot of the pile is fitted with a steel shoe which is tapered to allow for ease of penetration into the ground. The head of the pile should also be protected from damage by the drop-hammer. This can be done by fitting a helmet over the head of the pile. The space between the concrete and the helmet can be packed with plastic filling, sacking or rope.

The concrete must be a good-quality concrete. Specially rich mixes are often specified for the foot and the head of the pile to counteract the extra stresses which are created at these points.

These piles must also be lifted at points indicated by the designer as extra reinforcement has been placed at these lifting points. They should then be stacked so that the packing pieces are placed at the lifting points. This will ensure that excessive stresses are not created at any part of the pile.

Precast piles can be either concrete reinforced with mild steel rods or prestressed concrete. Concrete reinforced piles are cast in individual moulds with the steel being preformed into frames and cast in the concrete. The whole unit is thoroughly compacted by vibration.

Prestressed piles are reinforced with high-tensile steel wires placed in position and stretched by hydraulic rams to predetermined loads. The concrete is then poured around the wires, vibrated and allowed to set and harden. When the concrete has reached the required strength, the formwork is removed and the wires are cut off at each end of the pile. These piles are often cast in factories where *long line* systems are installed, so that quite a number of piles can be cast end-to-end and then separated when the concrete has hardened.

In general, prestressed piles are more satisfactory than reinforced piles, both for handling and resistance to breaking under the blows of the drop-hammer.

Sometimes a pile has to be cut off when it is too long for requirements. When this is necessary, they should be cut *across* the pile and not *down* the pile, especially if a pneumatic tool is used for the cutting.

The advantages of precast piles are:
1   The reinforcement can be placed accurately.
2   The concrete can be mixed and placed under good conditions and vibrated to give a high density.
3   The piles can be driven into water-bearing soils without the contamination of the concrete.

Bored piles
Bored piles are piles which are formed by boring a hole into the ground, placing the reinforcement, and then filling with concrete. There are a number of different types of these piles on the market. Some of them have their lining tube left in the ground and others have their lining tube withdrawn.

In a firm soil the hole can be bored without a lining tube and then filled with concrete. But this method is of little use in soft, water-bearing soils, as the hole is likely to collapse as it is being bored.

The advantages of bored piles with the lining tube left in are:
1   The concrete cannot become contaminated with water or earth.
2   The piling plant is generally lighter than the piling plant needed for precast piles.
3   There is no difficulty in removing the tube.

The advantages of bored piles with the tube withdrawn are:
1   The cost of the tube is saved.
2   The surface area of the concrete provides more frictional resistance between the pile and the ground. This in turn gives a higher bearing capacity than the piles with the tube left in where the pile is required to act as both a bearing pile as well as a frictional pile.

Pressure piles
Pressure piles are bored piles, but precast units are lowered into the borehole, and reinforcement can also be placed in these precast units after they have been put into position. A cap is then secured at the top of the tube and the concrete is forced under pressure into the tube and completely surrounds the precast units. This pressure also assists in the withdrawal of the tube. As the precast units and the tube can be supplied in short lengths, this type of pile can be used where there is limited headroom. The advantages of the pressure pile are:
1   There is little risk of the concrete being contaminated with water or earth.
2   The reinforcement is placed in its correct position.
3   The concrete being placed under pressure ensures a high density.
4   The cost of the tube is saved.
5   Piles can be driven with this method where there is limited headroom.
6   The piling equipment is lighter than that required for precast piles.

7 The concrete surface provides a good frictional resistance.

In situ piles

This type of pile is formed by first putting a plug of concrete in the bottom of a tube and then hammering the tube into the ground to the required depth. The plug is removed by hammering it downwards and pulling the tube upwards by means of the winch. When the plug is removed the concrete is poured and hammered into place with a steel ball while the tube is gradually withdrawn. This produces a very dense concrete, as well as hammering it into any soft patches of ground which may be surrounding the pile. This forms an excellent type of frictional pile. Great care, however, must be taken when using this type of pile adjacent to existing buildings as the hammering may be detrimental to them. Reinforcement can be used in these piles if it is needed. In this case, the concrete is compacted by raising and lowering the hammer inside the reinforcing cage.

Advantages of the *in situ* pile are:

1 The concrete must be of very stiff consistency and this, together with heavy hammering, gives a high density.
2 The concrete is hammered out into any loose pockets of soil. This gives an excellent frictional resistance between the pile and the ground.

After the piles have been driven, the heads are usually connected by means of ground beams and the slabs are then laid over these beams.

Self-assessment questions

1 What are the conditions that will largely affect the selection of the method of timbering for a deep excavation?

2 What are the four main types of timbering commonly used for deep excavations?

3 What are the main points which apply to all methods?

4 What is meant by a *tucking frame*?

5 What are the advantages of using horizontal sheeting?

6 With the aid of a neat sketch show how runners are used in timbering.

7 How is sheet piling placed in position?

8 Why is the inspection of timbering so important?

9 What are the main points to be observed when inspecting timbering?

10 Describe the method of backfilling excavations.

11 Describe the method of setting out for a heading.

12 With the aid of neat sketches show the following methods of timbering headings:
(a) box setting
(b) poling setting
(c) piling setting

13 By means of a neat sketch show a method of timbering for a shaft 6 m deep and 3 m^2 on plan.

14 What are the main groups into which piles may be divided?

15 Describe the main points that should be observed when handling precast concrete piles.

16 What are the main advantages of precast concrete piles over *in situ* piles?

17 Describe the method of sinking pressure piles. State their advantages.

18 Describe *in situ* piles in which the concrete is hammered down. State their advantages.

Chapter 9

Demolition and shoring

After reading this chapter you should be able to:

1 Have a good knowledge of the methods used for the demolition of buildings.

2 Have a good understanding of the safety regulations concerned with demolition work.

3 Know how to erect various types of shoring.

Demolition work

When contracts are being drawn up, the demolition of existing buildings is often a contractual requirement. This can be dangerous work which requires courage, skill and a sound knowledge of the construction of buildings to ensure accidents do not happen. The method of demolition is usually in the reverse order to the way the building was assembled. Once the salvageable items have been removed from the building, the shell of the structure can be demolished in one of the following ways:

1 By knocking down the walls piece by piece with pick and shovel or with pneumatic tools. This method, although comparatively slow, is often used on confined sites in city areas, to keep the amount of dust to a minimum and to reduce the possibility of accidents to people on the site or to passers-by.

2 By using a crane and demolition ball usually weighting about a metric tonne which is shown in Figure 103. The crane swings the ball at the wall and knocks it down in large pieces. This method is very useful for demolishing buildings which have a fair amount of space around them which allows for the swing of the ball and for the portions of brickwork to fall without risk of accidents.

3 By setting fire to the building(s) and then pushing the weakened structure down by means of a bulldozer. Alternatively a wire rope can be wrapped around the structure (or part of the structure in the case of a terrace of houses) and wound on to a winch. Sometimes the rope is attached to a bulldozer which pulls the buildings down, but often this creates heavy wear on the machine and it is generally better if a winch can be used for this type of work.

4 By cutting holes at strategic points in the walling and pulling the walls down with the aid of wire ropes which are taken round the building and attached to a winch or bulldozer.

5 By using explosives. This is a very efficient method, but the explosives must be handled by an expert who is well trained in this work and knows the exact type of charge to use, the quantity of explosive required, and where it should be placed.

Method 3 is particularly useful where there is a large area to be cleared, such as in slum clearance, or where the property may be infected with vermin. It must, however, only be used after consultation with the fire-prevention officer of the dis-

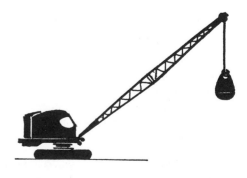

Figure 103 *A crane and demolition ball*

trict in which the demolition work is to be done. Every precaution must be taken to safeguard adjoining properties and to ensure the safety and welfare of people living in them. In addition to this, fires must be dampened down at the end of each day and hose-pipes must be available at all times while the fires are burning to prevent them from getting out of control and endangering adjoining properties.

Whichever method is used, however, there are certain points which should be observed during the demolition of any building to ensure that the work is carried out in accordance with the requirements of the Building Regulations, which include the following:

The Construction (General Provisions) Regulations

No. 1580, Part X, lays down the statutory requirements for the demolition of the whole or part of a building or other structure and includes the following:

Supervision. That a competent person who is experienced in this type of work must be in charge of demolition work.

Fire and flooding. That all precautions must be taken before the demolition work has begun to prevent any danger of fire or explosion through leakage of gas or vapour, and the danger of flooding.

Precautions in connection with demolition. No part of a building shall be overloaded with debris which would render it unsafe.

The following special operations shall be carried out only under the immediate supervision of a competent foreman or by a workman who is experienced in this type of work:

1   The demolition of a building where there is a special risk of collapse which would endanger employed personnel.
2   The cutting of reinforced concrete, steelwork or ironwork forming part of the building or other structure being demolished.

Before demolition has begun precautions should be taken by adequate shoring to prevent

the accidental collapse of any adjoining building or structure which would endanger any person employed. This requirement also applies during the progress of the work.

The following are special points which should be considered in demolition work to prevent accidents:

1   If a hole in a floor is covered over, a notice should be fixed on the cover stating that there is a hole underneath. This will prevent anyone from lifting up the cover and walking forwards with it. Alternatively an adequate guard can be put around all holes in floors.
2   *Traps* should not be left in boards or flooring, that is, where boards are overhanging holes to such an extent that when a person treads on them they are liable to fall.
3   Dust should be dampened down. This enables the personnel to see what they are doing and the work to be done without causing too much nuisance to owners or occupiers of adjacent buildings.
4   Pieces of timber with nails sticking up should never be left around. This is too common a hazard.
5   In urban areas the windows on the lower floors should be boarded over to prevent the escape of dust.
6   Warning notices should be put up wherever part of the structure is dangerous.
7   Every attempt should be made to keep the site as tidy as possible. This is extremely difficult, but a reasonable degree of tidiness can be achieved by experts in this field.
8   Unnecessary risks should never be undertaken on site by any of the personnel.
9   Chutes should be used to lower rubbish from one level to another; bricks and other debris will bounce from a heap of rubbish if they are thrown from a height which of course will be a dangerous hazard.

In addition to these points, it is sound practice to obtain, if possible, drawings of any alterations which may have been carried out to the building during its lifetime. This should foresee any possible hazards which might cause accidents.

B S Code of Practice no. 94 'Demolitions' is a

particularly useful reference for works of this nature.

Shoring

This is the term given to any system of bracing, usually composed of timber or steelwork, to give support to a structure, and to prevent any movement during other operations which are being carried out on, or adjacent to, that structure. Shoring should never be used to force back a structure which has inadvertently moved. It should only be used to prevent any possible further movement.

The main members of a shoring system should be placed so that they can provide as much direct resistance as possible to the load to be carried. Although it is often extremely difficult to calculate the loading which may have to be carried by each shore accurately these calculations should assume extreme conditions of loading, even though the walling of the structure may provide some degree of resistance to the loads. Therefore, large cross-section timbers are often used to prevent any chance of bending or failure in the members. It is much wiser to use a 'safe' size of timber rather than be sparing with it, as a failure in the system could result in the builder being eventually involved in much greater costs in repairing damage which may be caused to the structure.

Timber is used to a great extent in shoring because of its adaptability in cutting to shape and length and because of its large salvage value when the shores are dismantled.

Steel sections make useful members in a shoring system but usually they have to be purpose-made and are generally more expensive. They can, however, be provided with a jacking system. Screw jacks are ideal for this purpose as they provide a positive and uniform method of tightening up the whole system. The salvage value, in comparison with any initial cost, may be lower than the value of timber shores.

Each case must be carefully considered separately and the most economical method must be adopted. The stability of the structure and the safety of the personnel should always be taken into account.

Broadly speaking, shoring can be classified into three main systems:

Raking shores
Flying shores
Dead shores

But, the following points should first be considered generally:

1   Each shore must rest on a solid base to ensure stability in the system.
2   The timbers must be of adequate cross-sectional area to resist the loads that may be thrust upon them. It is usually better for the shores to be square or nearly square in cross-section.
3   The needles must be of adequate size in cross-section and securely held in or under the wall.
4   The system must be well-braced to prevent any movement once it is in position. The bracing is so placed that the members form triangles. This is a shape that cannot be distorted, unless any member is broken.
5   The shoring systems must be spaced sufficiently close together to prevent any possible movement of the structure between the shores.
6   In the cases of raking and flying shores, wall plates should be first placed against the wall and secured with wall hooks and needles which are short lengths of timber about 225×50 mm in cross-sectional area (Figure 104). The shores are placed against the wall plate so that the thrust is distributed over the face of the wall.
7   The angle of the shores in a raking system should not be too steep; less than 60 degrees to the horizontal plane would be ideal. However, this angle is sometimes difficult to maintain in urban areas, particularly where the width of the pavement may determine the extent to which the base of the shoring system may be taken.
8   When a timber shoring system has to be tightened, it should be tightened evenly and

gently, preferably with the crowbar or pinchbar. A shoring system should never be tightened by driving home wedges with a sledge hammer, as this is likely to jar the structure and cause further damage to a structure which may already be unstable.

9 It is advisable to give added resistance to the thrust of the shores by fixing cleats immediately above the needles. These cleats are often secured by timber spikes but they should, for preference, be housed into the wall plate to give added stability.

10 In the case of dead shores which are being used to support a wall in which an opening is to be cut, the needles must be placed above the height of the new beam or lintel to be fixed above the opening so that it will be possible to place the beam or lintel in position.

11 It is good practice to strut up all windows as this will help to stabilize the wall if there is movement in the structure.

Systems of shoring

Raking shores

These are inclined members placed against a wall to prevent it from falling outwards or making any lateral movement. They are erected in systems or frames, as shown in Figure 105.

The general design of these systems depends upon the following:

1 The height of the wall.
2 The thrust to be resisted.
3 The angle to the horizontal at which the shores can be placed against the wall.
4 The distance between the systems.

The timbers used for this class of work would usually be softwoods such as redwood, pine or fir, because of their straightness of grain and their long lengths.

These shores can usually be erected in the following way. However, there are no set rules as site conditions may have an effect on methods of erection or precise shapes of systems.

1 The position of the needles is first determined usually by the floor heights (Figure 105). The shores are then placed in the piers between window openings.
2 Holes for the needle which can be of 100×100 mm section are cut into the 225×50 mm or 225×75 mm wall plate.
3 Holes are also cut into the brickwork corresponding to the position of the needles in the wall plate. Great care must be taken to ensure that the hole is shaped so that the needle will have a good bearing on the wall when the load is applied through the shore. Sometimes this operation can be carried out after the wall plate has been placed against the wall and held in position by wall hooks (Figure 104). The holes are cut with a hammer and chisel through the holes in the wall plate to a depth of about 100 mm.
4 The base of the shores should be prepared while the wall plates are being fixed into place. If the shoring system is to rest on a natural ground base, the best method is to dig a hole and pour concrete in to form a solid bed. The sole plate should be pressed firmly into the top of the concrete which is then allowed to set and harden. The depth of the hole will depend upon:
   (a) The quality of the soil;

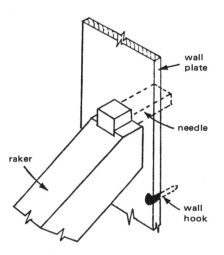

Figure 104 *Detail showing head of raker notched over the needle*

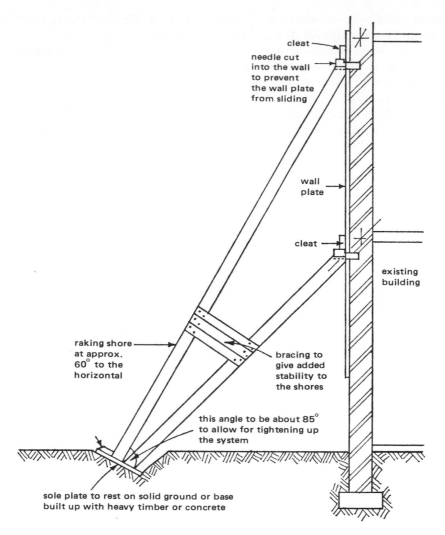

Figure 105   *Method of supporting a structure*

(b)   Whether the concrete has to be removed after the shores have been dismantled, or if it can be left in the ground and covered over with soil; and

(c)   The general weather conditions.

If the ground is saturated, it would be advisable to dig the hole deep enough to ensure the stability of the shores.

The thickness of the concrete will depend to a great extent upon the load which is to be carried. If the system is going to rest on a base which is solid, the sole plate should be placed to form a reasonable angle between the shores and the sole plate, and in such a a way that it cannot slide.

The angle of the sole plate should be at an angle of about 85 degrees to the slope of the outer raker (Figure 106). This will allow for the whole system to be tightened up with the aid of a crowbar.

5   The needles are placed through the mortises in the wall plate into the holes in the brick-

work, ensuring that there is good contact between the upper surface of the needle and the brickwork.

6 The first raker is then marked out and cut off to length. This can be done by pulling a line from the needle to the point on the sole plate where it will be resting. The length of the raker can be measured with a measuring tape, and the bevels of the cuts taken from the line to the wall plate and the sole plate. When the raker has been cut and prepared, the top should be notched so that it fits over the needle. The bottom should have a small notch so that a crowbar or pinchbar can be inserted. The shore should now be tightened to the underside of the needle (Figure 106).

7 A cleat should be fixed immediately above the needle to give added strength. This cleat can be spiked to the wall plate or it can be housed into the plate, as shown in Figure 105.

8 Each raker is fitted into place in turn, and the bottoms should be securely dogged or spiked into the sole plate.

9 The whole system is braced together with timber bracings which are spiked to each raker and to the wall plate. If the wall plate is wider than the shores, a packing piece should first be spiked to the wall plate and the bracings then spiked in turn to the spacer (Figure 107).

The chart shown in Figure 108 indicates the minimum cross-sectional area of raking shores

that can be required to support a wall. It is assumed that the shores are not placed at a steeper angle than 60 degrees to the horizontal. It must be emphasized, however, that the chart is to

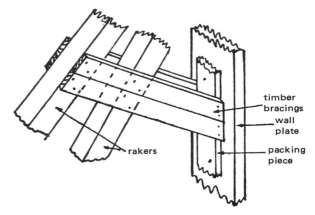

Figure 107

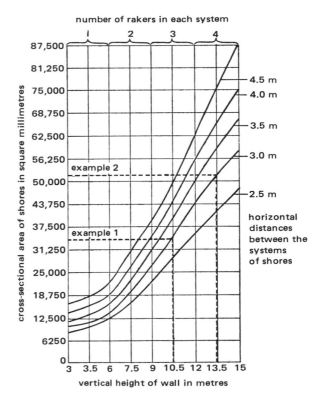

Figure 108

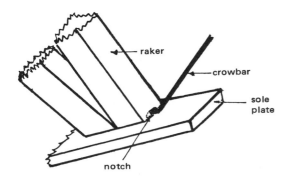

Figure 106   *Detail showing the foot of a raker*

be used merely as a guide. Each job must be designed according to the conditions on site and the load to which the shores may be subjected.

Example 1
Determine the minimum size of shores which should be used to support a wall 10.5 m high. It is expected that the shores will be placed at 3 m centres.

By referring to the chart shown in Figure 108, it will be seen that a line drawn from the 10.5 m point to the curved line representing 3 m centres will cut that line at a vertical height of 35,000 mm².

The size of shores can then be, say, 200×175 mm, as near to square section as practicable, with three rakers in each system.

Example 2
Determine the minimum size of shores which should be used to support a wall 13.5 m high. The shores are to be placed at 3.0 m centres. Again by referring to the chart in Figure 108, it will be seen that a line drawn from the 13.5 m point on the horizontal scale will cut the curved line representing the 3.0 m centres at a point showing 52,000 mm². This can be satisfied with a shore 230 mm² in cross-sectional area with four shores being used in each system.

Rider shores
If the system is erected with the method shown in Example 2, the outer shore will have to be about 15 m in length, which would make it rather excessive for ease of handling. The longer the shore the more likely that bending will occur. Therefore it is quite usual to place a shorter length of shore against the next lower shore and to fix it with dogs, a 'rider' shore is then placed on the top. A pair of folding wedges should be inserted between the two timbers so that the rider shore can be tightened up to the needle (Figure 109).

Flying shores
Flying shores are horizontal shores which are used to give temporary support to parallel walls. They are erected in systems with the horizontal shores placed at, or about, floor level, and raking

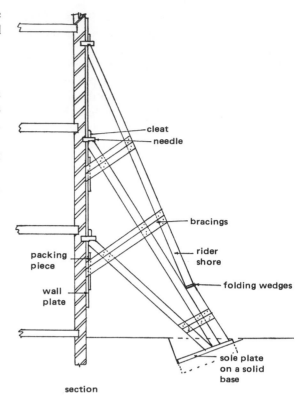

Figure 109 *The application of a rider shore*

shores used as struts from the shores to the faces of the walls (Figure 110). This type of shoring has special applications when a structure built between two other structures has to be demolished as flying shores can be erected between the two structures. This will stabilize them and safeguard against any movement while the demolition is in progress.

These shores are erected as follows:

1 The positions of the needles are determined.
2 The holes and wall plate are cut and fixed in the same way as the raking shores.
3 The horizontal shore is placed on the top of the first pair of needles, and cleats are fixed below the needles.
4 The top straining sill is fixed to the horizontal shore and the raking struts are placed in position between the end of the straining sill and the two upper needles. They are then wedged tightly in position.

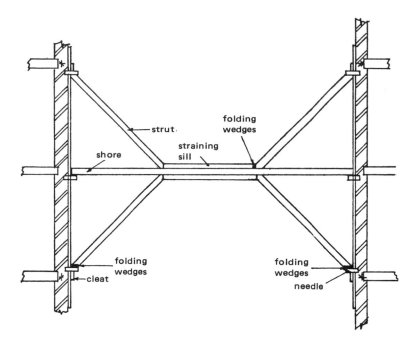

Figure 110 *Flying shores*

5 The lower strutting is fitted in position as the demolition of the building progresses. The lower straining sill is spiked to the underside of the shore and the lower raking struts are fixed from the lower pair of needles to this straining sill. The wedges in this case are usually placed immediately on the top of the needles to prevent their falling out as might be the tendency if they were placed between the straining sill and the strut.

When very tall buildings have to be shored up, horizontal shores can be erected in frames or systems. These should be well-braced together. Typical line diagrams are shown in Figure 111.

Dead shores

Dead shores are vertical members used to give temporary support to a structure, or part of a structure, while repairs are being carried out, especially if the lower parts or supports of the structure have to be removed.

These shores may be in the form of either *steel props* or *timber supports*.

The steel props are readily adjustable for vari-

ous heights by means of a screw thread and, in fact, are a longer version of the trench prop (see *Brickwork 2*, Chapter 1). The particular advantage of using these props is that they are recoverable for further use and therefore involve no waste. Great care must be taken, however, to ensure that the props are not overloaded, especially when they are extended to their full length.

Timber shores are readily adaptable to suit a wide variety of conditions and, of course, have to be cut and fitted to suit the situation which does mean that there will be some wastage of material.

Whichever form of support is adopted, the basic principles for providing dead shores are the same.

For example, when providing temporary support for a floor, a sole plate can be placed on the slab below and dead shores wedged up tightly to a head plate placed on the underside of the floor which is being supported (Figure 112). Folding wedges should be used under each shore to take up any irregularities between the slab and the floor. Dead shores should be braced together to prevent possible dislodgement.

In the case of walling, dead shores can be used

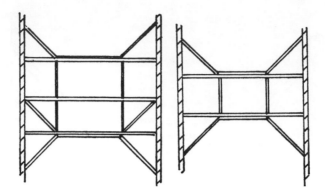

Figure 111   *Double and treble systems of flying shores*

if an opening at the lower part of the structure has to be cut out. For this type of work, the dead shores are used in conjunction with needles, as shown in Figure 113.

The shores should be placed underneath the brick piers and not under any windows in the wall. It is also advisable to fix struts in the windows while this work is in progress.

It is most important that the needles are positioned so that they are above the height of the new beam or lintel which will eventually be placed in position over the opening.

The method of erecting a system of dead shores can be carried out as follows:

1   The positions of the needles are determined, preferably not more than 1.5 m apart.
2   Holes are cut through the wall for the needles.
3   Sole plates are laid on each side of the wall,

allowing about half a metre for working space. The closer the shores are placed together underneath each needle, the less the moment of force exerted on the system. On the other hand, sufficient working space must be provided to allow for ease of handling heavy beams or lintels. The sole plate should be bedded solidly on a layer of stiff mortar to take up any irregularities in the base.

4   The dead shores are then placed between the sole plate and the needle and tightened up by folding wedges (Figures 112 and 113).
5   Each system is erected in the same way and the whole system braced together to prevent any possible lateral movement of the shores.

When the holes for the needles are cut away in the brickwork it is very difficult to ensure that the surface on the underside of the brickwork will be even. Therefore, some form of protection should be given to the needle to prevent the uneven brickwork from 'biting' into the needle. The surface against which the needle will be in contact can be evened over with a cement mortar (1:2) and left to harden. This will give a good bearing for the needle. Alternatively, a piece of timber packing can be inserted between the needle and walling.

If there is any possibility of the wall moving outwards while this work is in progress, it is advisable to place raking shores against the face of the wall in addition to dead shores.

Although the erection of shoring is usually the carpenter's responsibility, the bricklayer must

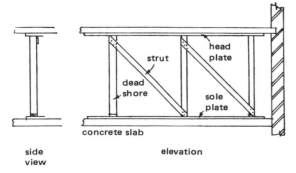

Figure 112   *An application of dead shores*

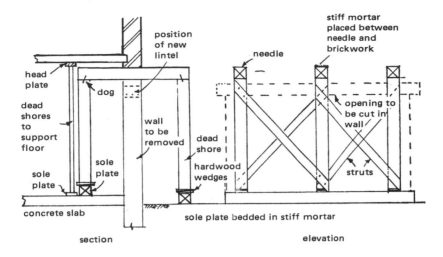

Figure 113 *Cutting out an opening in a wall*

have a good knowledge of the principles involved, as the cutting away of large openings in walling cannot begin until the bricklayer is quite certain that everything is thoroughly secure and there is no risk of movement or collapse.

Self-assessment questions

1 Describe three ways which can be used to demolish buildings and state the advantages of each.

2 State any special precautions that must be taken when using any of the methods described in question 1.

3 Outline the requirements of the Building Regulations regarding demolition work.

4 Outline some of the special points that should be observed in demolition work to prevent accidents.

5 Explain the term 'shoring'.

6 Describe the various systems of shoring and state their uses.

7 State the special points that should be observed when erecting shores.

8 Describe a method of erecting raking shores.

9 Determine the size of shores for a building which is 12 m high, when the shoring systems are to be placed at 3.5 m centres.

10 What is a 'rider shore'? Explain its use.

11 State the main points to be observed when placing dead shores in position.

12 What are 'flying shores' and where would they be used to great advantage?

Chapter 10

Drainage and sewerage

After reading this chapter you should be able to:

1 Understand what is meant by a catchment area.
2 Know the various materials used in the construction of sewers.
3 Have an understanding of the construction and operation of sewers.
4 Know how to construct tumbling bays, and the reasons for their use.
5 Know how to build manholes using water bond.
6 Have a sound appreciation of the method of testing sewers for soundness.
7 Understand the construction of settlement tanks, filter tanks, petrol interceptors and cesspools.

Catchment area

This is the name given to the area from which the sewage is collected before it is conveyed to the disposal unit for treatment. The size of the area will largely depend upon the type of terrain in which it is situated; for example, in hilly districts it may well be much smaller than in other districts where the slopes of the ground are much more gentle. The main aim of the catchment is to ensure that sewage travels to the disposal unit by gravity; otherwise the effluent would have to be pumped to the disposal unit which would greatly increase the cost of conveying the effluent.

A town may be divided into several catchment areas with each area served by a main sewer with tributary sewers. These tributary sewers are properly recorded on a sewer map by the local authority, and private sewers and drains all feed into the main sewer. When new towns or districts are amalgamated with established towns a very careful survey must be carried out to ensure that the existing sewers are large enough to cope with

the extra sewage and that the existing catchment areas will pick up with the new catchment areas. In addition to this, the new sewers will have to be readily connected without need for pumping.

It is, therefore, extremely important that the gradient of the sewers should not be too steep as water pressure will build up in the pipes if they are completely full and the sewer will have to be dug deeper into the ground which will make the pumping of the effluent out of the sewer at the disposal unit very expensive. The slope of a sewer need only be sufficient to allow the effluent to travel at a reasonable speed which will ensure that the drain is self-cleansing when operating under normal conditions of working. A normal velocity would be about 1–1.5 m per second but this, of course, would vary to suit local conditions.

Materials used for the construction of sewers

Sewers and drains can be constructed in a variety of materials depending upon the size of the sewer, the soil conditions, and any special methods of construction, such as the crossing of streams. These materials include the following:

Glazed vitrified clay pipes
Vitrified high-density clay pipes
Pitch-fibre pipes
Precast concrete pipes
In situ concrete
Cast iron pipes
Brick sewers

Glazed vitrified pipes

B S 65 lays down the minimum requirements for the manufacture of pipes and fittings (see *Brickwork 2*, Chapter 13). These pipes are available in diameters up to 1 m and in lengths up to 1.5 m.

Vitrified high-density clay pipes

These are made by extracting the air from the clay when moulding it under great pressure to form the pipes which are then subjected to very high temperatures.

These pipes are available in sizes up to 500 mm in diameter.

The resultant pipes are lightweight units which are usually supplied in lengths of 2 m, although 300 mm diameter pipes are available in lengths of up to 2.5 m. They are extremely durable and will readily satisfy the requirements of B S 65 and B S 540. They are connected together by means of flexible joints using styrene butadiene rubber (S B R) sealing rings. For special purposes, neoprene rings are obtainable.

Pitch-fibre pipes

B S 2760 relates to pitch-impregnated fibre drain and sewer pipes and specifies the minimum standards for their manufacture (*Brickwork 2*, Chapter 14). They are available in diameters up to 200 mm and in lengths up to 3 m.

Precast concrete pipes

These are made to B S 556, in diameters ranging from 102 to 1829 mm, by the following methods:

1   By casting vertically in a steel mould where the concrete is vibrated as it is poured into the mould while a revolving centre core is oscillated up and down.

This method will give a very smooth bore to the barrel of the pipe and is mainly used for smaller-diameter pipes.

2   By casting larger-diameter pipes into steel moulds and vibrating the concrete as it is poured, while the surplus water in the concrete is drawn off by a suction pump.

This method is commonly referred to as 'vacuum concrete'.

3   By casting the pipes in large open-ended cylinders.

These cylinders are placed on two sets of contra-rotating wheels. The wheels are set into motion and a concrete of wet consistency is fed into the cylinder at each end while the drum is revolving. When the required amount of concrete is loaded, the revolutions of the cylinder are then increased and the concrete is forced against the steel cylinder. Since aggregates and cement have a higher specific gravity than water, they are forced close to the mould while the water is left on the inside of the 'spun' concrete pipe. This surplus water then drains off at each end of the newly cast pipe while it is spinning. This method produces a very dense pipe. The inside of the barrel is usually smoothed off by hand while the pipe is still spinning.

4   Where a very high strength is required of 'spun concrete pipes' (for example, when they have to be placed close to a road surface) the pipes may be wrapped in a fibre-glass coating to give them added protection against damage through vibrations. When this is done the pipe is placed in a machine rather like a large lathe and revolved. Fibre-glass strands are then wound around the pipe as it revolves. When it is fully covered with fibre-glass strands the whole surface is then covered with synthetic resin. When this coating sets hard, it provides a pipe which has an extremely high resistance to deformation under load.

The British Standard no. 556 requires that each pipe shall be marked as follows:

1   The number of the British Standard (that is B S 556).

2   The letter 'R' if the pipe is reinforced.

3 The strength class, i.e. 1 to 5, or the letter 'H' to denote heavy duty cover slab or 'L' to denote light duty cover slab.
4 The letter 'S' to denote sulphate-resisting cement, or 'A' to denote high alumina cement, or 'X' to denote if super-sulphated cement has been used in the manufacture of the pipe.
5 The day, month and year of manufacture. For example, a typical marking on a pipe may be BS 556 R 4 A 10.9.83. This is interpreted as follows:

... to comply with the requirements of BS 556, reinforced, strength class 4 made with high alumina cement on tenth day of September 1983.

When ordering concrete cylindrical pipes the buyer should include the following information so the manufacturer knows exactly what the buyer needs:

1 The quantity and nominal sizes of the pipes.
2 The strength class of the pipes.
3 If the pipes are to be reinforced or not.
4 The strength class of the manhole cover slabs.
5 The type of joint required.
6 The type of cement which will be used.
7 If a sample of the aggregate is required.
8 The kind and number of tests required.
9 Whether any variation is to be allowed in the time of maturing.
10 Whether certificates are required as to compliance with this standard and date of manufacture.
11 Whether a test certificate is required for manhole chamber cover slabs.
12 Whether admixtures are prohibited.

In situ concrete
This concrete may be mass or reinforced, and is used mainly for the construction of very large ducts usually found at the outfall of a long sewer to a large city, or for culvert construction for the carriage of surface water (Figure 114).

Cast iron pipes
These are classified into three groups:

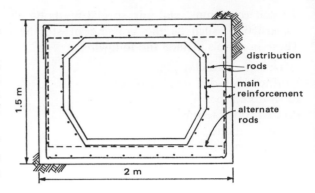

Figure 114 *A typical reinforced concrete culvert or outfall*

1 Cast iron pipes vertically cast in sand moulds (BS 78) which are made from 75–381 mm in diameter.
2 Cast iron spigot and socket drain pipes (BS 437) made from 50–229 mm in diameter.
3 Centrifugally cast (spun) iron pipes (BS 1211). These are made from 75–610 mm in diameter.

BS 78 covers cast iron pipes subjected to high pressures and requires that:

1 Each pipe shall be marked near the socket with the nominal diameter, the class letter (that is, A, B, C or D), the maker's identity, the last two digits of the year of manufacture and the number of this standard. For example: 152 C '. . .' 82, BS 78.
This means that the pipe has a nominal diameter of 152 mm, is a class C weight, the maker's identity, made in 1982 in accordance with the requirements of BS 78.
2 Each pipe shall be tested for straightness and uniformity of thickness.
3 Each pipe shall be tested hydraulically before coating.
4 Each pipe shall be preheated and coated, by immersion, with a tar-based or other suitably based composition.

BS 437 covers cast iron pipes subject to low pressures, and requires that:

1   The pipes are made from a suitable grade of pig iron with a mixture of clean scrap. The cast iron shall be dark grey on fracture and be soft enough to be easily drilled, tapped and filed.
2   The minimum weights of the various diameters shall not be less than those specified.
3   Each pipe shall ring clearly when struck with a light hammer.
4   The pipes shall be protected by being coated with a composition which has a tar base. The coating shall be smooth and tenacious.

BS 1211 deals with cast iron spun pressure pipes for sewage.

1   There are three classes:
Class B to withstand approximately 130 m head of water.
Class C to withstand approximately 200 m head of water.
Class D to withstand approximately 260 m head of water.
2   The pipes shall be totally immersed in heated tar-base composition for complete internal and external coating.
3   Each pipe shall be marked with its weight inside the socket, the maker's identification, the BS 1211, the last two digits of the year of manufacture and either the appropriate class letter or number as required. If numbers are used, the classes are indicated as follows:
Class B – 3
Class C – 2
Class D – 1

Brick sewers
Brick sewers are not common these days but they are still used where resistance to chemical attack is needed or very special shapes are called for in the sewer construction. Engineering bricks to BS 3921 are generally used for this class of work as they provide a very high resistance to wear and chemical attack. A single-brick sewer is shown in Figure 115.

Types of systems for sewerage

Sewers must be constructed to carry away two forms of effluent: foul water; and surface water.

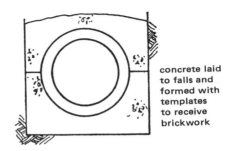

concrete laid to falls and formed with templates to receive brickwork

Figure 115   *Construction of a single brick ring sewer*

Both of these have a great influence on the design of the systems to be used. With foul water the amount of effluent that the sewer will have to carry will usually be equal to the amount of piped water that the town receives (about 140–170 l per head per day) whereas with surface water the amount of effluent is very indeterminate. Although there are several methods of calculating the amount of run-off from areas, there are so many variables that it is very difficult to design a system that can cope with a 'dry' weather flow and a sudden intense storm as well. These variables would include the following factors:

1   The variation in rate of rainfall intensity.
2   The degree of permeability of the area on which the rain falls.
3   The capacity of the sewer to 'store' sudden excess water above a normal flow.
4   The time it takes for rainwater to enter the sewer after it has fallen.

The systems that can be used for sewers are:

The combined system
The partially combined system
The separate system

The combined system
In this system only one conduit is needed to carry both foul water and surface water to the disposal unit. It is a system that is favoured by many coastal towns where the sewage can be discharged direct into the sea.

Advantages
1   It simplifies the connecting of house drains to

the sewer because it eliminates any possible chance of connecting the wrong pipes to the sewer.

2 Only one pipe has to be excavated for and laid for the system.

3 The sewer will be well-flushed out during heavy rainfalls or storms.

Disadvantages

1 The sewer will have to have a very large diameter to cope with the increase of effluent during heavy rainfall or storms.

2 If the system is connected to a disposal unit, the cost of treating the *combined* foul and surface water will be much more than the treatment of foul water alone.

3 Storm water overflows must be provided

because of the possibility of flooding the sewer. A typical construction of storm water overflow is shown in Figure 116. The storm water in some cases can be run into water courses but this is liable to cause pollution because of the foulness of the sewage. Therefore, in large cities, storm water is taken off into special storm water sewers and stored into large storm water tanks until the flow returns to normal. In the Greater London area, the storm water tanks in the disposal units can be several acres in area.

4 There is a possibility of the sewer silting up unless a satisfactory self-cleansing velocity is obtained with the peak foul water flow.

In general, this system is not used for new areas

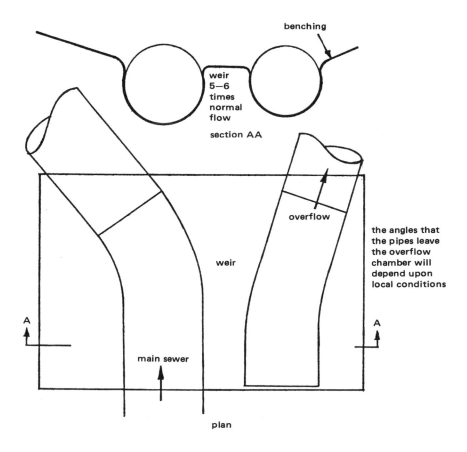

Figure 116   *An application of a storm water overflow*

because of these disadvantages which outweigh the advantages.

The partially combined system

This method is a compromise between the combined system and the separate system. Two sewers are used; one sewer carries the foul water and some of the surface water, which could be the run-off from a road surface or back roofs and yards of houses. The other sewer carries the rest of the surface water, which could be the run-off from the front roofs or other hard standings.

Advantages
1 The foul water sewer will be flushed at intervals by natural sources.
2 If the surface water from the roads is taken into the foul water sewer, the remainder of the surface water will be considerably 'cleaner', which means that there is less likelihood of river pollution if the surface water is discharged into water courses.

Disadvantages
1 Two pipe systems are required.
2 The disposal unit has to have extra 'capacity' of pumps and treatment tanks to cope with the surface water conveyed by the foul water pipe.
3 Storm overflows must be provided on the foul water sewer to act as a safety measure in case of heavy storms. This can cause pollution of water courses.

The separate system

This system requires two pipe systems, one for the conveyance of foul water and the other for the conveyance of surface water. The foul water is treated at the disposal unit while the surface water can be discharged into water courses.

Advantages
1 The disposal unit can estimate within close limits the amount of sewage to be treated.
2 Pumping and treatment costs are kept to the absolute minimum.
3 No storm water overflows are needed in the foul water system.

Disadvantages
1 Two pipe systems are needed which makes the installation more expensive.
2 The foul water sewer is not flushed during storms.
3 It may be necessary to resort to periodic artificial flushing.
4 It may be difficult to detect any errors which may have been made when the domestic drains were connected to the sewers and to trace a drain which is causing pollution because of incorrect connection.
5 The discharge of surface water into water courses can cause pollution because the surface water from roads and pavements is filthy.
6 If a number of drains are inadvertently connected to a foul sewer can cause flooding which would increase pumping and treatment costs at the disposal unit.
7 There would be additional costs in housebuilding because each house would need two pipe systems installed.

All these points must be carefully considered when a sewer system for a new or redevelopment area has to be selected by a local authority to ensure that the most economical and efficient system is installed.

Design of foul water sewers

The average amount of water which flows through a foul water pipe per day is 140–170 litres per head of the population. But the maximum flow will of course be considerably higher than average, because there are 'peak periods' during the day: for example, in the morning between about 7–9 am, at noon and in the evening. (The maximum flow can be assumed to be twice the normal flow.) The disposal unit can build up an extremely accurate picture of these peak flows by watching 'trends' in flows. It is therefore essential to allow for the peak discharge of a sewage at a much higher rate than the 'average' flow. For totally separate sewers, this allowance can be up to 5–6 times the average flow, and in combined and partially combined systems, the allowance is twice the average flow to cope with the maximum flow plus the allowance for the estimated surface water discharge.

Egg-shaped sewers

A rough estimate shows that about half of the domestic flow will be discharged at three peak periods during the day totalling 6 hours; the rest of the domestic flow will be even throughout the day. Therefore, in a town of 240,000 people the total effluent could be 36,000,000 litres per day. Half of this figure will be discharged over the 6 hour peak period; therefore the 'average peak' flow could be

$$\frac{18,000,000}{6} = 3,000,000 \text{ litres/hour};$$

whereas the average flow would be

$$\frac{36,000,000}{24} = 1,500,000 \text{ litres/hour.}$$

But there will also be 'low' average periods in the very early hours of the day and the sewer will have to be self-cleansing over a wide range of 'average' flows. Therefore, in the case of a normal circular pipe there may be insufficient flow in the pipe at the low periods to convey the solids. If the pipe is tapered at the bottom, the depth of water in the sewage in low periods can be maintained deep enough to enable the effluent to carry the solids along with it. This type of sewer is called an *egg-shaped sewer*. They are sometimes built in brickwork (engineering bricks are usually used for this work), but can also be made in pre-

cast concrete pipes. Examples of egg-shaped sewers are shown in Figure 117. Terra-cotta units are often used for inverts for brick sewers (Figure 118).

Egg-shaped sewers in brickwork can be made as follows:

1   A trench is dug to the required fall, and the bottom levelled and rammed.
2   A concrete bottom is then laid to falls.
3   The invert is always laid to a line regardless of whether it is a terra-cotta invert or a brick invert.
4   The brickwork on the sides of the sewer is then laid in courses with a line stretched between profiles or sections of brickwork. A template of the shape of the sewer is used to ensure accurate work.
5   Concrete is laid behind the brickwork as the work proceeds until the springing of the upper part of the sewer is reached.
6   A timber centring is then fixed inside the sewer and the brickwork built over it. This centring should only be 1.5 m long to enable the bricklayer to work inside the sewer in front of the centring. The centring is moved along as each section is completed (Figure 119).
7   The upper part of the sewer is then covered with concrete and then the trench can be backfilled in the usual way.

Egg-shaped sewers can also be made in another way, as follows:

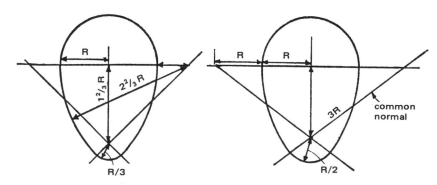

Figure 117   *Typical geometrical setting out for egg-shaped sewers*

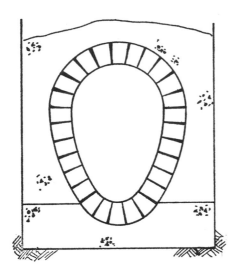
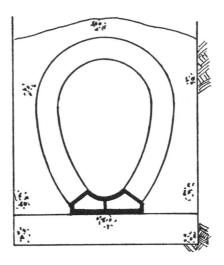

Figure 118   *Sections showing typical constructions for brick sewers*

1   The trench is excavated, levelled and rammed.
2   Formwork is set up inside the trench, ensuring that it cannot move upwards (Figure 120).
3   Concrete is then placed around the formwork so that it forms the invert to the sewer.
4   When the concrete has set hard the formwork is then removed.
5   The brick lining is then laid to falls by stretching lines from profiles or sections of brickwork.

The work is then continued as in points 6, 7 and 8 of the first method.

Ventilation of sewers

Adequate ventilation of sewers is extremely important to dilute gases liable to collect in the sewer and to prevent syphonic action if the pipe becomes full. When the flow lowers this creates a change in air pressure which might empty syphon

Figure 119   *Suitable centring for turning the brickwork over the sewer*

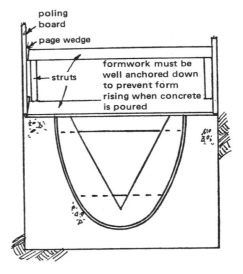

Figure 120   *Section showing the formation of concrete invert ready for brick lining*

traps. Domestic ventilation systems are usually used for ventilating sewers which means that intercepting traps do not have to be installed between the drains and the sewer. If intercepting traps are used, the sewer must be ventilated through manhole covers or ventilating pipes connected to the sewer at intervals. Concentrations of gases in sewers can be quite hazardous because there is a danger of explosion or noxious fumes to personnel who have to enter the sewers for maintenance and repairs.

Manholes

Manholes for sewers up to 1 m in diameter can be spaced at distances not exceeding 100 m, but on larger diameters this distance can be increased to 200 m.

Manholes should be provided at the following points:

1 Junctions of two or more sewers.
2 Changes of direction.
3 Change of gradient.
4 The head of the sewer.
5 Wherever the pipe diameter changes in size.

Benching

This is a very important item in the construction of manholes. The top of the benching should not be too steep (a fall of about 1–12 is usually quite sufficient) and should be at least level with the top of the outlet pipe to the manhole. This will prevent the fouling of the benching and guard against slippery conditions. The width of the benching must be adequate for a man to stand on, and in the case of large-diameter sewers of about 0.5 m or more the benching should be about 0.5 m wide. In larger and deeper manholes the benching must be wide enough to allow two people to stand in safety. In large systems it is advisable to provide safety barriers so that a person has adequate handhold when climbing down into the sewer invert to carry out maintenance work in the sewer. The step irons in the chamber should be positioned to provide direct access to the benching and not over the pipe itself.

For manholes up to 3 m in depth, 1-brick thick walls are quite adequate but for greater depths the thickness should be increased. Engineering bricks are recommended for this class of work and generally much skill is needed on the part of the bricklayer if a good output is to be achieved. Usually English bond is adopted for manholes on sewers, but sometimes a *water bond* is specified. This is a bond consisting of two ½-brick walls and the courses laid half-bond with each other both on plan and in cross-section (see Figure 121).

Once the manhole chamber has been constructed of adequate size, the access shaft need only be of a nominal size of about 850 × 675 mm, with the step irons (or step ladder) in line with the benching in the chamber.

Tumbling bays

Where a sewer has to be joined to another sewer at a considerably lower level, it is advisable to use a back-drop manhole or tumbling bay. This is a manhole which incorporates a vertical drop pipe and allows the effluent from one sewer to flow quite evenly into the other. The upper pipe is usually carried on through the wall of the manhole to provide a means of rodding should it become blocked. Figure 122 shows a typical example of this type of manhole.

A back-drop manhole can also be used with great advantage in a system which is installed in a hilly area where the gradients in the sewer are likely to be too steep to allow a steady flow of the effluent.

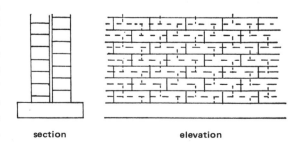

section   elevation

Figure 121   *Water bond*

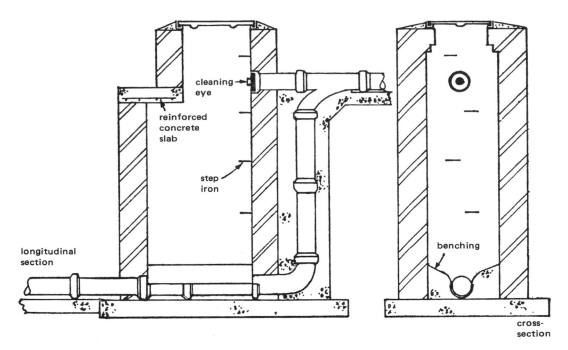

Figure 122   *Tumbling bay or drop manhole*

Testing of sewers

The principles of testing sewers are the same as the principles described in *Brickwork 2*, Chapter 13, for the testing of drains, except the stoppers are much larger in diameter and because of the greater pressures, are more elaborate in design.

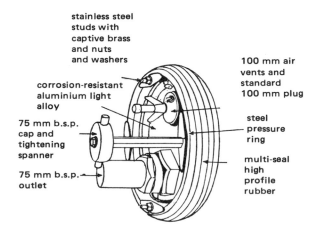

Figure 123   *Sewer plug*

Figure 123 shows a stopper suitable for diameters up to 1.2 m. Great care must be exercised when securing the stoppers in position to ensure that they are firmly secured.

Septic or settlement tanks

Septic or settlement tanks can be constructed in brickwork or with concrete pipes. They are tanks which are provided for the treatment of sewage from houses where public sewers are not immediately available. They can be of any capacity and, in the case of concrete, the pipes can be up to 2 m in diameter. Figure 124 shows a section through a concrete circular septic tank; access to the dip pipes is provided in the cover. In the small-diameter tanks the whole cover can be removed to provide access to the tank but in the larger diameter tanks the cover is usually provided with a manhole cover. In these settlement tanks, the accumulation of sediment at the bottom is quite slow, but the scum at the top of the effluent will have to be removed at more frequent intervals, depending upon the size of the tank and the usage. The scum at the top of the sewage is a

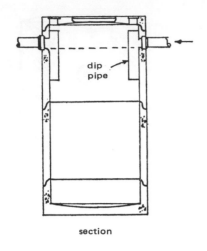

section

Figure 124   *Concrete septic tank*

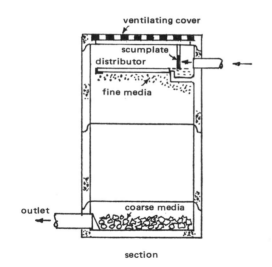

section

Figure 125   *Concrete filter tank*

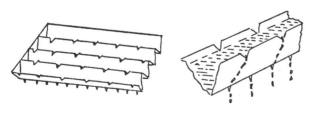

Figure 126   *Detail of distributor*

most important factor in the action of the septic tank, as it is in this scum that the bacterial action of 'digesting' the sewage takes place.

Filter tanks

The effluent from the septic tank can then pass into a filter tank which can be constructed of brickwork or concrete pipes. Figure 125 shows a section through a concrete filter tank. This type of tank contains filtering media through very large stones at the bottom which diminish in size to fine sand at the top. The effluent is distributed over the filtering media by means of troughs (Figure 126) which allow the water to overflow at the top of the trough and be distributed on to the filtering media by means of fine drops.

The filtering effluent from the filter tank can then be piped to a nearby water course.

Petrol interceptors

As it is illegal to discharge inflammable effluents into a sewer, suitable steps must be taken to extract such effluents from sewage by passing them through intercepting chambers. A typical inflammable effluent is petrol and garages in particular must ensure that this cannot escape into a sewer. This can be done by installing a petrol interceptor in the drainage system which consists of a brick-built unit of three impervious chambers, generally about 1 m² on plan (Figure 127).

The effluent discharges into the first chamber and the petrol floats on the top as it is of a lower specific gravity. The water will then escape through the outlet pipe into the second chamber and any petrol which has inadvertently escaped with the water will again float on the top. The water escapes through the outlet pipe into the third chamber and finally into the sewer. At this stage the effluent should be quite clear of petrol. The chambers must be cleaned out at frequent intervals, depending on the quantity of effluent which has to pass through the intercepting chamber.

Cesspools

Cesspools are different to septic tanks in that they

only contain the sewage for a period of time and have to be pumped out at frequent intervals according to their capacity and usage. Figure 128 shows a typical section through a cesspool which can be constructed in brickwork or concrete units. It is advisable to fix an interceptor at the end of the domestic pipe run before it enters the cesspool to prevent any possibility of unpleasant odours penetrating to the house through the pipelines.

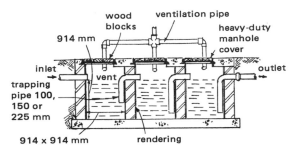

Figure 127 *Longitudinal section petrol interceptor*

Brickwork construction in sewers

Engineering bricks are used in sewers and in general this type of work demands a high standard of craftsmanship. Practical experience on work of this type is essential to gain some idea of the exacting requirements and it is worthwhile to remember that a skilled craftsman is very well paid for constructing brick sewers.

Self-assessment questions

1 Explain what is meant by a 'catchment area'.

2 Why is it undesirable for the sewers to be laid at too steep a gradient?

3 List the various materials which can be used in the construction of sewers.

4 What is meant by the term 'spun concrete pipes'?

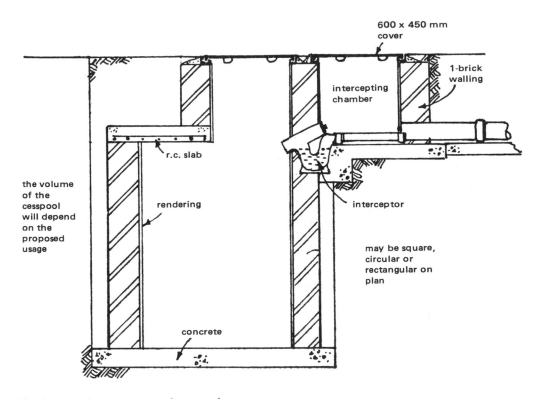

Figure 128 *Section showing a typical cesspool*

5   How can the strength of concrete pipes be increased?

6   Describe the various markings that should be displayed on a concrete pipe which is made in accordance with BS 556.

7   If a concrete pipe is marked as follows, give its interpretation: BS 556 R 3 H S 12.9.83.

8   State the three groups in which cast iron pipes are classified.

9   What types of bricks are suitable for the construction of sewers? Give your opinion of this type of work and how it should be constructed.

10   What are the three systems for the conveyance of sewage? Compare their usage.

11   State the variables that create difficulty in calculating the run-off from a catchment area.

12   Why are egg-shaped sewers used?

13   Describe the method that can be used to build a brick egg-shaped sewer.

14   Describe how the benching for domestic inspection chambers differs from the benching used for sewer construction. Give reasons for the difference.

15   By means of a neat drawing show the construction of a tumbling bay. State the purpose for which this type of construction would be used.

16   By means of a neat sketch show the construction of a settling tank and a filter tank.

17   State how the settling and filter tanks work. Where would these tanks most likely be used?

18   Sketch a typical section through a cesspool.

19   How does the operation of a cesspool differ from a septic tank?

20   Sketch a section through a petrol interceptor. Why are petrol interceptors used?

Chapter 11

General walling and brickwork construction

After reading this chapter you should be able to:

1 Have a good understanding of the strength of brickwork.

2 Appreciate the crushing strengths of bricks and the effects of mixes of mortars on the strength of brickwork.

3 Have a good knowledge of the mixes of mortars.

4 Have a good understanding of the effects of restraints on the strength of brickwork also the definition of 'slenderness ratio' and 'effective height'.

5 Have a sound understanding of the effects of eccentric and concentrated loads on walling.

6 Have an understanding of the Building Regulations concerning structural stability of walling; particularly regarding loading, heights of storeys and walls, lengths and thicknesses of walls.

7 Have a good knowledge of the construction of retaining walls and buttresses.

8 Know how to carry out underpinning to an existing building.

9 Know how to cut out a large opening in an existing wall and how to safeguard the structure against collapse.

10 Know how to repair cracks in brickwork or walling which has been damaged by continual wetting or sulphate attack.

Strength of walling is a technical term which means the capacity of the combination of bricks and mortar to resist crushing from the vertical loads imposed upon them.

The stability of walling is a term which refers to the wall's capacity to resist overturning by side thrusts due to wind or eccentric loading, such as roofs or floors and buckling due to excessive slenderness. This stability is largely gained by the strength of the combination of the bricks and mortar, the mass of the wall, and the frequency and effectiveness of the lateral supports both horizontal and vertical.

Strength of brickwork

Although brickwork has been used for thousands of years, detailed consideration to its strength characteristics has only been given in recent years.

In smaller types of buildings, walls which have been primarily built to resist weather conditions, or for thermal and sound resistance, have been quite adequate in strength for carrying normal loads. Therefore, it has not been necessary to actually *design* wall thicknesses for these structures.

By using known design factors in larger structures it has been possible to economize on the thickness of walling and more rational designs have been made.

Another important factor, however, is the introduction of lightweight materials which are used in many walls instead of bricks mainly for thermal insulating properties. The strengths of these materials, however, are generally below that of the bricks normally used. It is therefore essential to establish methods of designing walling where the strength of the wall can be related to the loads it is expected to carry. B S Code of Practice CP 111 has laid down provisions for design walling.

Brick strengths

It is quite a straightforward procedure to obtain the crushing strength of any type of brick. In many cases the brick manufacturers will supply this information on demand. B S 1257 lays down the methods that should be used for carrying out these tests. For clay bricks, B S 3921 lays down the requirements for their sampling and testing.

The suction rate should also be specified, as this can have an effect upon the adhesion between the mortar and the brick which, in turn, can affect the ultimate strength of the brickwork. The maximum rate should not exceed 20 g/dm²/min. This is a very simple test to carry out. The brick which is to be tested is first dried thoroughly and then weighed to the nearest gramme. Two rods or lengths of angle iron are placed in a shallow dish which is filled with water up to about 3 or 4 mm above the rods or angle iron. The brick is placed bed downwards on the rods and left for 60 ± 2

seconds. It is then removed, the surplus water is wiped off with a damp cloth and the brick reweighed.

Mortar strengths

The Building Research Station has carried out a considerable amount of investigation into the effect of mixes of mortar on the strength of brickwork. It has generally been found that there was no advantage in using a very strong mortar for brickwork; in fact, it was found that, where 50 per cent of the cement in a cement/sand mortar (1:3) was replaced by lime, which made a 1:1:6 cement/lime/sand mix, the strength of the mortar was reduced by over 40 per cent but the strength of the brickwork which was built with the mortar was only reduced by 4 per cent.

Table 12 shows the strength of brickwork built in 1:3 cement mortar, for the following ratios of lime:cement by volume.

In general, for any particular strength of brick there is a corresponding mortar strength which gives a maximum strength to the brickwork. Therefore, adding to the cement content will not make the mortar stronger and will not increase the overall strength of the walling.

The mortars which give this maximum are roughly outlined as:

1   For low strength bricks 1 cement 2 lime 9 sand
2   For medium strength bricks 1 cement 1 lime 6 sand
3   For high strength bricks 1 cement 3 sand (to which lime may be added to improve workability up to quarter of the volume of the cement)

Table 12

Proportion of cement and lime to sand (by volume)	All cement	50 : 50	60 : 40	70 : 30	80 : 20	90 : 10	All lime
1 : 1	—	72	70	66	58	47	—
1 : 1½	—	87	84	77	68	56	—
1 : 2	96	94	90	84	74	60	—
1 : 3	100	96	92	87	79	65	48
1 : 4	—	92	87	81	71	59	—

Cement:lime mortars are also valuable because they improve the resistance of brickwork to cracking and reduce the risk of efflorescence on the bricks.

As a general rule, therefore, it is not advisable to use a mortar which is stronger than necessary as it will not give added strength to the general walling.

Mixing of mortars

When thick walls or high strength walls are to be erected on site, great care must be taken to ensure thorough mixing of the mortar ingredients. In the case of *gauged mortars*, the mixing can be specified in one of three ways.

Cement:lime:sand

The cement, dry hydrated lime and sand can be mixed dry immediately before the water is added (preferably by weight, or if this is not convenient by volume using gauge boxes). On many sites, however, the permission of the site engineer should be obtained before using this method as there is always a possibility of the lime not being fully slaked (see *Brickwork 1*, Chapter 2).

Cement:lime putty:sand

Where gauged mortars are being made up with matured lime putty, dry hydrated lime must be added to water. Never add the water to the lime. Clean containers should always be used for the lime putty. Lime putty that has been made up from dry hydrated lime should be matured for at least 16 hours before use. Immediately before the mortar is mixed the cement and sand should be mixed dry, and the putty should then be added. The required consistency can now be obtained by adding water.

Cement:coarse stuff

Where gauged mortars are being made up with matured coarse stuff, ready-mixed lime:sand mortar should be obtained or made up by mixing dry hydrated lime, sand and water together in a mortar pan in the proper proportions. The coarse stuff should be protected from drying out.

Immediately before the mortar is to be used,

the gauging of cement should be added in the required proportions. Water is then added to give the correct workability.

Table 13 shows the mortar proportions for coarse stuff.

Table 13

Type	Mortar mix (volume)			Coarse stuff mix (volume)	
	cement	lime	sand	lime	sand
1	1	$0-\frac{1}{4}$	3	1	12
2	1	$\frac{1}{2}$	$4-4\frac{1}{2}$	1	9
3	1	1	5-6	1	6
4	1	2	8-9	1	$4\frac{1}{2}$

Table 14 shows the cement:coarse stuff proportions for mortar.

Table 14

Type	Mortar mix (volume)			Proportions (volume)	
	cement	lime	sand	cement	coarse stuff
1	1	$0-\frac{1}{4}$	3	1	3
2	1	$\frac{1}{2}$	$4-4\frac{1}{2}$	1	$4\frac{1}{2}$
3	1	1	5-6	1	6
4	1	2	8-9	1	9

Mortars should be used before the initial set takes place, normally within two hours of the cement being added. Any mortar left after this time should be discarded; on no account may mortars be reconstituted.

The effects of restraints on brickwork strength

If the wall or column is loaded uniformly without eccentricity, its loading capacity is dependent upon the individual strength of the bricks; the strength of the mortar; and the slenderness of the wall between effective lateral restraints which is basically the ratio between the height and width of the column. This can cause a problem for many complicated wall systems but this is overcome by adjusting the measurement of the height of the wall; this is called the 'effective height'.

The slenderness of a square column of height H and side D completely restrained at the top and the bottom is defined by the ratio H/D. As this ratio increases, so the strength decreases.

If the column is not restrained laterally at the top, which could mean that any tendency for sideways bending would not be controlled, the slenderness ratio is taken to be the same as that for a higher column held at top and bottom. For design purposes it is usual to say that the 'effective height' of a column unrestrained at the top is twice the actual height, so that the slenderness ratio is 2 H/D.

The effects of slenderness on the strength of walls are similar to those for columns except in the case of walling there is less possibility of buckling than there is with an isolated column. This can be allowed for by assuming an 'effective height', which is three-quarters of the height used in the case of a brick column. Therefore, for a wall supported top and bottom of height H and thickness D, the slenderness ratio is 0.75 H/D, and for a wall unsupported at the top, the slenderness ratio is 1.5 H/D.

The B S Code of Practice CP 111 specifies that the slenderness ratio determined in this way should not usually exceed 18. For buildings of not more than two storeys, this value can be increased to 24. When a lime mortar is used, the ratio should never exceed 12. Table 15 shows the slenderness ratio factors.

Table 15

Slenderness ratio	Factor
1	1.00
2	0.96
4	0.88
6	0.80
8	0.70
10	0.60
12	0.50
14	0.40
16	0.35
18	0.30
21	0.25
24	0.20

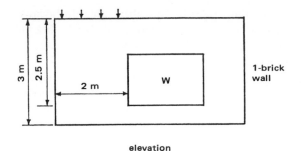

elevation

Figure 129   *Loading on walling*

A pier in a 1-brick wall is to carry a total load of 20 tonnesf (including the mass of the wall) (Figure 129).

The height of the wall is 3 metres and height from the sill 2.5 metres.

The pressure to be taken at the sill height.

The length of the pier is 2 metres.

Determine if the wall is safe to carry the load.

$$\text{Pressure} = \frac{20 \text{ tonnesf}}{2 \text{ m} \times 0.225 \text{ m}}$$

$$= \frac{20{,}000 \text{ kg}}{200 \times 22.5 \text{ cm}}$$

$$= \text{say, } 4.5 \text{ kg/cm}^2$$

$$\text{Effective height of wall} = \tfrac{3}{4} \times 3 \text{ m}$$

$$= 2.25 \text{ m}$$

$$\text{Slenderness ratio} = \frac{\text{effective height}}{\text{width}}$$

$$= \frac{2.25 \text{ m}}{0.225 \text{ m}}$$

$$= 10$$

Therefore the reduction factor is 0.6 (refer to Table 15).

A brick having a crushing strength of 10.5 kg/cm^2 and bedded in a 1:1:6 mortar can withstand a pressure of 9.8 kg/cm^2.

Therefore the safe load that this wall can carry is 9.8 kg/cm$^2 \times 0.6$ which is equal to say 5.88 kg/cm^2.

As the required pressure for the loading is only 4.5 kg/cm^2 then the wall is quite safe.

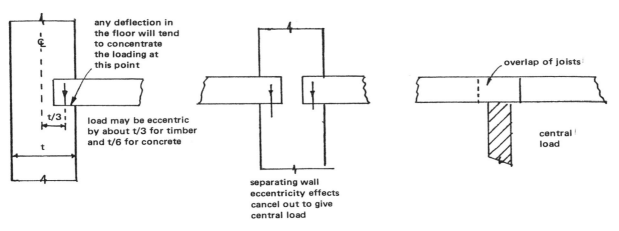

Figure 130   *Load-bearing partition*

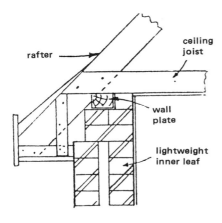

Figure 131   *Section showing a method of placing a wall plate centrally over a cavity wall to distribute the load more evenly*

Eccentric and concentrated loads

When walls are carrying floors, any deflection in the floor will concentrate the load on the inner edge of the wall. This will usually be greater with timber floors than, for example, with reinforced concrete floors (see Figure 130). This eccentricity should be avoided as much as possible because it has a marked effect upon the strength of the walling. Floor loads on partitions generally come from both sides of the walls and are therefore often assumed to be centrally loaded and therefore have less tendency to cause bending in the walling.

Another example of eccentric loading is the transmission of loads from the roof to the external walling. The loads are usually distributed along the length of the wall by means of a wall plate placed on the inner leaf of a cavity wall, or on the inside face of a solid wall. With brick walls this method is quite satisfactory as the brickwork is usually strong enough to resist bending, but when lightweight materials are used for inner leaves of cavity walls, the wall plate should be placed centrally over the wall, as shown in Figure 131. This will ensure that the load is taken by both leaves and the wall ties will play little part in strengthening the construction. On the other hand, where the load is carried by one leaf only, the wall ties play a most important part in assisting the leaves to resist any tendency to bend. It is therefore essential that the ties are correctly placed and that sufficient numbers are fixed in the wall (see *Brickwork 2*, Chapter 5).

Lateral support

Most external walls of a building have lateral support both along vertical sides by intersecting walls and along horizontal sides by floors at successive storey levels. Timber floors and roofs can give lateral support if the wall is securely tied to the floor by metal anchors (see Figures 132–135). The straps are screwed at one end to the floor joist and well built into the wall at the other end. These supports are not usually placed in small houses, but are very useful in multi-storey flats. They should be spaced approximately 1 m apart for walls carrying floor joists and 2 m apart for walls parallel to floor joists.

The Building Regulations (Schedule 7)

The Building Regulations (Schedule 7) lays down certain rules for satisfying requirements for the structural stability of certain walls. This schedule includes the following:

Loading
Where the wall forms part of the construction of a one or two-storey building, the bricks must have a

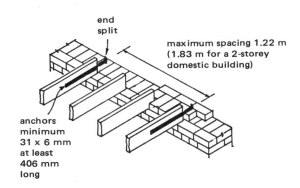

Figure 132   *Anchors for joists*

resistance to crushing (expressed in newtons per square millimetre of gross horizontal area) of not less than 5 N/mm² and for blocks 2.8 N/mm².

For all other walls the bricks or blocks must have a resistance to crushing of not less than 7 N/mm².

A brick or block is considered solid if the aggregate volume of solid materials is not less than 50 per cent of the total volume of the unit calculated from the overall dimensions. The units are considered hollow if the aggregate volume of solid material is less than 50 per cent of the total volume calculated from the overall dimensions.

Aerated concrete, and concrete made with lightweight aggregates, are considered solid material.

Measuring heights of storeys and walls
The height of a ground floor should be measured from the base of the wall to the underside of the floor above; the height of an upper floor should be measured from the underside of the lower floor to the underside of the upper floor (or to the top of the wall if there is no floor). In the case of a gable, the height is measured to half the height of the gable (Figure 136).

A separating wall is measured from its base to the base of the gable, or to the highest part of the wall (if it does not comprise a gable) excluding any parapet wall which is less than 1.2 m high.

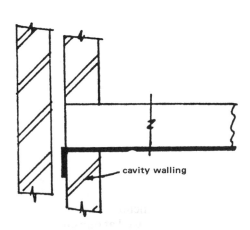

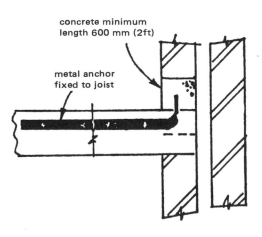

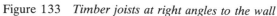

Figure 133   *Timber joists at right angles to the wall*

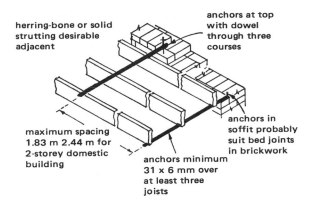

Figure 134 *Alternative arrangements of anchors for joists parallel to wall*

Measuring lengths of walls

A wall is divided into distinct lengths by piers, buttresses, chimneys or buttressing walls (Figure 137).

A pier or buttress must be extended to within a distance from the top of the wall equal to three times the thickness of the wall at its thinnest point. The distance it projects from the wall should be at least twice the thickness of the wall at that level and the horizontal sectional area should be at least 190 mm wide (see Figure 138).

A chimney must have a horizontal section of not less than the area required for a pier or but-

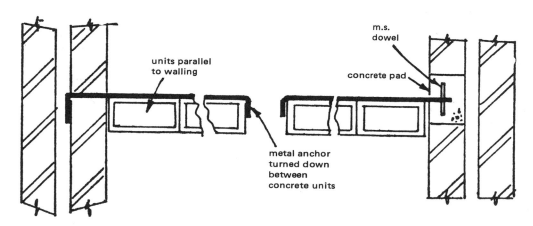

Figure 135 *Alternative methods of anchoring cavity walls to precast concrete floors*

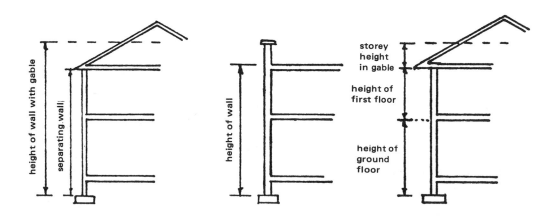

Figure 136 *Wall and storey heights*

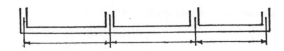

Figure 137 *Lengths of walls*

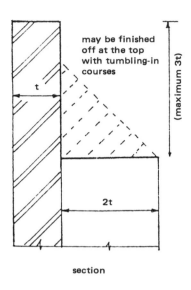

section

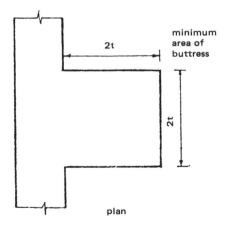

plan

Figure 138

tress (excluding any fireplace opening or flue) and an overall thickness of the wall to which it is attached. (For buttressing walls see *Brickwork 2*, Chapter 5.)

Any measurement of lengths of wall should be made from the centre of any pier.

Thickness of certain external walls and separating walls

This part of the schedule prescribes the minimum thickness for external walls of single storey buildings and other buildings where the imposed load on each floor above the ground storey does not exceed 2 kN/m².

No part of any wall or roof thereof is higher than 15 m above the level of the lowest finished surface of the ground adjoining the building.

The thickness of any part of a wall in any storey must be at least one-sixteenth part of the height of that storey. In the case of walls built with stone, flints, or clunches of bricks (that is, bricks which fused together when they were taken from the kiln) must be $1\frac{1}{3}$ times the thickness of a wall built with bricks or blocks. Table 16 shows the minimum thickness of various lengths and heights of walling.

For all other walling which is excluded from Table 16 the minimum thickness should be at least one-sixteenth of the height of the storey or 290 mm except the topmost storey which should be at least 190 mm thick.

Internal load-bearing walls should be at least half as thick as external walls.

There are other rules for the construction of brick walls for buildings higher than 12 m, but these buildings are usually constructed with reinforced concrete or steel framing. The walling is built as in-filling at each storey, which enables tall structures to be erected without extremely thick walls at the base, which are both expensive to build and take up too much internal space.

Retaining walls

Retaining walls are walls built to retain masses of water or earth. Walls which retain water are usually referred to as *dams* and walls which hold back earth are called *revetment* walls. Typical sections through retaining walls are shown in Figure 139. These can be constructed of brick, stone or reinforced concrete depending upon the weight of material which has to be retained and must resist the tendency to slide and overturn, when pressure is applied from behind them. Therefore, the wall must have sufficient weight, sufficient width of foundation to give adequate friction between the

Table 16

Height of wall	Length of wall	Thickness of wall
Not exceeding 3.5 m	Not exceeding 12 m	190 mm for the whole of its height
Exceeding 3.5 m but not exceeding 9 m	Not exceeding 9 m	190 mm for the whole of its height
	Exceeding 9 m but not exceeding 12 m	290 mm from the base for the height of one storey and 190 mm for the rest of its height
Exceeding 9 m but not exceeding 12 m	Not exceeding 9 m	290 mm from the base for the height of one storey and 190 mm for the rest of its height
	Exceeding 9 m but not exceeding 12 m	290 mm from the base for the height of two storeys and 190 mm for the rest of its height

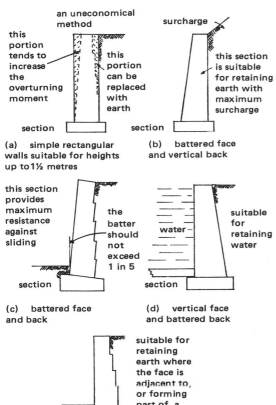

Figure 139

ground and the foundation, and be wide enough to resist shearing at any level.

Since the pressure behind the wall decreases as it gets nearer the top, the wall does not have to be as thick. This is usually done in half-brick offsets, but in some cases the face of the wall can be battered.

If there is water pressure behind the retaining wall, the wall can be relieved by putting large granular material or a line of porous pipes immediately behind it and building pipes through the wall to allow the water to escape (see Figure 140).

Where walls with battering faces are to be built,

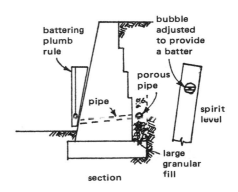

Figure 140

the wall is erected with a correct batter with the aid of a battering plumb rule (Figure 140). Alternatively, certain types of spirit levels which have adjustable vertical spirit tubes can be used. These can be adjusted until the bubbles register in the centre of the spirit tube. The straightedge is then leaning at the desired batter.

Buttresses

Where a wall is liable to be subject to lateral forces, which can make it bend or buckle in its length, buttresses can be built at intervals along its face to increase its stability. These buttresses must be properly bonded into the supported wall, and must also have an adequate horizontal cross-sectional area to resist the forces which can act upon the wall. These buttresses will generally have to resist greater stresses at the base of the wall than at the top of the wall. It is, therefore, more economical to build the buttress thicker at the base than at the top. The reduction can be done either by battering the face of the buttress (Figure 141) or by stepping the face back in regular offsets. These offsets must be constructed with plinth bricks (Figure 142) to ensure a properly weathered surface. Alternatively, a tumbling-in course can be used (see *Brickwork 2*, Chapter 6).

Underpinning

Whenever a new building is to be built in urban areas, it is quite common to have the foundations lower than the foundations of an adjacent building. It is therefore essential that the stability of the existing building is safeguarded by extending its foundations down to the level of the foundations for the new structure.

It is important to remember that care and forethought are essential if this operation is to be successful; the procedure is as follows:

1 The wall to be underpinned must be carefully inspected for any cracks or weaknesses and these carefully noted.

2 The wall should then be divided into a con-

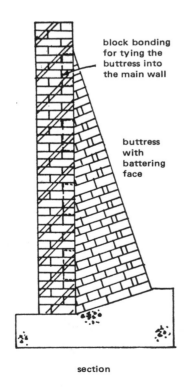

block bonding for tying the buttress into the main wall

buttress with battering face

section

Figure 141

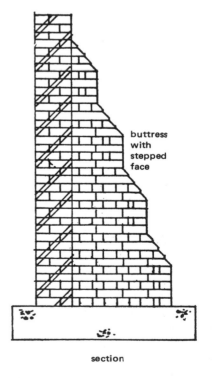

buttress with stepped face

section

Figure 142

venient number of working bays, generally not exceeding about 1.5 m, depending upon the quality and stability of the wall. These working bays should have sufficient room to enable a person to work inside them (Figure 143).

3 A batten should now be fixed along the face of the wall throughout its length to act as a datum.

4 A sequence of working which will often be determined by the conditions on the site and the accessibility of the working area adjacent to the wall should now be carefully outlined. No two adjacent bays must be excavated at the same time. If consecutive bays have to be worked in, it is essential that the first bay is fully completed and allowed to harden before work is begun on the second bay.

5 Each bay is excavated in turn, usually by hand. The earth is taken out at the front of the bay (Figure 144) which allows support to be given to the foundations for as long as possible, while this excavation is being dug. The earth is then dug out from underneath the foundations until the new level is reached (Figure 145).

6 The ground is now levelled and thoroughly rammed.

7 The projection arm of the foundations is cut off so that it is flush with the face of the wall.

8 The foundation concrete is laid to the required thickness, provided there is adequate projection on both sides of the wall (Figure 146). The level of the concrete is

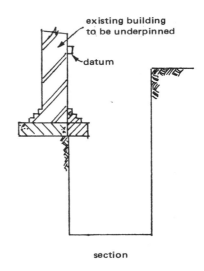

section

Figure 144 *Stage 1 – the excavation in front of the building is taken down to the required level, and footings and foundation projections cut off*

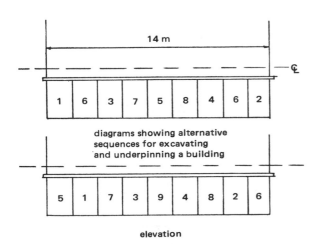

diagrams showing alternative sequences for excavating and underpinning a building

elevation

Figure 143 *Alternative sequences for excavating and underpinning a building*

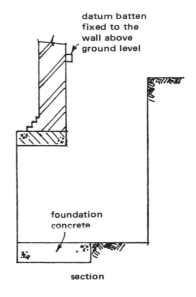

section

Figure 145 *Stage 2 – the earth is dug out from under the foundations*

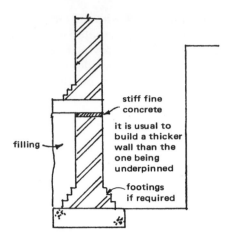

Figure 146   Stage 3 – the brickwork is built up solidly and solidly pinned up under the old foundations

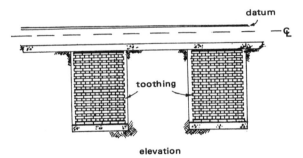

Figure 147   Two bays built which pin up existing building

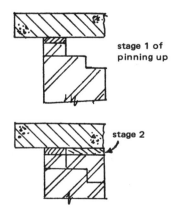

Figure 148

carefully measured down from the datum rod which was fixed to the face of the wall (Step 3). Any water in the excavation must first be pumped out.

9   The brickwork is built up in the working bay. If it is an end section, it will be toothed at one end, but if it is a portion in the middle of the wall, it will be toothed at both ends of the portion of brickwork (Figure 147). The brickwork must be built with good-quality bricks and a cement mortar (1:3 or 1:4). As each consecutive bay is connected up the toothings *must* be solidly filled in with mortar.

10   When the brickwork is nearing the underside of the existing foundation, great care must be taken to ensure that the work is thoroughly pinned up to the concrete. One method of ensuring a thorough job is to gauge the brickwork to allow about 25 mm gap between the top of the new brickwork to the underside of the existing concrete. This gap is then filled with a strong (1:2) cement grit mortar mixed in a very dry condition with just sufficient water to hydrate the cement. This mortar is then forced into the gap between the wall and the concrete and thoroughly rammed home with a thin stick. If the underside of the concrete is very rough, the gap may well be larger. If the wall is thick, this can be done in stages (Figure 148) to ensure that the foundation is well-pinned up. This final operation is the most important part of the work because if it is slipshod, there could be slight movement which would cause subsidence in the structure and cracking in the walls. Alternatively the gap can be filled by inserting pieces of slate or tiles in the mortar but this is an inferior method to the using of a strong dry cement mortar.

11   The gap behind the new wall can be filled in with hardcore or weak concrete as the new wall is being built. If the site concrete in the existing structure has to be supported, the backfilling must be carried out with great care.

12   The alternate bays are then filled in with

hardcore or weak concrete until the whole foundation is supported. Each bay is gauged down from the datum batten so that each bay is bonded soundly into the one adjacent to it. Remember that it is not possible to see from one bay to another, and it is therefore essential that some guide is available to ensure that the gauging of the brickwork is correct (Figure 147).

With all underpinning work it is important to do the work accurately and carefully and without undue haste. Ideally, the work in one bay should be left to set and harden before the work in the bay immediately adjacent to it is started.

Stabilizing the foundations of a building which is subject to settlement

The process described for underpinning can be used to stabilize a building, but an alternative method has been developed by the Frankipile Co Ltd. This is an extremely efficient method of carrying out this work and can be recommended where the work is to be carried out without vibration.

The pile is formed of precast concrete sections (Figure 149) successively jacked into the ground by a hydraulic jack until a pressure gauge indicates the required bearing capacity.

Each section has a steel-lined hole running through it; the steel lining helps the locating of the sections and ensures that they are all in line. The first section has a pointed steel toe-piece to make penetration into the ground easier.

Process
1 A hole is dug below the existing foundations of the structure.
2 The first (pointed) section is placed into position below the foundations.
3 A bearing plate is then positioned between the jack and the foundation.
4 The jack is then put between the first section and the bearing plate and the first section is forced downward by the hydraulic jack powered by a pump outside the excavation.
5 When the top of the first section is almost flush with the ground, the jack is removed and the process is repeated with the second and subsequent sections.
6 As each section is added, a length of steel tube is inserted into the hole and grouted into position to make an effective joint between the sections.
7 The operation is continued until the pressure gauge indicates sufficient penetration resistance to ensure adequate bearing capacity.

Formation of openings in existing walling

The formation of openings in existing walling needs greater care and skill to ensure that the structure does not collapse. There are several methods of carrying out this operation.

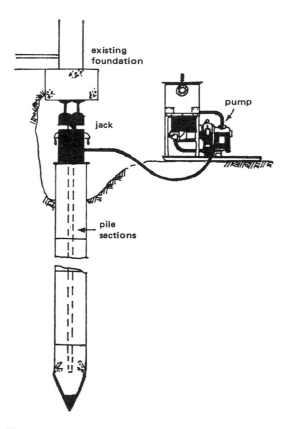

Figure 149

Method 1

The walling above the opening to be formed is shored up with dead shores (see Chapter 7). The needles must be placed above the height of the new lintel (eventually to be placed over the opening) about 1.5–2 m apart, depending upon the quality of the existing walling. The sizes of the needles will be determined by the span of the opening and the weight of walling which is to be carried. In some cases it is advisable to shore up under each floor to relieve the dead weight upon the needles. If the building has to be used while the work is in progress, a lining of hardboard, or similar material, can be fixed to the inside of the dead shores (Figure 150). The inner shores should be placed close to the wall but the outer shores should be about 1 m away to allow for working space between the shore and the wall. This is essential as the beam has to be pulled in this space and then lifted into position. This operation requires sufficient room to manœuvre and to prevent accidental dislodgement of any dead shore.

When the needles are well secured in place, the brickwork is cut away to allow the beam to be lifted into place. The space between the beam and walling above can now be thoroughly pinned up with the same method that was used for underpinning. When this work has hardened sufficiently the walling below the beam can be cut away. This cutting away must be skilfully done to ensure that the reveals on each side of the opening are square and cut with precision, as a ragged cutting away can cause a weakness. If the reveals are to be built up with new bricks, sufficient bearing must be provided for the new beam to ensure adequate support on the existing wall. The new bricks must of course be well-bonded into the existing walling (Figure 150).

When the whole of the new work has hardened, the needles can be removed and the holes can be made good.

It is important that this work is not rushed. Great care must be taken to ensure the stability of the structure and the safety of the people carrying out the work. Mistakes in this type of work can be very costly.

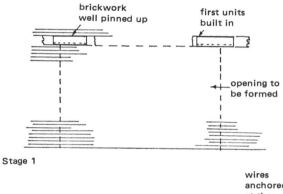

Stage 1

Stage 2

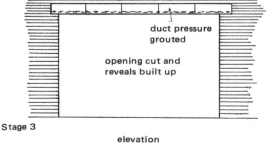

Stage 3

elevation

Figure 150

Figure 151

Method 2

No shoring is necessary with this method. Concrete units which eventually form the beam are built in one by one into the wall and each one is carefully pinned up to the work so that at no time is there more than 1 m of walling left unsupported. When the full length of the beam is built into the wall, high-tensile steel wires are threaded through the ducts provided in the concrete units. These wires are anchored at one end by special steel grips. A hydraulic jack is attached to the other end of each wire in turn and a force is then applied and the wires are stretched to a predetermined strain. These are then anchored at the end where the load is being applied and the jack is removed. The duct is filled with neat cement grout applied under pressure. When this has set the walling immediately below the beam can then be cut away with complete safety (Figure 151).

Method 3

This method is very similar to Method 2, but steel members are used instead of precast concrete. Each section is cut out and a steel member is built solidly into the wall; each section is then bolted to the adjacent section with high-tensile steel bolts. When the beam is secure, the walling below can be cut out as in Method 2.

Repairing brickwork

Brickwork which has been well constructed with good quality materials has ample protection against the weather and is not affected by other influences, will give excellent service for many years. Buildings which have been constructed in brick however, can suffer damage through accident or long neglect, also as a result of deficiencies in design, materials or workmanship. In such cases it is essential that before attempting to carry out any repairs remedial work must be done. For example, if a wall has been continually saturated through a leaking gutter or down pipe, then repairs to the plumbing work must be completed first before starting work on the brickwork.

Bed joints damaged through continual wetting

When a wall has been subjected to continual wetting this may result in the joints becoming softened or even eroded. In such cases the joints should be raked out to a depth of 15–20 mm or until a firm bed is found, then the facework repointed to match the surrounding brickwork (see Brickwork 1 Chapter 12).

In instances where the bricks themselves have become damaged, these should be carefully cut out either with a plugging chisel or by using a power drill with a masonry drill. Using this method allows for the brick to be re-used by reversing it and building the damaged surface into the interior of the wall.

Damage due to sulphate attack

In mild attacks the same method as described for continual wetting may be used, but in severe cases the affected part of the wall should be cut out and replaced with bricks having a low sulphate content and bedded in a mortar consisting of a mix of sulphate-resisting cement, hydrated lime and sand in the proportion of 1:1:6 and pointed with a mortar to match the surrounding walling.

Damage due to frost, causing spalling of the facework

Where bricks have spalled on their faces due to frost, these bricks should be cut out to a depth of at least 50 mm and replaced with queen closers (commonly called slips) cut with the aid of a mechanical saw from matching bricks and pointed to match the surrounding facework. This method will allow either two stretchers or four headers to be obtained from one brick. This is an important factor in instances where it is difficult to obtain matching face bricks.

Cracks in the wall

If the cracks run diagonally across the wall the bricks each side of the crack should be carefully cut out. The brickwork should then be built up using a mortar of 1:2:9 for normal walling or if a strong mix is required then 1:1:6 cement, hydrated lime and sand. If the existing walling had been built with a soft mortar then a mix of 1:3:12 would be quite adequate. Great care should be exercised to ensure that the joints are really solid around the replacement bricks.

The rule that should be observed when carrying out any repairs is that the mortar should never be stronger than the bricks which are being used for replacement.

Self-assessment questions

1 Describe the meaning of the terms 'strength' and 'stability' of walling.

2 Why is it necessary to introduce design methods into walling for small houses constructed with modern materials?

3 How does the suction rate of a brick affect its ultimate strength? How is this suction rate determined?

4 What is the recommended ratio of the strength of the mortar to the strength of the bricks in a wall?

5 State the mortar mixes which are generally suitable for low, medium and high strength bricks.

6 Describe the various methods which can be used to mix a cement/lime/sand mortar.

7 What is meant by the term 'slenderness ratio'?

8 How is the slenderness ratio affected by the loading in various walls or columns? What should be the maximum figures for this slenderness ratio?

9 Under what circumstances is it important that the wall ties are correctly placed in a cavity wall? State the reasons for this.

10 How can lateral support be given to a wall?

11 What are the minimum crushing strengths of bricks specified by the Building Regulations for
   (a) two-storey buildings
   (b) all other walls

12 When is a brick or block considered to be solid?

13 Describe how the heights and lengths of walls are measured.

14 State the thickness of a wall which is 12 m in height and exceeding 9 m in length.

15 State the methods that can be adopted to relieve any pressure that may build up behind a retaining wall.

16 Describe the method that can be used to ensure accuracy when building a retaining wall with a battering face.

17 Why are buttresses used? By means of neat sketches show typical methods of building buttresses.

18 A new building is to be erected immediately adjacent to an existing building. The foundations of the new building are to be taken 2 m below the foundations of the existing building. With the aid of sketches describe the method that can be adopted for this work. The length of the existing building is 10 m.

19 An opening 8 m long and 3 m high is to be formed in an existing brick wall, the thickness of the wall is 1½ bricks. The condition of the wall is fair and has been built with a cement/lime/sand mortar. The timber floors rest on the wall in which the opening is to be cut. Describe a method that may be used to carry out this work. State the particular points at which special care must be taken.

20 Describe the method of repairing a wall which has become damaged through continual wetting where the joints have softened and some of the bricks have spalled.

Chapter 12

Circular work

After reading this chapter you should be able to:

1 Have a good knowledge of the construction of large span arches and understand what is meant by a skew arch.

2 Understand the setting out and construction of vaulting.

3 Know how to set out and construct a niche.

4 Have a knowledge of the setting out and cutting of arches which are circular on plan, and those which are both circular on plan and in elevation.

Large-span brick arches

Large-span arches are not very popular nowadays, but when they do have to be constructed great care must be taken to ensure both their stability and the stability of the work above the arch. Centring must first be provided to give temporary support to the arch while it is being constructed.

This centring can be formed with built-up ribs (see *Brickwork 2*, Chapter 7) or, alternatively, solid ribs can be used, as shown in Figure 152. These ribs should be housed into the ties and secured together by straps or dogs.

The large-span arch is usually made with several arch rings which are sometimes built separately; that is, each ring is laid over the whole

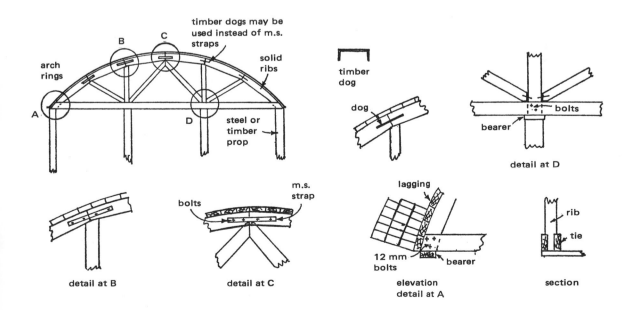

Figure 152 *Large-span arches*

span, grouted in, and the next ring built on the top. This method has the disadvantage of having to have working platforms at various heights especially in the case of tall rises in church construction and having to have the arches excessively wide with, for example, bridge construction. Each ring would have to be walked on to supply material and allow the work on the next ring to be done, and this would dislodge the bricks in the lower ring. This type of work is therefore usually built by bringing round all of the arch rings at the same time, and working from each side of the span to prevent accidental dislodgement or distortion of the centre.

Skew arch

The skew arch is usually chosen for places where the arch is neither perpendicular or at right angles to the springing lines (Figure 153). The construction for this arch is similar to the construction for any large-span arch but the courses are *not* parallel to the springing lines. They are instead perpendicular to the face of the arch so that the courses run in a spiral fashion across the formwork. This is to ensure that the whole of the arch has a direct springing. If the courses were taken parallel to the springing lines, this would mean that two parts of the arch would not be properly supported (Figure 154).

Intersecting vaults

Intersecting vaults are not often seen nowadays but an excellent example of this type of work has been completed in recent years at the Hampshire County Council offices at Winchester.

Intersecting vaults are formed where two or more barrel vaults meet at right angles or at an acute angle. They are constructed on centring in the same way that any other type of arch is constructed. Great care must be taken at the mitre between the two barrel vaults as it is important to remember that the bricklayer is working from the top side of the vault and the accuracy of the bricklayer's work will not be seen until the centring is removed. The stability of the work will also depend greatly upon the accuracy of the mitre. When hard bricks are used for the construction of these vaults an actual mitre should be formed at the junction. If a mechanical saw is used, a perfectly good joint can be made. On the other hand, if soft bricks are used, special shapes can be made so that a bonding arrangement can be formed. The straight joint at the mitre will not then be necessary, but this is an expensive and tedious method as each course has to be cut with a different shape. It is largely a question of 'cut and fit'.

A small amount of sand can be placed in the

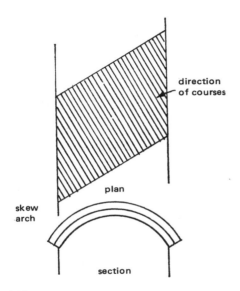

Figure 153

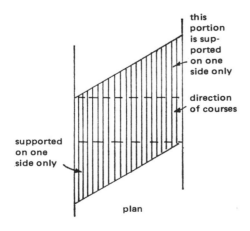

Figure 154

joint before laying the mortar to facilitate the pointing of the joints when the work is finished. This sand must be thoroughly brushed out from the joints when the centring is removed and the work is ready to be cleaned up. Figures 155–157 show typical plans and intersections of different types of vaults.

The niche

This type of work has little to do with the general stability of walling as it is simply decorative, but in spite of this it must be constructed carefully so that it does not form a weakness in the general walling. An elevation, vertical section and plan of a semi-circular niche are shown in Figure 158. The lower part of the niche is called the *body* and the upper part is the *hood*. This type of niche would normally be constructed with very soft bricks such as red rubbers so that the shapes can be easily cut.

Method for cutting and setting the body

1   The plans of the body are set out full-size and the bonding for each course drawn.
2   Templates are produced for the brick shapes (Figure 159) and secured in a cutting box (Figure 160).
3   A full-size plywood template is made to the shape of the inside curve of the body (Figure 159).
4   When the bricks have been bedded, squared and sawn (see the cutting of gauged arches in *Brickwork 2*, Chapter 7) they can be bedded in place by using the template to check the accuracy of the work, and ensuring that each course is level by being lightly rubbed down

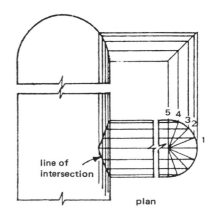

Figure 156

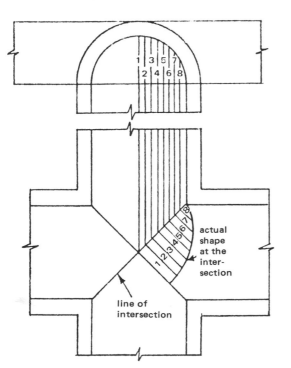

Figure 155

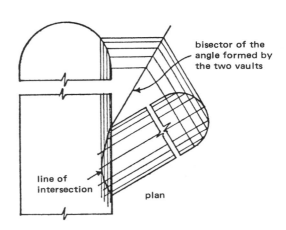

Figure 157

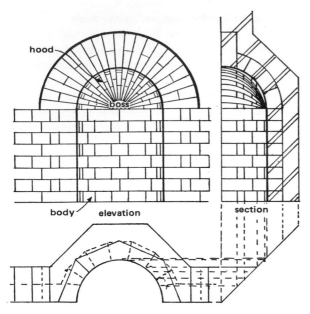

Figure 158 *Plan showing alternative courses*

with a carborundum stone which will take out any irregularities. The bricks can be bedded in a lime putty but a white lead and shellac is preferable as this provides a neater joint.

5 The body is built up to the springing of the hood.

Method for cutting and setting the hood

1 The hood must be built on a mould, and this mould can be made by cutting out two templates in the same shape as the inner curve of the hood. The templates should then be fixed together at right angles to each other (Figure 161) and strutted together for stability.

2 A plywood template is cut out to the shape of the curve, and a piece of zinc or other soft metal is fixed around a nail at one end. This nail is then driven into the vertical template of the mould (Figure 162).

3 Some expanded metal is then fixed over the struts; this holds the vertical and horizontal members of the mould together.

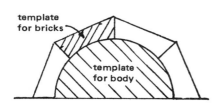

Figure 159

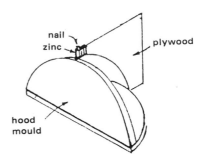

Figure 161

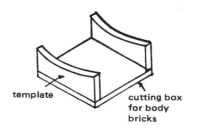

Figure 160

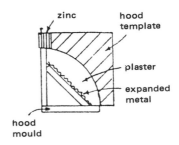

Figure 162

4 Plaster is then spread over the expanded metal and built up to the shape of the mould; a perfect shape is obtained by the plywood template which is rotated over the plaster (Figure 162). The plaster mould is then allowed to set.

5 The courses are marked off on the front edge of the mould by measuring the distances between the bricks on the *intrados*. When the distances are determined the course lines are then projected right over the mould with a flexible straightedge or straight piece of soft metal.

6 Because of the difficulty of cutting the bricks to these fine limits a boss is usually provided at the centre of the hood; this boss will also be set out on the mould.

7 When the course lines are marked, a piece of tracing linen or paper is then placed over any two adjacent lines and the two lines are marked on the linen. This should be checked by placing the linen over other pairs of lines on the mould. A piece of timber of sufficient width and length is then cut out to the shape of the curve of the mould (Figure 163) and the tracing linen is then glued on to the centre of this timber. The timber is then reduced to the shape of the tracing linen; this is called the *soffit mould*.

8 The cutting box is then prepared by fixing two lengths of timber to a base board. The shape and length of these timbers will be equal to the distance from the *extrados* of the hood to its springing as seen in elevation; the width will be equal to one course (Figure 164).

9 The soffit mould is fixed into the cutting box (Figure 164) and the positions of the hood courses are marked on to this soffit mould.

10 The bricks which were cut to the same shape as those for the body of the niche are now used for cutting the hood. These are placed in their correct position in the cutting box and then reduced to the required shape with a bow saw (*Brickwork 2*, Chapter 7).

11 The correct angle is then applied to the lower and upper edges of the hood voussoirs. This should be marked with a bevel and the

angle on the bricks should be adjusted with a file (Figure 165). This is the final cutting operation.

12 The hood mould is now firmly placed into position.

13 The boss is cut to the required shape and is usually hollowed out by a small piece of carborundum to fit over the hood mould. The shape of the hollowed portion of the boss should fit the template which was used to build up the body of the niche.

14 The boss is bedded into place; the hood voussoirs are then carefully bedded around the mould, working from both sides of the

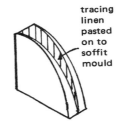

tracing linen pasted on to soffit mould

Figure 163

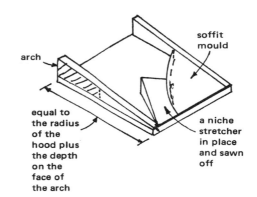

arch

soffit mould

equal to the radius of the hood plus the depth on the face of the arch

a niche stretcher in place and sawn off

Figure 164

bevel

Figure 165

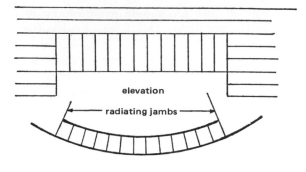

elevation

radiating jambs

Figure 166

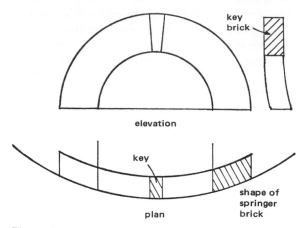

key brick

elevation

key

plan

shape of springer brick

Figure 168

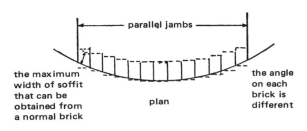

parallel jambs

the maximum width of soffit that can be obtained from a normal brick

the angle on each brick is different

plan

Figure 167

mould, and also ensuring that each course coincides with the course marks on the hood mould.

15 When the hood courses have set, the final step is to remove the hood mould carefully; take great care with this operation as the hood mould is fairly heavy and it is very easy to chip the bricks which have been bedded in the niche. The face of the niche is then cleaned with the aid of a fine piece of rounded carborundum stone.

Much skill is needed for this work and great care must be taken at every stage to ensure accuracy. When this work is done well it looks most impressive.

Circle on circle work

A great deal has been written on circle on circle work but a practical application cannot often be given to the drawings and descriptions. In some cases arches which are circular on plan can be

readily set out and cut in boxes; for example, a *soldier* arch which is curved on plan and built over an opening having *radiating jambs* (Figure 166) is a simple arch to set out and cut. But in buildings it is most unusual for radiating jambs to be used in openings and it is far more likely that parallel jambs are used. In this case the simple soldier arch curved on plan now becomes quite complex as shown in Figure 167.

Each brick is, of course, different and, unless special sizes of bricks are ordered, the soffit of the springer brick is quite narrow if it is to be cut from standard bricks.

A number of bricks should be placed on end in a true curve, and an arc marked out with a trammel or tape.

The same principle applies to a camber arch, but if red rubber bricks are used, they must be available in widths which will permit a suitable soffit. Here again the setting out of this work is difficult. If radiating jambs are used, the arch can be cut quite simply by calculating the true length of the arch on plan; the bricks can then be cut as for a normal camber arch (see *Brickwork 2*, Chapter 7) and then cut a second time to suit the radius of the curve. However, if parallel reveals are needed, the second operation is largely cut and fit.

This procedure applies to all arches which are curved in *elevation* as well as curved on plan. For example, Figure 168 shows a semi-circular arch curved on plan with parallel jambs. A study of Figure 168 will show that the springer brick is curved on face but the key brick is straight and the angle of the face to the soffit is different in both cases. There is therefore no simple method of cutting these arches unless some elaborate jigs are erected, which would normally be much too costly for this work. They are usually 'cut and fit'. There are, however, many excellent examples of this work and the craftsman's skill in cutting and setting them deserves great credit.

Self-assessment questions

1 Describe a method of building a large-span arch.

2 What is meant by a *skew* arch and why is this type of arch used?

3 Describe the method of constructing intersecting vaults. State how provision can be made for pointing the work on completion.

4 Describe the method of preparing and building the body of a niche.

5 Describe a method of obtaining a hood mould for a niche.

6 Describe the method of forming the cutting box for the voussoirs of a niche hood.

7 Show by means of a neat drawing the method of setting out a soldier arch which is curved on plan, and has radiating jambs. The span of the arch is 1 m and the radius of the curve 3 m.

8 Explain why it is so difficult to cut arches which are curved on plan in openings with parallel jambs.

Chapter 13

Flues and ducts

After reading this chapter you should be able to:

1 Have a sound knowledge of the construction of chimneys for industrial purposes.

2 Know the various methods of lining tall chimneys.

3 Have a knowledge of a typical method of constructing tall chimneys in brickwork.

4 Have an understanding of the erection of pre-cast concrete chimneys.

5 Have a knowledge of the refractory linings used in furnaces also the use of refractory concretes.

6 Understand the uses and construction of Se-ducts; U-ducts; and refuse chutes.

Flues for industrial appliances

All flues must be fitted with an insulating liner. This will provide a smooth bore for the gases to pass through and will protect the surrounding brickwork or stonework against damage which might be caused by the condensation of the flue gases. *Brickwork 2*, Chapter 9, deals with the provision of linings for flues for domestic appliances. Water vapour is one of the chief products of combustion and it has been estimated that for every kilogramme of fuel burned the amounts of water vapour outlined below are produced:

Solid fuel   0.4 kg of water vapour
Oil   1.2 kg of water vapour
Gas   1.33 kg of water vapour

Therefore the concentration of water vapour is least for solid fuels and highest for gas, facts which, in turn, mean that the flue temperatures must be kept at a higher level for gas-fired boilers, if condensation is to be avoided. In order to achieve this, the flue liner must be insulated by a cavity between the liner and the surrounding brickwork. This cavity should be either hol-low or filled with a lightweight insulating material, such as exfoliated mica (Figure 169). This will prevent the heat from being transferred through the liners into the surrounding structure. The gases will then remain warmer and consequently the amount of condensation will be reduced. It is also most important to ensure that there is no possibility of any rain getting in between the brickwork and the liners, which would drastically

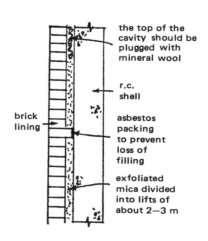

the top of the cavity should be plugged with mineral wool

r.c. shell

brick lining

asbestos packing to prevent loss of filling

exfoliated mica divided into lifts of about 2–3 m

Figure 169

impair insulation. Therefore, the chimney stack must provide good protection against the penetration of rain with properly constructed cappings, suitable flashing and a damp-proof course.

Flues should be as straight as possible. Bends and offsets increase heat losses from the gases and reduce the available flue draught, which increases the risk of condensation. If bends are necessary (for example, where the boiler output pipe is connected to an external chimney) the angle that the pipe makes with the horizontal should never be less than 45 degrees.

Firebrick linings

The larger type of flue can be lined with firebricks (*Brickwork 1*, Chapter 1). These linings are usually a ½-brick or 1 brick in thickness. This work can be done with either dense refractory firebricks or the lighter type of Fossalsil flue bricks. B S 1758 covers the requirements for fireclay refractories which include:

The chemical composition, the silica and alumina content laid down as follows:

Classes K1, K2, L and M all containing 78 per cent silica
Class N 28–35 per cent alumina
Classes P1 and P2 35–40 per cent alumina
Classes Q1, Q2 and Q3 40–45 per cent alumina
Classes K1 and K2 are of a special purposes type

Dimensional tolerance. 95 per cent of the bricks taken for testing should not vary from their stated dimensions by more than 2 per cent. Their concavity should be not more than 3.2 mm in 305 mm and their convexity should be not more than 1.6 mm in 305 mm for class K and not more than 3.2 mm in 305 mm for other classes.

Conditions and workmanship. Bricks and shapes shall be true to form and have sharp edges. They shall be free from deleterious cracks, laminations, cavities and black core.

Identification. Suitable means shall be provided to identify the class of all consignment of bricks and shapes.

Refractory linings

Firebricks can generally be divided into various categories in accordance with B S 1758 as follows:

Q1 High-duty firebricks. These contain about 40–42 per cent alumina and are capable of withstanding severe operating conditions. They are exceptionally resistant to slag attack and erosion by grit-laden gases at high temperatures. These would have a cold crushing strength of about 211 kgf/cm².

P1 Medium firebrick. These have a slightly higher silica, and a little lower alumina content. They are a first-class brick for general purposes and are able to withstand rapid thermal changes without cracking. They would have a cold crushing strength of about the same as for the high-duty firebricks.

N General-duty firebricks. These are a general-purpose firebrick where conditions are not severe enough to warrant the use of aluminous firebricks, but where the volume stability and high mechanical strength of these bricks can be used to advantage. The cold crushing strength of this group is about 246 kgf/cm².

The second and third group would generally be suitable for the lining of chimneys. These are bedded with a powdered fireclay mixed with water to a soft consistency. It is usually 'buttered' on the brick rather than having the bed spread on the bricks which have already been laid, as for normal brickwork. The mixed fireclay is better handled if it is put into shallow boxes rather than attempting to put it on a mortar board. The joints should be kept as thin as possible, though well-filled with fireclay.

Fossalsil linings

These bricks should be stored under cover and kept dry until needed. They must not be exposed to frost if they have inadvertently become wet.

These bricks should be soaked for about an hour before they are laid. The bricks are set in a mortar consisting of four parts Fossalsil powder to one part Portland cement by *volume*. No sand should be added to this mix. The mortar should be applied to the brick which is being laid rather than spreading it along the wall, as for normal brickwork. The joint should be kept as thin as possible to ensure a sound joint; 3 mm is all that is necessary. The consistency of the mortar should be somewhat wetter than ordinary mortar and

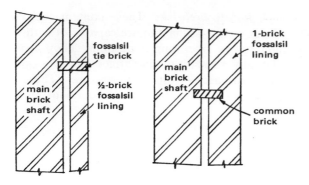

Figure 170   *Tying-in a Fossalsil lining to the main shaft*

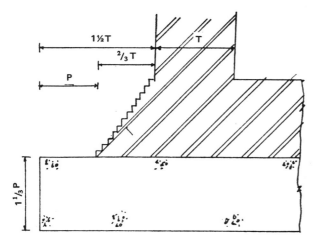

Figure 171   *Detail showing typical foundations for a tall chimney*

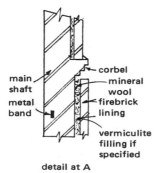

detail at A

Figure 172   *Allowing for expansion and protecting the cavity*

should be placed in a shallow sided box rather than put on a mortar board.

For estimating purposes, 152.4 kg of Fossalsil powder is required per 1000 Fossalsil bricks. 609.6 kg of cement are required for each 1016 kg of Fossalsil.

In frosty weather, Fossalsil work must be covered up overnight, and in severe conditions a fire can be lit at the bottom of the flue to keep the work warm and free from frost attack.

It is quite usual to 'tie in' the Fossalsil flue brick lining at intervals with the main brickwork. In the case of $\frac{1}{2}$-brick linings, these ties will be done with Fossalsil bricks, but where the lining is 1 brick in thickness, the ties can be done in common bricks, provided the common brick tie is not nearer to the face of the Fossalsil lining than the thickness of a half brick (Figure 170).

Tall chimneys

Tall chimneys can be constructed of:

Brickwork
In situ concrete
Precast concrete blocks

Brick chimneys

These can be constructed in accordance with the 'deemed to satisfy' clauses of the Regulations, which include the following:

1   The bricks must be either hard, well-burnt clay or Class A sand lime. In either case they should be properly bonded with mortar.
2   For circular or regular polygon plan the width at the base must be at least one-twelfth of the height.
3   For rectangular plan, the width at the base must be at least one-tenth of the height.
4   The thickness of the brickwork should not be less than 1 brick (200 mm) at the top, for not more than approximately 6 m, and should then increase by a $\frac{1}{2}$ brick for each additional 6 m or part thereof.
5   The shaft should have a batter of 125 mm in every 6 m.
6   The footings shall project not less than two-thirds of the thickness of the brickwork at

the base and be not less than $1\frac{1}{3}$ times their projection in height (Figure 171). They can be in regular offsets or in one large offset and should be built solid to the level of the base of the shaft.

7 The projection of the concrete from the base of the shaft should be not less than 1.5 times the thickness of the brickwork at the base.

8 The thickness of concrete at the base should not be less than $1\frac{1}{3}$ times the projecting arm from the footing courses or from the base (Figure 171).

9 Where openings are formed in the side of the shaft, the jambs must be thickened to maintain the strength.

10 Any structural steel or reinforcement must be protected against heat or corrosion.

11 The shaft should have a lining of insulating bricks bonded to the structural brickwork or an independent lining of firebrick, carried to a sufficient height to protect the shaft from damage, and separated from the structure by a cavity of at least 25 mm wide. The lining should be covered at the top and allowance made for expansion (Figure 172).

The bonding usually adopted for the building of brick chimneys is English garden-wall bond since the courses diminish because of the batter of the shaft. Therefore, it is difficult to 'maintain the perpends' and English garden-wall bond lends itself to this type of construction better than other bonds.

Plumbing points kept 'plumb' with a battering plumb rule should be maintained all round the shaft. Another method of ensuring the uprightness of the shaft is to drop a plumb-bob from the centre of the shaft at the top until it reaches a mark at the bottom. This should be checked at frequent intervals, at least every scaffold lift. A theodolite can also be used for this purpose, but this would normally be used by a site engineer.

Most chimney shafts are built overhand with the scaffold erected on the inside and all the materials hoisted inside the shaft.

Lightning conductors must be fixed to the chimney as soon as it has been built. These are usually of copper and form a good conductor between the earth and the clouds. The conductor should be connected to a terminal which may extend to about 2 m above the highest point of the chimney; it is then taken down to the ground and diverted horizontally to a convenient spot where good moist earth is available to provide a good 'earthing terminal'. The conductor should then be connected to a copper plate, the size of which will depend upon the amount of moisture in the ground; the drier the ground, the larger the plate. The minimum size is usually about 1 m². This plate is taken down into the ground about 2 m and surrounded with ashes or powdered coke. The lightning conductor should be kept as straight as possible and sharp bends should be avoided (Figure 173).

In situ concrete chimneys

These are built of reinforced concrete. The work is usually conducted from the inside of the chimney, but a scaffold platform is generally attached to the formwork on the outside of the chimney. As the formwork is raised, the platform is also lifted. The formwork also has to be adjusted in size at each lift to allow for the batter of the chimney. The accuracy for uprightness can be checked in the same way as the accuracy of brick chimneys is checked.

Concrete chimneys are generally lined with brickwork to protect the concrete from damage by the products of combustion. This lining is usually made with engineering bricks, as they have a high bearing capacity and are greatly resistant to the effects of flue gases.

Precast concrete chimneys

These have a rather more pleasant appearance than the *in situ* concrete chimneys, as they can be constructed with stone-faced blocks which enables features to be made of the joints (Figure 174). Various decorative shapes can be made with this method thereby providing pleasant architectural features. The chimneys are lined with brickwork, and are usually constructed with vertical sides as it is difficult to achieve economically a batter with precast units.

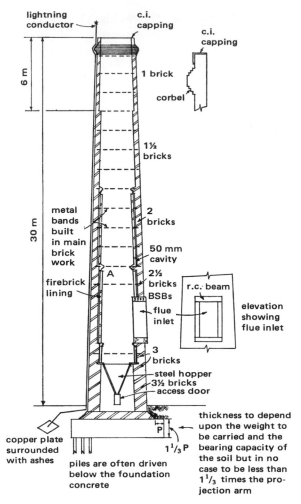

Figure 173 *Typical section through a tall chimney*

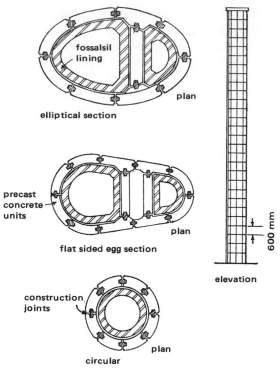

Figure 174 *Typical precast concrete chimneys produced by John Ellis & Sons Ltd, Leicester*

Furnace linings with refractory concrete

Refractory concrete has to withstand high temperatures, thermal stresses, abrasion, corrosion and slag attack. It is therefore essential that no further loads should be placed upon it, so superimposed loads should be kept to a minimum. Tensile and bending loads must be avoided, as it is almost impossible to reinforce refractory linings in the same way as structurally reinforced concrete. Heavy reinforcement expands at a greater rate than refractory concrete at high temperatures and can therefore disrupt the concrete and cause severe cracking.

Despite the fact that heavy structural reinforcement is not suitable, the modern practice of lining furnaces monolithically with relatively thin walls of refractory concrete sometimes makes it necessary to support the linings from the furnace casing or other structural framework.

Metal anchors are commonly used for this purpose. If these are positioned so that each anchor has one end fixed to the steelwork exposed to air, the other end protected from the furnace temperature by a suitable cover of refractory concrete with a relatively low thermal conductivity, the anchor will remain relatively cool and will afford effective support. A typical arrangement is shown in Figure 175.

The lining of steel chimneys and other cylindrical vessels is shown in Figure 176. The mesh should have the largest practicable openings to allow thorough compaction of the refractory concrete. The metal anchors are usually given a coat of bituminous paint before installing the concrete.

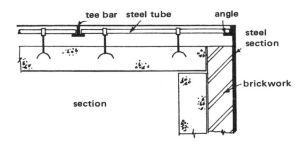

Figure 175 *Typical methods of suspending refractory concrete by means of patent anchors*

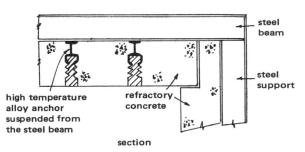

Figure 177 *Suspending refractory concrete*

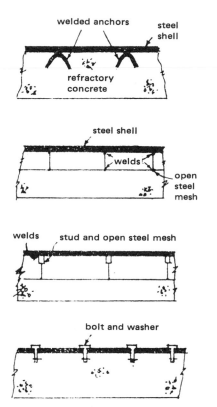

Figure 176 *Various methods that may be used as anchorages for refractory concrete linings in steel shells, door frames, steel chimneys, etc.*

Figure 178 *Hot (or as cast) joint*

Figure 179 *Cold joint*

forms of firebrick anchors are on the market. Figure 177 shows a typical anchor of this type.

Joints in refractory linings

For furnaces which operate at temperature of about 1000°C it is usually possible to dispense with expansion joints. If a wall is cast chequer-fashion in butt-jointed bays about 1 m² each butt joint may open slightly when the structure cools after the first firing. The thermal characteristics of refractory concrete are responsible for this. These joints will, however, close when the furnace is again at operating temperature. It is important that sand or scale particles do not become lodged in these joints as they may cause spalling in the refractory concrete. The joints, therefore, must be designed to prevent this from happening. Figures 178 and 179 show typical types of joints used for this work.

This paint will burn off when put into service which will leave a very slight gap to allow for differential thermal expansion.

High-temperature alloy steel anchors are also obtainable for special duties and various patented

Refractory concrete arches

These may be given any profile the designer chooses. Generally arches in refractory concrete can be built with much less rise than arches built with firebricks.

Transverse butt joints are usually provided at every metre run and arches are usually divided by longitudinal butt joints at the third-points or mid-point of the span. These joints are rebated as shown in Figures 180 and 181.

If an arch has a rise of less than about 50 mm per 300 mm of span, it is usually treated as a flat arch and suspended in sections, as outlined for ordinary refractory linings.

All refractory concrete should be compacted thoroughly. Vibrators should be used, if possible, to ensure that the concrete is well consolidated. Refractory concrete should not be trowelled too early or too excessively as this may result in a powdery surface.

The refractory concrete should be kept cool and wet for 24 hours after placing. Formwork should be removed after about 6–8 hours after casting and the exposed surfaces sprayed with a fine mist spray, or covered with wet sacks or hessian.

Refractory concrete is ready for use 24 hours after placing, but there will still be a considerable amount of water remaining in the concrete at this stage. Therefore, the firing should be quite 'gentle' at first to expel this water. For thick units, the temperature should be restricted to about 50°C

per hour until the concrete has reached about 600°C.

Repairs to firebrick work

A mix of one part of high alumina cement to two and a half parts of 3 mm to dust of firebrick can be used where thin joints are not needed in the repairs. But for laying or pointing firebrick work a finer mix of one part high alumina cement to two parts of 2 mm to dust firebrick should be used. If more plasticity is needed then raw fireclay up to 20 per cent of the weight of the cement can be added.

For stopping cracks or leaks in firebrick work the following mix can be used:

one part high alumina cement, one part of firebrick dust 2 mm down, one part raw ground fireclay, quarter part short asbestos fibre

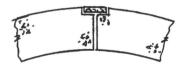

Figure 180   *Refractory concrete butt-joint*

Figure 181   *Refractory concrete butt-joint*

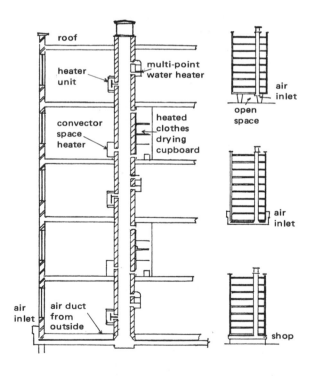

Figure 182   *A typical Se-duct installation showing how the various sealed appliances can be arranged. The flanking drawings show alternative air inlet arrangements*

The dry ingredients are thoroughly blended, and water is added to give the required consistency.

The Se-duct

The Se-duct is a flue system which has been designed specifically for the installation of gas appliances in multi-storey buildings. The system consists of a single vertical duct of rectangular section (Figure 182) open at the top and bottom to which appliances with sealed combustion-chambers are fitted as required on any floor. There is a free flow of air through the duct so that the air for combustion for the appliances is drawn from it. The appliances also discharge the products of combustion into the same duct.

The size of the duct is related to the number and type of appliances connected to it. This is to ensure that there is sufficient air for satisfactory combustion of each appliance (Figure 183). The duct must function independently of any other ventilation system in the building.

The Se-duct is constructed from units which are composed of dense refractory concrete. The ends are rebated so that alignment is facilitated during erection. The joints should be made with a gauged lime mortar or a plasticized fireclay compound. Surplus material at each joint should be thoroughly cleaned off and the joint should be well-filled with the jointing compound so that there is no possibility of leaks in the duct, as it is essential that the ducts are air tight.

The ducts should be clad with lightweight or clinker clocks which in turn should be finished with at least two-coat plasterwork (Figure 184).

The duct should be finished at the outlet with a terminal block preferably extended to at least the height of the parapet wall or of any roof construction, such as a lift motor room or a water tank near the duct. The terminal should be fitted with a weather- and bird-proof inlet, and should have outlets on all four sides (Figure 185).

The inlet to the duct may be from an open area at the base of the building or through horizontal ducts with vertical inlets (Figure 182). Plans showing the positioning of these inlets in multi-storey buildings are shown in Figure 186.

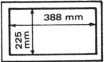
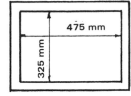
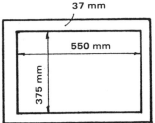

Figure 183 *Sections of Se-ducts*

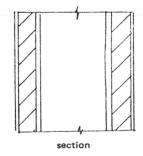

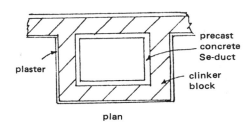

Figure 184 *Typical construction of a Se-duct*

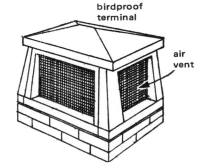

Figure 185 *A typical Se-duct terminal on a modern block of flats*

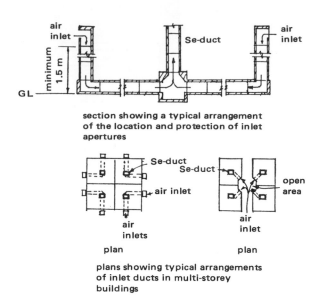

section showing a typical arrangement
of the location and protection of inlet
apertures

plans showing typical arrangements
of inlet ducts in multi-storey
buildings

Figure 186   *Plans showing typical arrangements of
inlet ducts in multi-storey buildings*

The U-duct

The U-duct is similar to the Se-duct. It is used
where the inlet is difficult to obtain at the base of
the building. As the name suggests (Figure 187) it
is taken from the top of the building, and conveyed down one limb of the U-duct and the gas
heating appliances are connected to the rising
limb of the U (Figure 188). The convection cur-
rents are created by the difference in densities of
the air in the two limbs due to the higher temperature in the rising limb.

Each limb of the U-duct should be usually
about 25 per cent greater in cross-sectional area
than the corresponding Se-duct. Therefore, the
total area will be two and a half times as great.

The ducts are generally built side by side either
in a composite unit or in separate ducts.

The outlet terminal should be kept at a higher
level than the inlet terminal to prevent the possibility of recirculation of the flue gases (Figure
189).

Refuse chutes

These are built in multi-storey buildings and are
intended for the conveyance of refuse from upper

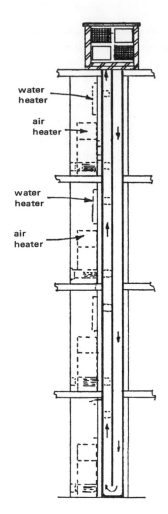

Figure 187   *Section through a four-storey U-duct*

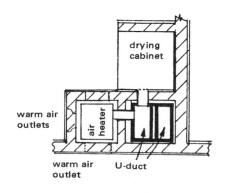

Figure 188   *Plan showing methods of connecting gas
appliances to the U-duct*

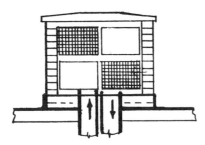

Figure 189 *The inlet and discharge of a U-duct terminal are positioned to avoid recirculation*

floors to large storage containers at the bottom of the chute. Great care must be taken to ensure that there is no risk of fire with hot ashes and that no foul odours are allowed to escape.

The Building Regulations state that refuse chutes shall be:

1 Constructed of suitable non-combustible material.
2 Constructed so that the inner surfaces are impervious to moisture.
3 Constructed so as to prevent the lodgement of any refuse within the chute.
4 Circular in cross-section with an internal diameter of not less than 375 mm.
5 Fitted with adequate means of access for inspection and cleansing.
6 Fitted for the insertion of refuse with hoppers which should be situated in a place which is freely ventilated or has adequate means of mechanical ventilation.
7 Ventilated to the external air by a shaft or pipe which shall not be less than 17,500 mm^2, so constructed that the outlet is protected against the entry of rain, and be taken to such a height and positioned so as not to be a nuisance or prejudicial to health (Figure 190).
8 Fitted at its lowest extremity with a shutter capable of closing the outlet of the chute (Figure 190).

The hoppers shall be:

1 Constructed of suitable non-combustible material.
2 Installed to discharge the refuse in an efficient manner to the refuse container.

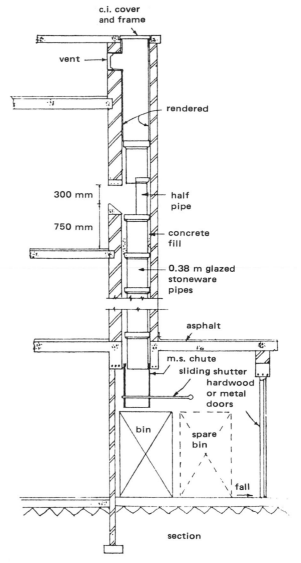

Figure 190 *Section showing the construction of a refuse chute*

3 Incapable of remaining in any position other than fully open or closed positions (Figure 191).
4 Capable of preventing, as far as possible, any emission of dust or foul air from the refuse container or the chute.
5 Constructed so as not to project into the chute.
6 Not situated within a building.

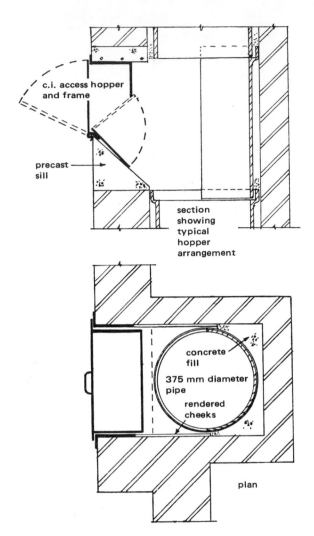

Figure 191   *Detail of hopper*

The refuse storage chamber should be constructed so that:

1 The walls, floor and roof are made of suitable non-combustible material.
2 The inner surfaces of the chamber are impervious to moisture.
3 The floor of the chamber is laid to a fall towards a trapped gully.
4 It is fitted with a flush door which shall be situated in an external wall (Figure 190).
5 It is fitted with a flyproof ventilator or be provided with a ventilating pipe or shaft.

Self-assessment questions

1 Why should flues be lined?

2 Explain why condensation can be so harmful to chimneys.

3 State the various classes of fireclay refractories.

4 Describe the usual method of laying firebricks.

5 How should Fossalsil bricks be stored on site?

6 Describe the method of laying Fossalsil bricks.

7 State how Fossalsil brickwork may be tied in to the main chimney structure.

8 State the minimum width of the base for a circular chimney 36 m high and a rectangular chimney 30 m high, that would satisfy the Building Regulations.

9 By means of a neat drawing show a vertical section through a brick chimney 25 m high.

10 Show the minimum foundations that would be necessary for the chimney in question 8.

11 Describe a method that can be used to keep the chimney 'plumb'.

12 Describe a method of fixing a lightning conductor to a tall chimney.

13 How are concrete chimneys protected from corrosion by the products of combustion?

14 What is a Se-duct? For what purpose is it used?

15 Describe the method of constructing a Se-duct.

16 What is a U-duct? Under what circumstances would this type of duct be used?

17 Describe the method of constructing a U-duct.

18 Describe a method of constructing a refuse duct.

19 Outline the main requirements of the Building Regulations regarding refuse chutes.

20 By means of a neat sketch show a typical hopper for a refuse chute.

21 How should a refuse storage chamber be constructed?

22 By means of neat sketches show how refractory linings may be supported.

23 Describe a method of lining steel chimneys.

24 Describe typical mortars that may be used for repairing firebrick work and also for filling cracks in firebrick work.

Chapter 14

Floors

After reading this chapter you should be able to:

1 Have a sound knowledge of the various types of floors used in construction.
2 Know the minimum time that should elapse before removing formwork.
3 Have an understanding of the meaning of 'prestressed concrete'.

There are many ways of constructing floors in buildings and each way has its own particular advantage. But every method of floor construction, however, must satisfy certain requirements laid down by the Building Regulations. These regulations include the following points:

1 The floor must be capable of withstanding all dead and imposed loads for which it is designed to carry and satisfy the requirements for fire resistance.
2 The floor must have adequate thermal insulation.
3 The floor must be constructed to provide adequate resistance to the transmission of airborne and impact sound.

Types of floors

The following are six main types of floors used in construction:

Timber joist floors
Solid concrete slab cast *in situ*
Precast solid concrete slabs
A slab of concrete beams and hollow in-filling blocks of clay or concrete
A slab of hollow concrete beams
Filler joist floors

Timber joist floors
To satisfy the minimum requirements for sound insulation in the case of timber floors constructed in offices or blocks of flats, boarding should be nailed to battens. The battens should be laid to

float upon a layer of glass fibre or mineral wood quilt and capable of retaining its resilience under imposed loading. The layer is draped over the wooden joists. The ceiling below the joists should be constructed of a metal lath and plaster ceiling, 18 mm thick, and with a minimum weight of 0.0085 kgf/cm². If plain edge boarding is used, this construction would give a fire resistance of about half an hour; if tongued-and-grooved boarding is used and the thickness of plaster is increased to 21 mm, the fire resistance would be increased to about one hour (Figure 192).

The size of the joists would depend upon the span of the floor and the loads to be carried.

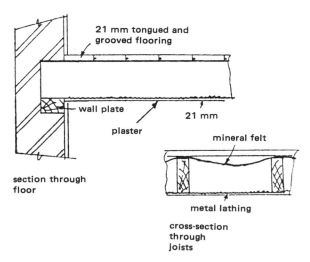

Figure 192 *Timber floor to give a fire resistance of one hour*

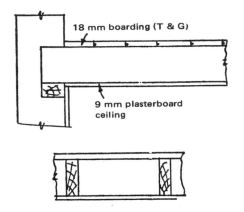

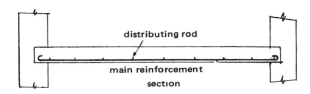

Figure 193 *Timber floor to give a fire resistance of half an hour in a two-storey house*

Timber floors in other types of buildings (for example, two-storey houses) need not have the mineral felt layer because the insulation of sound is not critical and the minimum fire resistance is only half an hour. Therefore, the construction may be much simpler and may consist of plain edge boarding with 12 mm plasterboard or 8 mm of gypsum plaster on metal lath, tongued-and-grooved boarding not less than 18 mm thick, and with 9 mm plasterboard ceiling or gypsum plaster on metal lath 15 mm thick (Figure 193).

Solid concrete slabs cast in situ

These can be broadly divided into two groups:

Simply supported
Continuous slabs

Simply supported slabs

These slabs are supported on all sides and are completely independent of any adjacent slabs. With these slabs the reinforcement can be composed of welded fabric or rods wired together to form a mat. The sets of rods are placed at right angles to each other (Figure 194) in the lower part of the slab. Where the slab is rectangular on plan, the thicker rods would generally be placed on the narrow span. Therefore, the smaller rods would act as distributing reinforcement (see *Brickwork 2*, Chapter 16).

Continuous slabs

These are slabs which are supported on intermediate supports, such as walls, columns or beams; the reinforcement would, therefore, have to be placed in the lower and upper part of the slab according to where the tensile stresses are likely to occur (Figure 195). The rods which are

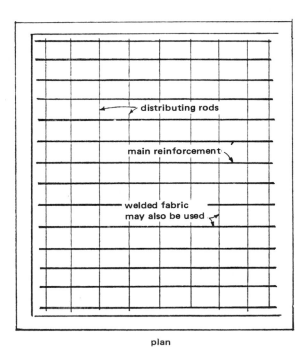

Figure 194 *Reinforced concrete slab*

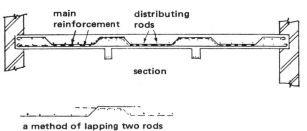

Figure 195 *Continuous slab*

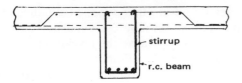

Figure 196 *Section through a beam and continuous slab showing how the beam and slab reinforcement may be tied together*

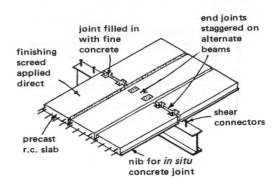

Figure 197 *Parcast precast composite system*

placed at right angles to the main reinforcement act as distributing rods. The stirrups of a reinforced concrete beam can be tied into the floor slab, as shown in Figure 196.

Both of these types of slabs need formwork before the concrete can be laid. This concrete must also be allowed to set and harden before the formwork can be struck which may mean a delay of 10 days (see Table 17). This, in turn, would delay production as the erection and dismantling of the formwork takes time. This method of construction has, however, the advantage of being flexible in design and easily adjustable to any shape required.

Precast solid concrete slabs

This type of construction is usually a *composite* construction, which means that it has a precast unit on the lower side and *in situ* concrete on top. This has the advantage that formwork is not needed, thereby saving erecting and dismantling

time. The slabs will, however, need lifting equipment to hoist them into position. The slabs can be constructed with reinforced concrete or prestressed concrete.

Figure 197 shows a detail of a Parcast precast composite system which is built of reinforced concrete slabs. Figure 198 shows a detail of a Bison solid plank (composite) floor, which is made with prestressed units.

Slabs of concrete beams and hollow in-filling of clay or concrete blocks

These have the advantage of being speedy in construction and lighter in weight than solid floors. Some types can be erected without formwork, although others need formwork before they can be constructed.

Table 17 *Period before formwork should be removed (in days)*

Formwork	Ordinary Portland cement concrete		Rapid-hardening Portland cement concrete	
	Cold weather (just above freezing)	Normal weather about 15°C	Cold weather (just above freezing)	Normal weather about 15°C
Beam sides, walls and columns	6	2	5	1
Slabs (props left under)	10	3	7	2
Beam soffits (props left under)	14	7	10	4
Removal of props to slabs	21	7	14	4
Removal of props to beams	28	16	21	8

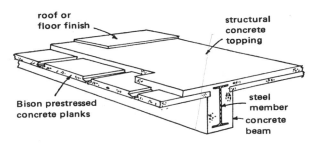

Figure 198   *Bison solid plank composite floor*

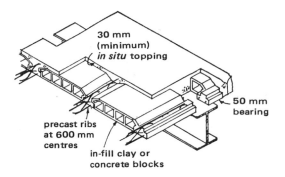

Figure 201   *Triad composite floor*

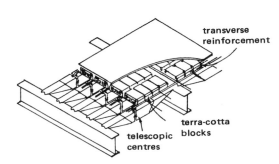

Figure 199   *Smith's fireproof floor*

Types which do need formwork

The formwork is first erected, but this only needs to be in skeleton form. For example, the Acrow adjustable steel floor centres or Trianco telescopic centres are ideal for this type of work (Figure 199). These centres are supported by the wall or beam sides or by temporary strutting. The hollow concrete or terra-cotta blocks are then placed across the adjustable steel centres and reinforcing rods are placed accurately in position between the rows of blocks. The whole floor is then concreted over.

Types which do not need formwork

These are usually comprised of precast concrete joists with concrete or terra-cotta blocks used as in-filling units between the joists. The whole is then covered with a concrete screed. Figures 200–211 show typical examples of these types of floors.

The joists can be constructed of either reinforced concrete (Figures 200, 201 and 202); prestressed concrete (Figures 203–210); or prestressed terra-cotta units (Figure 211).

Terra-cotta slips are usually inserted between the rows of terra-cotta blocks to prevent pattern staining in the ceiling when the building is completed. Pattern staining occurs because of the difference in densities between the concrete ribs and the terra-cotta blocks. Warm air will contain dust; if you look at the area of ceiling immediately above an electric light bulb, you will see the discolouration caused by dust particles. This is because dust particles are released as the air cools

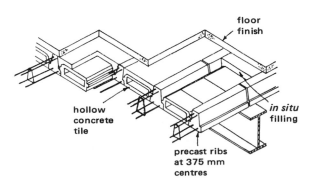

Figure 200   *Tilecast floor*

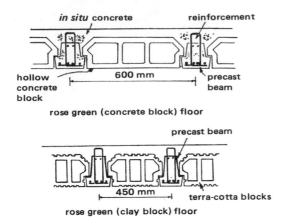

Figure 202   *Rose green floors*

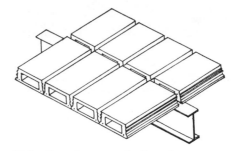

Figure 205   *Stuart's precast hollow floor*

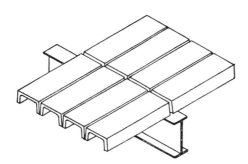

Figure 203   *Bradford precast trough floor*

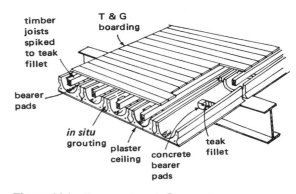

Figure 206   *Truscon type 2 floor unit*

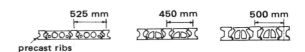

Figure 207   *Pierhead prestressed concrete floor*

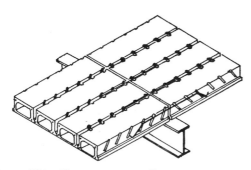

Figure 204   *Siegwart precast floor*

down. If one surface cools the air down more
rapidly than the other, this will attract more dust
which will eventually cause long narrow streaks
where the concrete ribs are situated, because of
the accumulation of the dust particles.

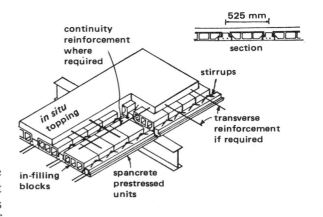

Figure 208   *Spancrete prestressed composite floor*

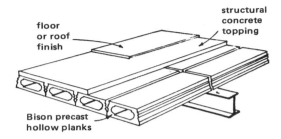

Figure 209 *Bison hollow planks*

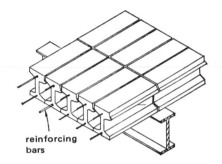

Figure 210 *Rapid floor*

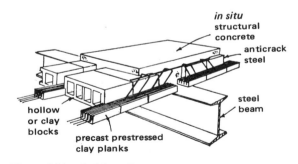

Figure 211 *Stahlton floor*

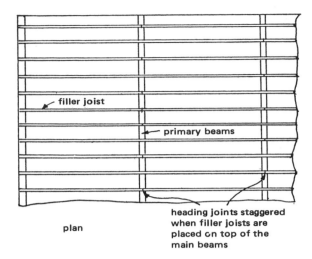

Figure 212 *Filler joist floor*

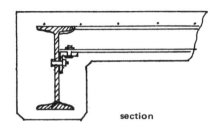

Figure 213 *Detail of fixing a filler joist*

Slabs of hollow concrete beams

There is wide variety of this type of floor unit on the market and it is a very popular form of floor construction. This is because the units are comparatively light to lift into position and the floor is quickly constructed. In many cases it can be used almost as soon as it is laid and the mortar or fine concrete jointing or infilling has set. Figures 204–210 show typical examples of these floors.

Lifting equipment is, however, necessary for raising the units and lowering them into position.

Filler joist floors

This type of floor is used on steel-framed construction and is generally intended for carrying heavy loads or where a high fire resistance is necessary.

The floor consists of main steel beams with smaller beams (filler joists) spaced at centres of about 600 mm (Figure 212). The fillers can be fixed to the web of the main girder, where the depth of beam visible below the ceiling would be kept to a minimum. This method does, however, require the use of angle brackets and holes must be drilled through the web of the main beam (Figure 213).

Alternatively the filler joists can be placed on the top of the main steel beams. This means that the filler can be bolted direct to the flanges of the main beam and that the fillers can be jointed at alternate main beams (Figure 214). But if this is done the full depth of the main beam will protrude below the ceiling. If false ceilings are used, it has no great disadvantage; in fact, it can have the advantage of providing more room above the ceiling to house any services that may have to be installed.

Prestressed concrete

An explanation of the term 'prestressed' concrete is now needed. Normal reinforced concrete is provided with mild steel rods placed at the various places in a beam or floor slab where tensile stresses are likely to occur (see *Brickwork 2*, Chapter 16). Therefore, it is assumed that, in the case of a beam, the steel will take all the loads in *tension* and the upper half of the concrete will take all the loads in *compression*, assuming that the lower half of the concrete is doing 'no work' in taking any loading. For ordinary purposes, this is quite a satisfactory method of working. But where high stresses are likely or great loads have to be carried, it is much better to use the whole of the load-carrying capacity of the concrete, which will ensure a much more economical use of its strength. This can be achieved by applying a load at each end of the beam; just as you would when lifting a number of bricks off a lorry, that is, by pressing hard at each end of a number of bricks,

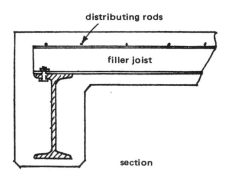

Figure 214   *Detail of fixing a filler joist*

thereby forming a beam which would carry some weight; once the load was released, the 'beam' would break down. This principle can also be applied to concrete but if mild steel rods were used, these would stretch and lose their strength. To prevent the concrete from breaking down, the reinforcement must be of a high-quality steel. This would be similar to spring steel in that it would have great strength to resist tensile stresses.

In order to create the load at each end of the beam a predetermined load is applied to the reinforcing wires by hydraulic jacks. The wire is stretched and the concrete is then placed around these wires and allowed to set and harden, when the stressing wires will be gripped by the hardened concrete. The load being exerted by the jack on the end of the wires is eventually released and transferred to the concrete. The whole of the cross-sectional area of the concrete is now working and much heavier loads can be placed on the beams. This method of prestressing is called *pre-tensioned, prestressed concrete*, that is, the wires are stretched before the actual concrete operations have begun.

Alternatively, the concrete can be placed into the formwork and allowed to set and harden. Small ducts are formed in the concrete from one end to the other. The number and size of these would depend upon the size of the beam and the load which is to be carried. When the concrete has reached a minimum strength, the prestressing wires are then threaded into the ducts. One end of each of the wires is then anchored to the concrete beam by means of patent grips, and the other end is stretched by means of a hydraulic jack. When the required load is reached, the wires at the jacking end are also anchored to hold the wires in position. Finally, cement grout is forced through the duct until it is solid and is then left to set and harden. This method is called *post-tensioned, prestressed concrete*.

Both methods are very efficient and each has certain advantages. For example, the floor joists which have been described in this chapter can be cast on a 'long line' principle, that is, the casting bed can be approximately 100 m in length and the wires could be stretched from one end to the other. A load can then be applied with the aid of large hydraulic jacks. When the required loading has been reached, the concrete formwork is then placed around the wires all along their length and the ends of each formwork is cut or formed over the wires which will seal off each unit. The concrete is poured into each formwork along the whole of the length and allowed to set and harden. When the concrete has reached the required strength, the prestressing wires are cut off (usually with oxyacetylene torches) between each concrete unit. The stress originally created by the hydraulic jacks is now transferred in the various concrete units.

In the case of the Stahlton floor the same principle is adopted but formwork is not used. Terracotta units are instead placed along the bed and the wires are placed in the grooves in the blocks. The wires are stretched and finally fixed in position with fine concrete. The prestressed planks are then cut off to the required lengths.

In all of this type of work, it is essential that the concrete is of a high-quality because it will have to carry great loads. Careful control must be maintained throughout. One bad batch of concrete would ruin a whole beam.

Prestressed concrete allows extremely long spans to be bridged with concrete; it would be impossible to use ordinary reinforced concrete because it could break down under its own weight. Alternatively, if reinforced concrete was used the spans would have to be greatly reduced. This would make work like bridging motorways very difficult.

Self-assessment questions

1 What are the general requirements for floors?

2 State the main types of floors.

3 By means of a neat sketch show a suitable construction for a timber floor in a block of flats.

4 How can timber floors in a block of flats differ from floors used for a two-storey house or a single dwelling?

5 State the two main groups of solid floor slabs. Compare the methods of reinforcing both types of slabs.

6 Why should the formwork be left under slabs? State how long this formwork should be left under beams and slabs. State what other action should be taken when the formwork has been dismantled.

7 Describe the two main types of precast solid floor slabs, and state their differences.

8 Describe the methods of erecting a hollow block floor slab.

9 What is meant by 'pattern staining'? How may it be prevented in floors constructed with hollow terra-cotta blocks?

10 What are the advantages of using hollow concrete beams? By means of a neat sketch show a typical example of a floor of this type.

11 Why are filler joist floors used in buildings? How may the filler joists be secured to the main girders?

12 What is meant by 'prestressed concrete'?

13 Why would mild steel rods be unsuitable for prestressed concrete?

14 Explain the difference between *pre-tensioned, prestressed concrete* and *post-tensioned, prestressed concrete*.

15 What is meant by casting on 'a long line system'?

Chapter 15

Concrete

After reading this chapter you should be able to:

1 Have a good knowledge of the function of 'The Agrément Board'.

2 Have a good knowledge of the various types of cements used in construction and their uses.

3 Know the various types of concrete and their uses.

4 Know the various types of lightweight aggregates in use.

5 Have a good understanding of the mixes and uses of refractory concretes.

6 Know what precautions that should be taken when concreting in cold weather.

7 Have a good understanding of 'prescribed mixes'.

Special concretes

Special concretes are concretes produced for specific purposes. The nature of this concrete can be determined by the type of cement used as the matrix or the characteristics of the aggregates.

The minimum standards of many of these concreting materials can be determined by the British Standards Institution, which publishes Specifications and Codes of Practice laying down minimum requirements for the quality of the materials and their applications.

The Agrément Board

This is a Board set up by the Ministry of Public Building and Works in 1965 for testing new products which were not covered by British Standards or Codes of Practice. They also issue certificates stating the results of these tests which are valid for three years and are allowed one renewal. The Agrément Board maintains close co-operation with the British Standards Institution and the Building Research Station, and its offices are at Lord Alexander House, Waterhouse Street, Hemel Hempstead, Hertfordshire.

New products can be tested by the Board for a prescribed fee payable by the manufacturer. If the product is up to standard, a certificate is then issued covering the following points:

1 The intended use of the product.
2 Its construction.
3 The method of erection or use.
4 Its function.
5 An opinion as to whether the product will satisfy the requirements of the Building Regulations.

The certificate will, of course, be made out to the manufacturer stating the works at which the product was produced.

The British Standards Institution is concerned with the general standard of materials; the Agrément Board is concerned with specific items produced by manufacturers. The two bodies therefore play a most important part in ensuring a good standard in the quality of materials and their application.

Cements

Cements are composed of a variety of chemicals produced by burning stones or clays at high temperatures. Among the foremost of these chemicals or elements are calcium, alumina, silica and ferric oxide. Different compounds are formed by variation in the ratio of these elements. These compounds create the various characteristics of the cements which give them their differing properties.

Care must always be taken when using a special cement to ensure that it is the correct material for the purpose for which it is intended. The manufacturer's instructions for its application must always be obeyed.

The setting and hardening process of cement is the result of the formation of complex chemical compounds which are set into motion as soon as water has been added. A detailed knowledge of chemistry is essential to fully comprehend these complex processes. There are, however, certain basic conditions which can be readily understood without a detailed knowledge of the actual chemical changes which take place. These are loosely termed the *setting* and *hardening* of cement, and are part of *one* continuous process of the chemical combination of the elements and the water although they are often thought to be *separate* processes. This is known as the *hydration* of the cement. During this process, the movement of the chemical elements in forming the compounds causes heat to be generated.

The speeds of the setting and hardening of cements will depend upon the rates at which the various compounds are formed. Some are more rapid than others.

Setting rate

The setting rate of cement is usually in two quite distinct stages which are classified as the *initial* and *final* setting times. These stages are comparatively rapid, as chemical compounds are quickly formed due to the fluid nature of the cement when the water is added. As the cement gets progressively harder, the formation of the compounds is gradually slowed down.

Hardening rate

The hardening rate of cement is a much longer process than the setting rate. In most cases the point at which it reaches its ultimate strength cannot be accurately determined, but it has been estimated that concrete made with Portland cement will keep increasing in strength for many years after it has been laid. This indicates that chemical changes are still taking place though only at an extremely slow rate. For general design purposes, the strength at twenty-eight days for ordinary Portland cement is taken as the hardening time; Figure 215 gives an indication of the gain in strength of cements over a period of twelve months.

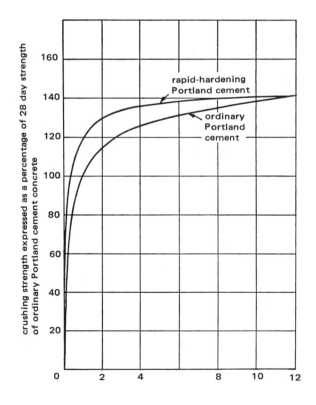

Figure 215 *The trend of the increase in strength of concretes made with Portland cements*

Types of cement

Ordinary Portland cement (BS 12)

This is a matrix which is suitable for most general concrete work, and if handled correctly it will produce concretes of high qualities and strengths (see *Brickwork 2*, Chapter 16).

The initial setting time of ordinary Portland cement should not be less than 45 minutes after it has been mixed with water, and not more than ten hours for the final set.

It is a usual requirement in specifications that concrete should be placed before the initial set has taken place.

Rapid-hardening cement (BS 12)

Rapid-hardening cement is very similar to ordinary Portland cement except its chemical composition is slightly different and it is ground more finely. Although its initial and final setting times are exactly the same as ordinary Portland cement, its rate of hardening is much faster; therefore it achieves the same strength in about half the time, that is, the strength of rapid-hardening cement at seven days will equal the strength of ordinary Portland cement at fourteen days. But both types of cement will eventually achieve the same strength usually about six months after mixing.

Concrete that is mixed with this type of cement has the advantage of being put into use more quickly than concrete which is mixed with ordinary Portland cement. This means that formwork can be struck at an earlier stage, which will enable more uses to be obtained from the formwork.

Portland blast-furnace cement (BS 146)

This consists of a finely ground mixture of Portland cement, clinker and water-quenched granulated blast-furnace slag. It has a slightly slower rate of hardening than ordinary Portland cement, but this has the advantage of not generating the same amount of heat. Therefore, it is extremely useful for use in very thick walls, slabs or mass foundations. It eventually achieves the same strength as ordinary Portland cement at twenty-eight days. Because it has a slower rate of hardening than ordinary Portland cement its curing times should be longer than fourteen days. This type of cement has greater resistance to heat, sea-water, and dilute acid than ordinary Portland cement.

White or coloured cements

These are on the market in ordinary and rapid-hardening varieties. They are largely used for precast concrete products and reconstructed stone, and have strengths a little lower than the strength of ordinary cement. They are made from clays with less than 1 per cent iron oxide content. The coloured cements are produced by mixing white cement with about 4–8 per cent of chemically inert pigments (BS 1014) and a dispersing agent but it is important to remember that, if these pigments are used, the cement content must be increased by 10–15 per cent to compensate for the reduction of cement in the concrete mix.

These cements are particularly useful for concrete work requiring a decorative finish, coloured pointings and renderings as they have a non-staining property and are very uniform in their colouring.

Sulphate-resisting cement

This has a slightly different chemical composition from ordinary Portland cement, although it will satisfy the requirements of BS 12. This type of cement is used mainly for concretes likely to be subjected to soils which contain mineral sulphates but it is also used for concretes which come into contact with subsoil water, sea water, factory effluent and sewers. It is frequently used in humid, industrial areas.

Accelerators, such as calcium chloride, would not be added to sulphate-resisting cement as they might reduce the durability of the concrete and cause corrosion of any steel reinforcement that may be present.

Water-repellent Portland cement

This is mainly used in renderings to check moisture penetration. When used in concretes it is most important to control the composition of the mix and the mixing time, or too much air can be entrained which will seriously impair the efficiency of the cement.

Ultra high early strength cement

This has a higher proportion of gypsum than ordinary Portland cement and its initial development of strength is much more rapid. There is, however, little increase in strength after twenty-eight days. It generates a lot of heat at the early stages and is therefore very useful when concreting in cold weather.

High-alumina cement (BS 915)

This is not a Portland cement, but is made by burning a mixture of limestone and bauxite at a very high temperature and grinding the resulting clinker to a powder. It is capable of achieving a high early strength and concrete made with this type of cement can be subjected to full designed loading 24 hours after placing, although it is generally better to leave the concrete for 48 hours before subjecting it to full loading conditions, if possible.

Although this cement is rapid-hardening, it is, however, slow-setting compared to ordinary Portland cement, as it has an initial setting time of between 2 and 6 hours, and the final set takes place within 2 hours after the initial set. Once the final set has been reached, the cement develops its high strength with great speed (Figure 216).

Concretes made with this type of cement must be kept comparatively cool. The heat which is generated within the concrete must be dissipated by curing with cold water as soon as the surface can withstand it without defacement but preferably not more than 6 hours after placing. Timber side forms of beams should be stripped as soon as possible and the sides sprayed with water. Deferred or ineffective curing is detrimental to the ultimate strength of the concrete.

Other types of cements must not be mixed with high-alumina cement, as this will cause a *flash set*, that is, the mix will set almost as soon as the water is added. This characteristic, however, can be used to advantage when plugging a small leak or affecting a minor repair, or fixing brackets which have no great weight to support. Mixing with other cements can also have a detrimental effect on the ultimate strength of the concrete.

All tools and plant should be kept quite free from lime, plaster or other types of cements before being used with high-alumina cement. If the work on the site requires concretes made with both ordinary and high-alumina cements, the batches must be kept completely separate and the mixer washed out thoroughly before changing from one type of cement to the other.

Concretes made with high-alumina cement have a very high resistance to many types of chemicals, such as the chemicals listed in Table 18.

They also have a high resistance to high temperatures and can be used as a refractory concrete if suitable aggregates are used with the cement. Table 19 shows the approximate temperatures that can be resisted by these refractory concretes.

Refractory concretes made with high-alumina cements have a very good resistance to the exhaust gases from most industrial furnaces. They can also resist condensation which can take place when plant is shut down; similarly, at the top of a chimney stack, where condensation with a high acid content can develop.

The firebrick aggregate and the cement must be of good quality if good results are to be obtained with refractory concretes.

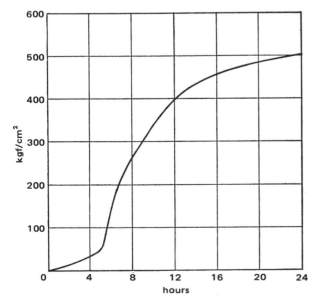

Figure 216 *The trend of the increase in strength of a 1:2:4 concrete made with high-alumina cement*

Table 18

Acid	Type of construction on which acids are found
Sulphuric acid	Gas washing plants. Sewage works where chemical treatment is carried out
Sulphurous acid	Bleaching chambers, which can be constructed with high-alumina concrete or in engineering bricks bedded with high-alumina mortar and rendered with a similar mortar
Butyric acid	Breweries
Carbonic acid	Natural mineral waters. Aerated water industry
Tannic acid	Tannery works
Sugar	Confectionery
Animal wastes	Abattoirs, factories dealing with waste products

Table 19

Aggregate	Type of concrete	Approximate maximum service temperature limit deg C
Siliceous sand and gravel	Structural	250
Limestone	Heat-resistant	550
Fine-grained basic igneous rock (e.g. traprock and some whinstones)	Heat-resistant	700–900
Clay brick or tile	Heat-resistant	1000
Slag	Heat-resistant High strength Abrasion-resistant	1150
Crushed firebrick	Refractory	1350

Advantages

The advantages of the use of refractory concretes made with good-quality crushed-alumina silicate firebrick include the following:

1   It is versatile and can be adapted for precasting shapes or 'gunning-in' *in situ*. This method is carried out by blowing the concrete on to a surface by a pressure gun which forms a refractory skin.
2   It is equally useful for new work or repair and modification work in general.
3   It can be formed to great accuracy.
4   It is formed with no joint or a minimum number of joints.
5   It is ready for use 24 hours after casting.
6   It is stable at temperatures up to 1350°C.
7   It has a high resistance to spalling and to attack by products of combustion.
8   It has approximately the same dimensions at 1000°C as it had when it was cast, so that no elaborate arrangements for expansion are necessary.

Refractory concretes are in great use for all furnace work, tall chimneys, kilns, retorts and

Table 20   *Mix proportions by volume*

| Type of mix | High-alumina cement | Firebrick aggregate | | | Recommended use |
		3 mm to dust	9 mm to 3 mm	18 mm to 9 mm	
Mix A	1	2	—	3	Concrete thicknesses 150 mm and over
Mix B	1	2	2	—	Concrete thicknesses 36 to 150 mm
Mix C	1	2½	—	—	36 mm and less

domestic firebacks and flue linings.

The mixes of refractory concrete are shown in Table 20.

The combined aggregate gradings should be as shown in Table 21.

Disadvantages

When concreting in hot weather with high-alumina cement care must be taken to ensure that the amount of heat in the mixes is kept to an absolute minimum and the following points should be observed:

1 The mixing water should be kept as cool as possible.
2 Mixing water which has been allowed to stand for long periods in the sun should never be used.
3 Aggregates should be shielded from the sun and sprayed with water to cool immediately before use.
4 Steel formwork which has become hot in the sun should also be sprayed immediately before the concrete is placed in it.
5 Attention should be paid to stripping or easing away wooden formwork. Cooling water should be applied to the concrete surfaces at the earliest possible time. Steel formwork can be sprayed on the outside of the forms, as this will cool down the concrete due to the good conduction of heat through the steel.
6 The maximum thickness of slab or lift should be kept at about 0.25 m.
7 In very hot weather the newly hardened concrete should be shielded from the direct sun until it is 7 days old.

Concreting

Concreting in cold weather with high-alumina cements

The degree of total heat released by high-alumina cement is approximately equivalent to the degree of heat that is generated by ordinary Portland cement, but it is released over a much shorter time; therefore, the temperature rise is greater. This characteristic, however, can give concrete made with high-alumina cement great protection against frost. The mix must not freeze for at least 4–6 hours after placing, that is, until the generation of heat has begun. Richer mixes than normal can be used to great advantage in cold weather work. On no account must additives like calcium chloride be added to high-alumina concretes.

If the aggregates are frozen before mixing, hot water can be added to the mixer, or the aggregate can be pre-heated, but it is important that the temperature of the concrete on discharge from the mixer should not exceed about 32°C. When hot water is used for mixing, the aggregates should be added to the mixer first, then the hot water, followed by the cement.

Exposed surfaces of the concrete should be protected against frost damage by covering with waterproof paper, hessian or sacking, for at least the first 6 hours after mixing.

Table 21 *Combined aggregate gradings for crushed firebrick*

	Percentage by weight passing BS sieves		
Sieve sizes	20 mm down	10 mm down	3 mm down
20 mm	100	—	—
10 mm	70	100	—
5 mm	48	70	100
2.36 mm	35	50	95
1.18 mm	25	35	65
600 μm	20	25	45
300 μm	15	20	30
150 μm	10	15	15

Concreting in cold weather with Portland cements

Unless some form of heat is applied to the concrete and it is adequately protected after placing, it is advisable to stop concreting when the temperature reaches about 8°C on a falling thermometer. With special precautions, however, concreting can be continued at freezing temperatures; these precautions include the following:

1   The temperature of the concrete at the time of depositing is at least 5°C.
2   The concrete is kept at as high a temperature as practicable, and in any case above 2°C until it has thoroughly hardened.

During frosty weather when the temperature rises above freezing point, it is sufficient to use extra rapid-hardening cement, or a rapid-hardening cement with calcium chloride added. The calcium chloride should not exceed 2 per cent by weight, and protective coverings should be put over the exposed surfaces of the concrete.

During severe spells of cold weather further methods of protecting the concrete must be adopted by:

1   Warming the formwork and reinforcement and removing snow and ice from the inside of the formwork; this can be done with the application of steam.
2   Heating mixing water to a temperature not exceeding about 80°C; a rise in water temperature of about 4°C will increase the temperature of a 1:2:4 mix with a 0.5 w/c ratio by 1°C.
3   Pre-heating the aggregates by perforated steam-pipes laid under the stock piles.
4   Ensuring that the temperature of the concrete when deposited is at least 5°C; the temperature when mixing should then be at least 15°C.
5   Mixing the water and aggregates thoroughly in the mixer. The Portland cement can then be added when the temperature of the water and aggregates does not exceed 32°C.
6   Covering the deposited concrete completely to protect it from frost and to prevent any loss of heat.
7   Not removing props or formwork without the permission of the site engineer.

Types of concrete

Ready-mixed concrete (BS 1926)

Ready-mixed concrete is not necessarily a special *type* of concrete; it is a special way of having concrete delivered to a site. This method of obtaining concrete can be used for all concreting work on site, or supplementing the concreting plant on site which may be inadequate for the requirements of the work schedule.

Ready-mixed concreting plants will usually supply any mix of concrete using any specified type of aggregates and cements. Where very special aggregates are required, however, sufficient time must be given to allow the plants to obtain an adequate supply. The plants can be put under contract to supply concrete at a specified rate to a site, and will normally go to great lengths to prevent letting a site down. This method of obtaining concrete has several advantages over mixing concrete on site which are outlined below.

Advantages
1   Uniform mixes can be assured.
2   It is not necessary to install large mixing plant on site.
3   Where concreting operations are intermittent on site, it allows work to be carried out without having constantly to transfer the mixing gang to other work.
4   The storage space that would be required for aggregates and cements is saved. This is particularly useful on confined sites.

Disadvantages
1   There is always the possibility of delays due to traffic hold-ups, or breakdowns.
2   This method is costly when only small batches of concrete are required. It is therefore better to have a small mixer on the site to provide small amounts of concrete.

Lean-mix concrete

This consists of a mix of one part of Portland cement to between fifteen to twenty parts of aggregates, usually of the 'all-in ballast' type. The mixing for this type of concrete should be done in pan-type or paddle mixers and not in the ordinary drum-type of mixer where the concrete might build up or ball together, especially if the aggregate contained more than 45 per cent of material passing a 5 mm sieve.

Lean-mix concretes are used for road construction and provide excellent road bases where bituminous surfacing is to be used. This concrete is generally laid by hand and compacted by rolling with vibrating rollers.

Another form of lean-mix concrete is made with face gravel, hoggin or all-in ballast which contains a large percentage of fines, and would generally be classified as 'dirty' materials compared to ordinary concreting grit. This is mixed, laid and compacted in the same way as lean mixes but the mixing must be carried out in pan mixers or paddle mixers. This is because there is a large proportion of fines. This type of concrete is called cement-bound granular-base material and it is used for road bases.

No-fines concrete

This concrete can be made with either a lightweight or a heavyweight aggregate. The usual grading for the aggregate is 18 to 9 mm with not more than 5 per cent passing a 9 mm sieve. The usual mix is 1:8 by volume for heavyweight aggregate and 1:6 for lightweight aggregate. Only sufficient water is necessary in the mix to ensure that the cement paste completely coats the aggregate.

To prevent the cement 'balling' in the mixer, half the water should be put into the mixer at first, then the aggregate followed by the cement, and the remainder of the water added after the aggregate and the cement have been partly mixed.

This type of concrete is used for the construction of low rise blocks of flats and houses. The honeycomb nature of the concrete makes it impervious against the penetration of water and also gives greater heat insulation than ordinary dense concrete.

Lightweight concretes

These are concretes which are produced for providing good heat or thermal insulation to buildings but are also used for lightweight partitions and walling. Over-cementing of these concretes is unnecessary and uneconomical, as these concretes usually only have to carry their own weight, or at the most, light floors or roofs. These concretes are ideal for making blocks which can be used in the building of inner leafs of cavity walling. They can also be easily cut and nailed and form a good base for internal plastering or external rendering. Generally their fire resistance properties are very good and usually better than the resistance properties of dense concrete.

The strength of lightweight concretes varies over a wide range from about 8 kgf/cm^2 to about 320 kgf/cm^2, according to the density and type of aggregate.

The drying shrinkage of lightweight aggregates is generally higher than it is for dense concrete, but suitable curing and drying will keep the movement to a minimum. Lightweight concrete blocks should always be stored under dry conditions and should never be allowed to become saturated.

Aggregates used for lightweight concretes
Clinker (BS1165)

This is the residue which comes from coke or coal which has been completely burnt and fused or sintered in lumps. Blocks made with clinker are often referred to on site as 'breeze blocks', but this term is incorrect as breeze is a finely divided coke and is not recommended as an aggregate for concrete.

Fly ash

This is the residue which comes from pulverized coal burnt at high temperatures. Excellent precast blocks have been produced from this type of material which at one time was considered just a waste product. Some types are produced by mixing the fly ash with water, forming it into pellets and then firing it at a high temperature.

Foamed slag (BS 877)

This is an excellent material and probably one of the principal lightweight aggregates in use in this country. It is produced by treating molten slag with controlled amounts of water. The conversion of the water into steam expands the slag so that it forms a porous material. The foamed slag is crushed and screened to the sizes required for use as an aggregate.

Expanded clays and shales

These are produced by heating at high temperatures where they generate gases which cause the material to expand and become cellular. This porous and cellular structure is retained when the clays and shales are cooled down and form a stable lightweight material.

Expanded vermiculite

This is a material resembling mica and is mined chiefly in America and Africa. When heated to temperatures between 650°C and 1000°C, it expands by exfoliation of the thin plates of the vermiculite to give particles resembling small 'concertinas'. It is used extensively in plasters, lightweight concrete screeds, partition blocks, slabs and cavity filling.

Pumice

This is the natural lightweight material in common use. It is of volcanic origin and is mainly imported from Germany but in only very limited supplies.

Sawdust

This is stabilized by an additive and then mixed with cement to produce excellent precast blocks for internal use.

Air-entrained concretes

These are produced by introducing additives into the mix. These additives form minute bubbles which are so small that they cannot be seen by the naked eye, and are evenly distributed throughout the concrete.

Air-entrainment gives added protection to concrete against frost attack. It can also reduce the permeability of concrete and therefore increase its resistance to chemical attack.

The air-entrainment will slightly reduce the compressive strength of the concrete, but this can be offset by the fact that air-entrainment makes the mix more cohesive and workable. Therefore, less fines and water are needed for the same

workability, which means that the concrete gains in strength. The additives should be evenly distributed throughout the concrete mix. This can be done by adding the air-entraining agent to the mixing water. The amount of air-entrainment will depent upon the requirements for strength and the use to which the concrete will be put; but the amount of air-entrainment should be about 5 per cent of the volume of the concrete.

Waterproofed concretes

These can be produced by introducing additives in Portland cement concretes. These additives are usually in powder form and great care must be taken to ensure that the correct amount is added to each mix, particularly on windy days when the powder is liable to be blown away before it has been added to the concrete mix. These additives must also be thoroughly mixed into the concrete to ensure even distribution. Manufacturers' instructions must always be carefully read and followed when using any type of additive.

Retarders

These are applied to the face of the formwork and are only intended to retard the setting action of the cement on the skin of the concrete. This allows the skin of the concrete to be easily removed which provides:

1 A surface of exposed aggregate, which forms a pleasant concrete finish.
2 A surface which is suitable for plastering upon without having to hack the surface to provide a key.
3 A good surface for forming a good construction joint between two sections of concrete.

The retarders are applied to the inner face of the formwork, and as soon as the formwork is struck the surface of the concrete should be brushed to remove the skin. If this is left for a few days, the skin will harden and become difficult to remove.

Placing concrete

It is important that concrete is placed in its final position before the cement reaches its initial set. The concrete should normally be compacted in its final position within half an hour of leaving the mixer, and once compacted, it should not be disturbed.

Before placing the concrete, the inside of the formwork should be thoroughly cleaned out, so that no shavings, pieces of wood, or cigarette ends are left in to contaminate the concrete. The concrete should be spread evenly in regular layers and thoroughly consolidated by vibrators as it is poured (*Brickwork 2*, Chapter 16).

Pumping concrete

Considerable quantities of concrete can be readily transported from the mixer to the place of deposit by pumps, provided the receiving end is capable of taking large amounts of concrete. This is a very economical way of transporting concrete from the mixer.

The pipelines are easily laid and joined by special couplings which can be quickly connected and disconnected.

The concrete can be pumped to a height of about 30–35 m and to a horizontal distance of about 300–350 m. On some sites where the place of deposit is not visible from the mixing plant, 'walkie talkie' radio sets can be used to great advantage between the concreting gang and the mixing plant operator. This will prevent too much concrete from being deposited.

When work is started on the pipeline a batch of cement mortar grout (1:2) is pumped through the line to act as a lubricant. At the end of the day's work the pipeline must be thoroughly cleaned out usually by compressed air and water or by pumping a plug through the lines and then flushing the lines with water.

Concrete used for pumping should be very workable; lean mixes should not be pumped, and care should be taken to ensure that there are no stoppages once pumping has started, as the pipeline would have to be blown out and lubricated before pumping could go on. If possible, there should be no sharp bends in the pipeline where friction could build up and cause wear and tear on the pipelines themselves.

Preferred mixes, materials, and workability

In order to avoid the confusion which arises from the multiplicity of concrete specifications and duplication of mixes, Tables 22 and 23 list the preferred mixes, materials and workabilities recommended for general use.

Prescribed mixes

The Code of Practice no. 110 recommends prescribed concrete mixes which replace the volume-based 'nominal' mixes. These prescribed mixes were introduced to eliminate the vagueness of the nominal mixes, which were simply quoted, for example, as 1:2:4 or 1:3:6.

In using prescribed mixes, it is only necessary to quote the concrete grade 7, 10, 15, 20, 25 or 30;

Table 22 *Preferred designed mixes*

Designed grade	Cube strength (N/mm^2) at 28 days
C15	15.0
C20	20.0
C25	25.0
C30	30.0
C35	35.0
C40	40.0
C45	45.0
C50	50.0

Table 23 *Preferred prescribed mixes*

Prescribed grade	Cement content kg/m^3	Approximate equivalent nominal mix by volume
P150	150	1 : 4 : 8
P175	175	
P200	200	
P225	225	1 : 3 : 6
P250	250	
P275	275	
P300	300	1 : 2 : 4
P325	325	
P350	350	1 : 1½ : 3

Table 24 *Prescribed mixes*
Weights of cement and total dry aggregates in kg to produce approximately one cubic metre of fully compacted concrete together with the percentages by weight of fine aggregate in total dry aggregates

	Nominal max. size of agg. (mm)	40		20		14		10	
Concrete grade	Workability	medium	high	medium	high	medium	high	medium	high
	Limits to slump that may be expected (mm)	50 to 100	100 to 150	25 to 75	75 to 125	10 to 50	50 to 100	10 to 25	25 to 50
7	Cement (kg)	180	200	210	230	—	—	—	—
	Total aggregate (kg)	1950	1850	1900	1800	—	—	—	—
	Fine aggregate (%)	30–45	30–45	30–50	30–50	—	—	—	—
10	Cement (kg)	210	230	240	260	—	—	—	—
	Total aggregate (kg)	1900	1850	1850	1800	—	—	—	—
	Fine aggregate (%)	30–45	30–45	35–50	35–50	—	—	—	—
15	Cement (kg)	250	270	280	310	—	—	—	—
	Total aggregate (kg)	1850	1800	1800	1750	—	—	—	—
	Fine aggregate (%)	30–45	30–45	35–50	35–50	—	—	—	—
20	Cement (kg)	300	320	320	350	340	380	360	410
	Total aggregate (kg)	1850	1750	1800	1750	1750	1700	1750	1650
	Sand:								
	Zone 1 (%)	35	40	40	45	45	50	50	55
	Zone 2 (%)	30	35	35	40	40	45	45	50
	Zone 3 (%)	30	30	30	35	35	40	40	45
25	Cement (kg)	340	360	360	390	380	420	400	450
	Total aggregate (kg)	1800	1750	1750	1700	1700	1650	1700	1600
	Sand:								
	Zone 1 (%)	35	40	40	45	45	50	50	55
	Zone 2 (%)	30	35	35	40	40	45	45	50
	Zone 3 (%)	30	30	30	35	35	40	40	45
30	Cement (kg)	370	390	400	430	430	470	460	510
	Total aggregate (kg)	1750	1700	1700	1650	1700	1600	1650	1550
	Sand:								
	Zone 1 (%)	35	40	40	45	45	50	50	55
	Zone 2 (%)	30	35	35	40	40	45	45	50
	Zone 3 (%)	30	30	30	35	35	40	40	45

Where necessary the aggregates for grades 7, 10 and 15 may be batched by volume in which case the bulk density of the damp aggregate may be taken as 1500 kg/m^3 and one whole bag of cement may be taken as weighing 50 kg

the maximum size of aggregate, the workability – medium or high; and the limits of expected slump.

The prescribed mixes are based on:

1 The aggregates which comply with B S 882 or B S 1047.
2 Cement complying with B S 12 or B S 146. If other cements are used, the advice of the cement manufacturers should be sought.
3 A natural sand complying with the requirements of B S 882 (see *Brickwork 2,* Chapter 16).

The amounts of aggregates by weight of cement in kilogrammes are given in Table 24.

Self-assessment questions

1 Outline the work of the Agrément Board.

2 What is meant by the *hydration* of cement?

3 Outline the meanings of setting and hardening rates of cements.

4 How do ordinary and rapid-hardening cements differ?

5 How does Portland blast-furnace cement differ from ordinary Portland cement?

6 For what purpose is low heat cement used? What special point must be kept in mind when this cement has to be used on a site?

7 What special precaution must be taken when using coloured cement in concretes to ensure that the concrete will be of adequate strength? Explain why this is done.

8 What type of cement would be recommended for use where concrete is to be laid in foundations which are situated in a soil likely to contain a fairly large percentage of mineral salts? State the precautions that should be taken when using this type of cement.

9 What precaution should be taken when using a water-repellent Portland cement?

10 State how the characteristics of ultra-high early strength cement differ from ordinary Portland cement.

11 How do high-alumina cements differ from Portland cements? What special advantages have high-alumina cements over Portland cements?

12 What are the special requirements for the curing of concrete made with high-alumina cements?

13 State the advantage of the use of refractory concretes. What mix would be recommended for a refractory concrete lining 150 mm thick?

14 What precautions should be taken when laying high-alumina concrete in hot weather?

15 Describe the method of concreting in cold weather with
(a) high-alumina cement
(b) Portland cement

16 What are the advantages of using ready-mixed concrete on a site?

17 What is meant by a lean-mix concrete? For what purpose would this type of concrete be used?

18 What is a no-fines concrete? Where would this concrete be used?

19 Describe the various types of aggregates that can be used in lightweight concretes.

20 What is meant by air-entrained concrete? What are its advantages?

21 Explain the meaning of a *retarder* in concrete. How would it be used and why?

22 What special precautions should be taken before placing concrete in formwork?

23   What should be done at the start of the day's
     work when pumping concrete?

24   What other special precautions should be
     taken when installing a pumping line on a
     site?

25   How are prescribed mixes specified?

Chapter 16

Accident prevention

After reading this chapter you should be able to:

1 Realize the importance of obeying the rules of safety and avoiding accidents on site.

2 Have an appreciation of the causes of accidents.

3 Have an understanding of 'The Health and Safety at Work etc. Act'.

4 Be able to identify the responsibility of all members on site regarding safety.

5 Have an appreciation of the costs incurred as a result of accidents.

Accident prevention is most important to everybody engaged in industry, but particularly in the building and civil engineering industry because they have high accident rates. In the whole of the industry the annual number of reportable accidents is usually about 200,000 which includes between 600 and 700 fatal accidents. Out of this number, approximately 40,000 accidents occur in the construction industry and these include about 200 fatal accidents. Reportable accidents are accidents which are serious enough to necessitate the victim having at least three days off work, in which case the factory inspector must be notified of the accident. Although it might be argued that, statistically, this is a low figure when compared to the total number of people employed in the industry (approximately 3 per cent), this figure should be analysed.

It has been estimated that for every reportable accident there are seven times as many accidents which go unnoticed as the victim does not lose more than three days' work. Therefore, in the construction industry, the estimated total number of accidents would be in the region of $40,000 \times 7 = 280,000$. If a figure of 30 times as many accidents cause injury but little or no time loss, this would reach an incredible total of $280,000 \times 30 = 8,400,000$ accidents. If the number of 'near misses' is considered, this figure

would reach unbelievable astronomical proportions which, although incredible, must be carefully considered.

If the number of normal working hours per year is taken as 40×50, the number of accidents per working hour is approximately $\dfrac{8,400,000}{2000}$, which is equal to 4,200 accidents per hour and one fatal accident every 10 hours.

The number of accidents in the construction industry is therefore far too great and will only be reduced when everybody realizes their responsibilities and take greater care.

If the number of accidents is to be reduced, the full co-operation of *every* person associated with the industry must be achieved. This applies to employers, engineers, subcontractors, foremen, safety officers, charge hands, craftsmen and operatives. Every section must play its part to the full.

Accidents are a constant drain on the industry's resources in manpower, finance, production and time, resources which the industry can ill afford to lose.

A typical analysis of annual accidents in the construction industry shows the following pattern:

Persons falling	27 per cent
Handling materials	26 per cent
Striking against an object	11 per cent
Machinery	8 per cent
Struck by falling objects	8 per cent
Hand tools	8 per cent
Transport	6 per cent
Others	6 per cent

Causes of accidents

It is important to remember that accidents do not just happen; there is always a *cause*. The human element of error is the main cause of accidents and whenever there is an accident it is worthwhile to consider how it happened and what could have been done to prevent it.

The number of silly risks that are taken by experienced craftsmen and operatives on site is quite incredible. The Chief Factory Inspector's annual report, or any of the publications of the Royal Society for the Prevention of Accidents (RoSPA) quote typical examples of accidents as follows:

1   Falling from a roof because the crawling ladder was insecurely held at the ridge of a roof; for example, by attempting to hold a crawling ladder on a half round ridge tile with only a small piece of wood fixed at the end of the ladder.
2   Being buried in a trench where no timbering has been installed.
3   Scaffold cranes being erected on scaffolding which has not been strengthened or stabilized.
4   Temporary stagings which have not been properly secured, supported or braced.
5   Removing formwork or struts before work has had time to set or harden properly.
6   Subjecting construction work to stresses before it is properly hardened. For example, an accident was caused by an operative placing a ladder against a newly built bungalow chimney only 450 mm^2 and climbing to the top. The chimney collapsed and knocked another man on to the floor below where he was partly buried by bricks.

7   Cutting large openings out of existing walling which weakened the structure to the point of collapse.
8   Dismantling scaffolding without proper authority.
9   Not wearing correct protective clothing or equipment.
10 Not securing guards on machinery; also using machines without guards.
11 Failing to carry out thorough inspections on machinery or equipment.

These are only a *few* of the causes.

The Health and Safety at Work etc. Act

The purpose of this Act is to provide the legislative formwork to promote, stimulate and encourage high standards of health and safety at work.

The aim must be to promote safety awareness and effective safety organization and performance by schemes designed to suit the particular industry or organization.

The Act consists of four parts:

Part 1 relating to health, safety and welfare in relation to work.
Part 2 relating to the Employment Medical Advisory Service.
Part 3 amends the law relating to Building Regulations.
Part 4 contains a number of miscellaneous and general provisions.

These regulations are the law of the land and must, therefore, be obeyed by everyone – employers and employees alike. Laws and regulations, however, will not in themselves prevent accidents; their observance will only do this. The regulations are essential to bring home to *all* personnel the responsibilities that each and every one has to keep accidents to an absolute minimum.

They embrace all operations on site and will inevitably reduce the number of accidents on site if operations are carried out in accordance with the requirements of the Act.

The responsibilities of site personnel

The employer

The employer has the responsibility of ensuring that all machinery and equipment is in good order and kept well-maintained. Although providing protective equipment and clothing can be expensive, the employer should realize that accidents can be very much more expensive and costly to production. Some firms take a pride in having accident-free sites whereby they actually make money because of the reduction in their insurance premiums. Furthermore, their staff are directly responsible for application of the requirements within the Act and can, therefore, be a direct asset to their company.

Employers must prepare a written statement of their general policy with respect to the health and safety at work of their employees and the organization for carrying out that policy.

Site engineers and agents

Site engineers and agents must ensure that the company's policy on safety is understood by all their subordinate supervisory staff: that all work must be carried out under safe conditions, and that disobedience of the rules will not be tolerated. Full support should be given to safety officers on sites; they should be helped in their work. Resist the temptation to assume that safety measures cut down production and only add to on-site costs.

Most site personnel will respond to the will of site managers if their policies are sound and they are determined to enforce it. The site manager should realize that if a great number of accidents happen on a site the personnel quickly lose confidence in management, production soon drops to a low level, and disputes result; this has an adverse effect on the efficiency of the running of the site. The site manager should also try to maintain a clean and tidy site as an untidy site tends to cause accidents more than one which is kept in a tidy state. The site manager should also ensure that all personnel are aware of correct hand signals when operating cranes and hoists and insist that the hand signals are used on site (Figure 217).

The safety officer

The safety officer has the responsibility of ensuring that the requirements of the Health and Safety at Work etc., Act are fully understood and applied to the site. The safety officer must also ensure that all registers and records are kept up-to-date and accurately completed and check that all machinery is in good order and is being operated correctly. In addition to this, the safety officer must investigate all accidents which do happen and compile an accurate report.

Where protective clothing and equipment have to be provided and worn, the safety officer must ensure that all personnel wear such protective clothing and use protective equipment; for example, the wearing of a safety helmet on site, wearing goggles when using grinders or cutting away concrete and wearing face masks under very dusty conditions and also the wearing of safety belts and lifelines (Figures 218 and 219). The safety officer should also encourate all personnel on site to wear protec-

Figure 217 *Recognized crane hand signals*

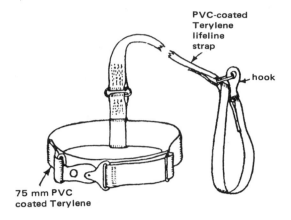

Figure 218 *Surelok all-weather belt (produced by Abbott Birks & Co Ltd)*

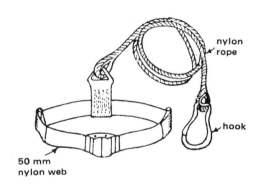

Figure 219 *The gripper endless belt*

tive shoes or boots; for example, footwear with steel toecaps and in some cases with steel soles (as a protection against the penetration of nails). Any incorrect procedure must be reported to the site supervisory staff immediately. The safety officer must maintain good discipline at all times, very often without real authority or site management for support. Good safety officers have a difficult task, but they can be a tremendous asset to a company, particularly if the sites under their control are completed without any accidents happening.

The safety representative
The safety representative may be appointed by a recognized trade union on site and shall represent the employees in consultations with the employer on all matters of health and safety.

Craftsmen and operatives
Craftsmen and operatives very often perform actions on impulse. In many cases they are a danger to *themselves*, as they often underestimate the dangers which abound on site, and take chances which do not make sense to the onlooker.

Everybody on site should take notice of the safety officer or the safety representative when they give advice on any matter concerning safety.

The practical joker is a menace on the site and should never be tolerated. Similarly, the 'know-all' who convinces others that they are not very manly if they wish to take precautions against accidents is also a menace. The safety officer and safety representative should carefully watch out for such practical jokers and know-alls.

The conscientious craftsman is often the victim of accidents through being anxious not to waste time by:

1 Waiting for a proper scaffold to be erected.
2 Putting timbering in a trench.
3 Altering a guard on a machine 'because the job to be done will only take as long as altering the guard'.
4 Working on an asbestos roof without proper crawling ladders.
5 Over-reaching from a ladder to save time by going down and moving it along.

Although there is always sympathy for a victim, it is important to remember that there would have been no victim at all if there had been some forethought.

The following points are causes of accidents attributable to carelessness or malpractice:

1 Removing part of a scaffold without permission or consulting the person responsible for that work.
2 Not placing adequate covers over holes in floors.
3 Omitting to place warning notices where there is danger.
4 Operating machinery which is unsafe.
5 Failing to use proper electrical connections.

6 Walking across insecure gangways.

7 Removing guard rails or toeboards from a working platform.

8 Leaving nails sticking up in pieces of timber; not putting the timber in tidy stacks or heaps.

9 Using ladders which are not properly secured, or in good condition.

10 Personnel not using ladders for moving from one platform to another and clambering down scaffolding.

11 Not wearing safety belts when working in dangerous places and not rigging and using lifelines properly.

In addition to these points, it is important to remember that when working overhead, all other personnel are not allowed underneath, if there is a danger of objects falling on them. Alternatively, tools, materials or equipment should not be placed where they can fall from the working platform.

The cost of accidents

Accidents are costly to firms, victims and their families, and to the other employees.

The firm

The following items are typical costs that a firm would have to expect in the event of a serious accident happening on site:

1 Transporting the injured person to hospital.

2 The time lost by other employees in assisting the injured person.

3 Additional time loss through other employees stopping work out of sympathy or out of curiosity.

4 The cost of the work being seriously disrupted, especially if the injured person is a key worker in a gang.

5 The cost of supervisory staff investigating the accident.

6 Re-planning the work.

7 Preparing accident reports and attending investigations or inquiries into the accident.

8 Repairing and possibly replacing damaged equipment and/or work.

9 Time lost in repairing plant.

10 The delay in the progress of the work and consequent increase in site costs.

11 The cost of training a new worker to replace the injured person.

12 Increased insurance premiums.

Victims and their families

1 The suffering of pain and shock.

2 The loss of direct earnings.

3 The loss of earning ability (capability of working in the future).

4 In the event of a death, the complete loss of the wage-earner to the family.

5 The extra expenses that are incurred when someone is ill, for example, travelling to and from the hospital, special foods.

The other employees

1 The possible loss of bonus due to the delay in the work, or the possible loss of a key person.

2 The loss of morale. This is difficult to assess in terms of money, but it has an adverse effect on production.

Therefore, accidents only cause trouble for everyone and add to site costs, as well as causing a great deal of human suffering for the victims and their families. So *always* take great care and do not invite accidents to yourself or to other people who are employed on the site.

Self-assessment questions

1 Explain how accidents can be prevented on site.

2 Whose responsibility is it to prevent accidents on site?

3 State the most common forms of accidents in the construction industry.

4 Give typical examples of causes of accidents on site.

5 State the title of the regulations which lay down the various rules which are concerned with safety on the site.

6 How can the safety officer and the safety representative ensure that accidents are kept to a minimum on a site?

7 How can the site agent assist the safety officer and the safety representative in their work of keeping accidents to a minimum?

8 How can site operatives assist in the prevention of accidents?

9 Explain why accidents are a serious matter in the industry.

Index